W9-BIP-610

Donated to
SAINT PAUL PUBLIC LIBRARY

Klan-Destine Relationships

Klan-Destine Relationships

A Black Man's Odyssey
in the
Ku Klux Klan

Daryl Davis

New Horizon Press   Far Hills, NJ

Copyright © 1998 by Daryl Davis

All rights reserved. No portion of this book may be reproduced or transmitted in any form whatsoever, including electronic, mechanical, or any information storage or retrieval system, except as may be expressly permitted by the 1976 Copyright Act or in writing from the publisher.

Requests for permission should be addressed to:
New Horizon Press
P.O. Box 669
Far Hills, New Jersey 07931

Davis, Daryl
Klan-Destine Relationships
A Black Man's Odyssey in the Ku Klux Klan

Library of Congress Catalog Card Number: 97-066564

ISBN: 0-88282-159-8

Interior Design: Network Typesetting, Inc.

New Horizon Press

Manufactured in the U.S.A.
2000   1999   1998   1997 /   5   4   3   2   1

Author's Note

These are my actual experiences and history, and this book reflects my opinion of the past, present, and future. The personalities, events, actions, and conversations portrayed within the story have been reconstructed from my memory, tape recordings, documents, press accounts, and the memories of participants. In an effort to safeguard the privacy of certain individuals, I have changed their names and in some cases, altered otherwise identifying characteristics and locations. Events involving the characters happened as described.

Contents

Part IV: Stereotypical Kluxers and Other Right-Wingers

Part V: Self-Destruction of a Klan

Part VI: Klan-Destine Relationships

Dedication

This book is dedicated to Emmett Till and Michael Donald, whose murders by Klansmen should never be forgotten. They did not die in vain. Also, to the daughters of Imperial Wizard Chester Doles and Imperial Wizard Roger Kelly. I hope the lives of these two children are not as racially impacted as mine and those of their parents. My wish for them is by the time they reach my age, they and others will have been able to make this a more harmonious universe. Last but not least, to my eight-year-old goddaughter, Adia Wright, the right to live, create and die in a world of equality.

Acknowledgements

I would like to thank the following people, without whom this book would not be possible:

My mother and father: Bill and Iris Davis for their influence in bringing me up to seek the inherent good in all people and not be judgmental based on one's race, religion, creed, etc., but on one's actions. It was my parents who took me all over the world and exposed me to many different people and cultures.

The Klanmembers and former Klanmembers: Roger Kelly, Vernon Naimaster, Anthony LaRicci and his wife, Frances, Robert White, Thomas Tarrants, Chester Doles, David Black, Gary Nigh, Conrad "Bull" Robinson and his wife, Fay, Daniel Wantz, Roy Frankhouser, John Baumgardner, Rick Milsted, Donald Toms, Karen, Jimmy Mitchell Rosenberg, Thom Robb, Bill Donovan and William Hoff.

Others from the Right-Wing and Left-Wing and places in between: Tom Metzger (WAR), Paul Goldstein (Lyndon LaRouche), Mark Thomas (Christian Identity), Dr. Robert Brock (Black Separatist), Kwame Toure (Stokely Carmichael), Michael McGee (Black Panther Militia), Joseph Fields (White Racist), David Lynch (White Power Skinheads and National Alliance),

John Nugent and Willis Carto (Liberty Lobby), Dr. Edward Fields (National States Rights Party and New Order of Knights of the KKK), Kirk Lyons (Right-Wing Attorney).

Law enforcement officers: Lee Ordway, Chester Claggett, Linda Krieger, Michael Brooks, Regina Anderson, Michael Rising, Bob Crouch, Jeffrey Clewer.

Media: Karen Allyn, Bill Lancaster, Mike Ahlers, Judd Duvall, Sally Holland, Ellyn Wexler, Deb Riechman, Julia Robb, Sondra Bishop, Geraldo Rivera, Jim Abraham, Tony Wilbert, Steve Chrzanowski, Robert Moore, Farai Chideya, Margie Hyslop, CNN and Maryland Public Television.

Friends: Mary Barber, Claire Wilson, Mimi Segal, Kim Fenton, Ina Barke, Tony Fasolina, Alice Dey, Aaron Saidman, Jeff Herman and his wife, Deborah Adams-Herman, Linda Gaiachino, Paula Wolfson, Mary Marcum, Don Montagna, Myrna Taylor, Washington Ethical Society, Joan Dunphy and her staff at New Horizon Press. Thank you for believing in me.

Mentors: Patsy Sims, Grace Halsell, Jack Nelson and James Cameron. The writings of these authors should be read the world over. Chuck Berry, Elvis Presley, Pinetop Perkins, Johnnie Johnson, Jerry Lee Lewis, Little Richard, B.B. King. These and many other musicians are the reason I became one myself. I am thankful my music allows me to perform all over the country spreading harmony and meeting people from all walks of life.

Information Specialists: Mira Boland, Anti-Defamation League of B'nai B'rith, Klanwatch of the Southern Poverty Law Center.

There are probably many friends and acquaintances I have inadvertently not listed due to oversight. Your contributions, encouragement, concerns and warnings are greatly appreciated. Please accept my thanks. There are also some people on the fringe and those working undercover in law enforcement whose names I have intentionally omitted at their requests. You know who you are. Please accept my thanks.

Introduction

KKK History from a Black Perspective

Before the Civil War, Giles County, Tennessee had many slaves and blacks made up fifty percent of the population. After the war, the freedom of these Blacks made many Whites nervous. The tension had increased in 1865 when a severe cyclone ruined many of the plantations. According to the Freedman's Bureau, the town became the scene of sporadic violence and economic chaos.

On Christmas Eve 1865, in Pulaski, Tennessee, six bored Confederate Civil War veteran officers, Richard Reed, Calvin Jones, James Crowe, John Lester, Frank McCord and John Kennedy, who had recently returned to their homes, got together. The group decided to form a secret social fraternity in which its members could have fun, make mischief and pranks on the public. With the exception of being on a small scale and being secretive, it was structured similarly to groups today such as the American Legion and the VFW (Veterans of Foreign Wars). The original members took the Greek work for circle, "kuklos", and derived ku klux. All six being of Scottish-Irish heritage, they took the word "clan" and spelled it klan for uniformity. Thus was born the KKK or the Ku Klux Klan. The men who formed the organization created mystic names for the titles of its officers.

Originally, the Ku Klux Klan was not designed to be a hate organization. Its members simply wanted to get together, share camaraderie and amuse themselves. That idea caught on and the six members began to receive letters from young men in nearby towns and even from Alabama, asking if they could establish other Klan clubs. As membership in the original Klan began to grow, it included Jews, Catholics, and in fact, any White person who believed in the ways of the South before the abolition of slavery.

On the first excursions of the KKK, its members paraded through town in the middle of the night on horseback, dressed in white sheets with holes cut out for eyes. Their horses were dressed in similar attire. No violence or cross-burnings were committed. Nonetheless, this type of spookiness on a night other than Halloween generated surprise and curiosity as to whom these white-clad figures were, much to the delight of the "ghosts" who had no intention of revealing their identities. Many early Klansmen wore different colored robes, as well as white, with no significance attached. It wasn't until later that certain colors designated a Klansman's rank. Ironically at this point, the color white was deemed the lowest.

While the curious White townspeople were trying to find out who and what was behind this charade, the newly freed Black slaves who came from a land of witch doctors and voodoo wanted to know anything but. Playing on those superstitions, the Ku Kluxers told the former slaves that they were dead Confederate soldiers returning to haunt them. Having achieved the desired reaction from playing a frightening joke on someone, the Klansmen continued with their pranks of scaring unsuspecting Black people into "staying in their places."

What we have come to believe as the real purpose, the dark secret and the true motivation of the Ku Klux Klan began to manifest itself as Northern Carpetbaggers began coming in greater numbers to the South to rebuild it and to strip it of its former morals, values and cultures. The riots in Memphis in 1866 increased the atmosphere of chaos.

As membership in the secret society increased, opportunists saw the possibilities of using their shock tactics and designated themselves keepers of law and order, ironically through lawlessness and violent vigilante activities. Blacks were the main recipients of lynchings, beatings, dismemberments, gang rapes, murders, house bombings and other atrocities. Whites, who committed crimes or immoral acts, such as cheating on their spouses or wife-beating or who showed any opposition to the Ku Klux Klan, were also on the receiving end of punishment. These acts of lesson-teaching were mostly implemented by men under pointed hoods, in white sheets, hiding behind white masks. Sometimes, these nightriders wore black robes in order to blend in with the darkness of night while committing their acts of terrorism.

In April of 1867, the original members of the Klan called an organizational meeting at the Maxwell House Hotel in Nashville. George Gordan, a former brigadier general for the Confederacy, headed the meeting. He was elected Grand Dragon of the Realm of Tennessee. A former slave trader and controversial confederate officer by the name of Lieutenant General Nathan Bedford Forrest was elected to hold the highest ranking office. He was given the title "Grand Wizard." Some of today's modern Klan groups have broken with tradition and renamed this position "National Director" hoping to shed the negative image of the Klan, even though their ideologies may remain the same. The prefix "Grand" designates state level while the prefix "Imperial" designates national level. A state is also referred to as a "Realm." The prefix "Great" designates county or province level while the prefix "Exalted" designates a district level within a county or province.

The organization of the local groups was left as the original, but above them was imposed a military hierarchy for "the

Daryl Davis

lovers of law and order, peace and justice" and was "affectionately" dedicated "to the shades of the venerated dead." However, nowhere in the prescript did the name Ku Klux Klan appear. Two major changes were heightened secrecy within the organization and political goals.

After this meeting, the Klan began to go public, holding a daytime parade in Pulaski and announcing meetings in the newspapers elsewhere in Tennessee. Meanwhile, the August 1867 elections in which Blacks were given the vote, were about to take place. General Forrest warned others of the animosity between the Blacks and "the Irish people" of Memphis, which might cause the Irish to offer strenuous interference if Tennessee Blacks voted in abundance. However, they did and the Republicans won. Thereafter, the Klan became a vigilante army.

With more elections coming up in 1868, violence became the Klan's chief method of gaining submission to their will. This method, according to Brevet Lieutenant Joseph Gelnay, who was sent to investigate the Ku Klux Klan and reports of mutilations, floggings, lynchings and shootings, successfully instilled fear in many people and helped the Klan to expand. As the secret Klan continued spreading from Tennessee through the South, it became impossible for a central group to control it.

Grand Wizard Forrest, disgusted by its new sprawling form, which was not the "honorable and patriotic organization" he had envisioned, issued General Order Number One telling his members to disband and refrain from committing night-riding terrorism in the name of the Ku Klux Klan. Despite his words, most members continued their covert activities and the political basis of the Klan grew.

By 1870, the Klan throughout the South, as well as menacing Blacks, also cowed Southern Republicans, law officers and the military. Then in May of that year, Republicans passed the Reinforcement Act to enforce the Fifteenth Amendment and prohibit interference with voting. In the South, more violence and riots occurred.

Finally, President Grant addressed Congress on the Ku Klux Klan problem. Radical Republican Congressman, Benjamin Butler, had drafted a bill on the Klan and a revised version was given to the House. Congressman Robert B. Elliott of South Carolina, a Black man, eloquently defended it and then Butler, describing a long list of atrocities by the Klan, asked for its passage.

The Bill was passed by both the House and Senate. Despite this, more violence broke out in York County, South Carolina where Governor Scott asked for help in handling the Klan. Major Lewis Merrill was dispatched to York County. Although Merrill gathered much evidence and tried to work within the Court system, he found the Court would not indict Klan members and intended to discredit him. Finally, President Grant suspended the Writ of Habeas Corpus and the United States Army stepped in. In South Carolina, the Ku Klux Klan was dissolved.

However, because of budgetary and manpower constraints, the huge number of Klan cases couldn't be prosecuted. By 1873, the Federal Government's Enforcement Policy was in general collapse. The Enforcement Acts were at a standstill by 1874. Though the Klan had been ruined in South Carolina, lawlessness and violence against Blacks continued.

Grant, now in his second term as President and with diminishing support, tried to stop the quenching of Black Civil Rights, but without success. In 1875, Republicans passed another Civil Rights Act; however, the Democrats had gotten control of the House of Representatives the year before. The new Act was not enforced and the Blacks in the South were second class citizens, unable to vote or advance and without civil liberties.

During the next twenty years, while support for the Klan diminished, not only did Republicans forget the Southern Blacks, but the Supreme Court eliminated almost all provisions of the Enforcement and Ku Klux Klan Acts. The Civil Rights Act was declared unconstitutional. Then the Court legitimized racial segregation (Plessy & Ferguson, 1896). Afterward, the South enacted many segregation laws. Blacks in the South were denied political, social or economic power.

This set the stage, during Reconstruction, for a 1915 revival of the Ku Klux Klan by William Joseph Simmons. Simmons, a Methodist minister, had became a Methodist circuit rider in Alabama and Florida. Unable to support himself, he wandered from job to job, finally becoming a promoter for a Fraternal Order called the Woodmen of America. At this point, he began to dream of a new organization, using the letters "KL." This evolved into his fantasy of reviving the Ku Klux Klan.

Increased interest in the Klan had been spurred on during this time by a newly released book novel titled, "The Clansman," by Thomas Dixon and shortly thereafter, the release of filmmaker D.W. Griffith's movie "Birth of a Nation," based on the novel. Then on April 27, 1915, in Georgia, a fourteen-year-old girl, Mary Phagan, was raped and murdered. Her employer, Leo M. Frank, who was Jewish and a Northerner, was arrested, tried and convicted in a trial that many civil liberty groups denounced as unjust. When the Governor of South Carolina commuted the sentence to life, Frank was lynched by men calling themselves "The Knights of Mary Phagan." Two months later they burned a giant cross on Stone Mountain, Georgia. Simmons' dream of reviving the KKK became a reality when he, with thirty-four others, signed an application to the state for Georgia to charter the Knights of the Ku Klux Klan, of which he would be the Imperial Wizard. Others soon joined and Simmons got a local company to make their white-hooded uniforms.

Charter member Jonathan Frost, proclaiming White Supremacy on a wider scale and social vigilance, stated: "We avow the distinction between races of mankind as the same that has been decreed by the Creator, and we shall be ever true to the faithful maintenance of White Supremacy and will strenuously oppose any compromise thereof in any and all things."

By the summer of 1921, one hundred thousand members had enrolled in the reconstituted Klan.

Simmons was forced out of office by another aspiring Klan leader named Hiram Evans. By conspiring with and making promises to other members, including those close to Simmons, he was able to gain the Imperial Wizard slot after numerous lawsuits and countersuits. This type of ousting and splintering among the rank and file with the Grand Dragons all vying for the purple robe (Grand Dragon is designated by the color green, and Imperial Wizard by the color purple) continues to this day. In addition, during the ensuing years many Klansmen have accused their leaders of misusing Klan funds for their own personal gain and have become disgruntled with the lack of violence perpetuated by their group; others have become disgruntled with the abundance of violence. These reasons, sometimes along with personal ego, have led to some members splintering off and forming their own organizations.

During the Simmons-Evans era, the Klan continued to grow, as did terrorism against its enemies. The list now read: Blacks, Jews, Catholics, Mexicans and immigrants, but also Whites, such as Protestants and women branded immoral or traitors to their sex or race. By 1922, the Klan had two million members. In Washington, D.C., forty thousand Klansmen marched down Pennsylvania Avenue to advocate White Supremacy.

In the 1930's the Klan membership began to shrink as the nation dealt with the Great Depression. This continued in the 1940's and early 1950's while segregation was the unwritten law of the South. However, when the Supreme Court ordered school integration in 1954, social tension increased in the South. Southerners opposed to the law vowed to maintain segregation.

Again the climate was ripe for Klan growth. Eldon

Edwards, who the previous year had formed one of the splinter Klan groups, the United States Klans, began to add members to his organization after the largest Klan rally in many years.

In 1960, after Edwards' death, Robert M. Shelton formed the United Klans of America. A new era of violence had begun.

During this period, Black and White freedom riders were viciously beaten. Violent confrontations occurred on university campuses, senseless killings were perpetrated, including those of Civil Rights' workers and educators. In a singularly horrific act of violence, four adolescent girls were killed at church.

In 1964 the FBI began to secretly fight the Klan and, the following year, because of the violence of the Klan, President Lyndon Johnson and Georgia Congressman Charles L. Weltner called for a congressional probe of the organization. The House of Representatives called up seven Klan leaders, including Robert Shelton, for contempt for refusal to turn over Klan records. The seven men were indicted and found guilty. Shelton and two others were sentenced to a year in jail.

Then another quiescent period began. Membership in the organization again declined, but its leaders continued spreading a message of racial prejudice.

In the mid 1970's, dapper and articulate David Duke, a former neo-Nazi, formed the Knights of the Ku Klux Klan. Largely due to his utilization of the media to broadcast his message, Klan membership began to rise once again. Duke and others, such as California Klan leaders Tom Metzger and Don Black tried to translate their popularity into political success. During this same period, Invisible Empire Wizard Bill Wilkinson, an avowed militant, and his two machine-gun toting bodyguards were shown in the newspapers boasting, "These guns ain't for killing rabbits, they're for wasting people." In an act which outraged most people, Wilkinson set up a Klan camp for children. In Texas, Louis Beam, a Grand Dragon in David Duke's organization, instructed his Texas Knights in guerrilla warfare.

Not only the Klan organization, but another growing White Supremacist faction, the neo-Nazis, who revered Adolf Hitler, were spreading their militant messages across America.

Some Klan leaders, such as David Duke and Don Black, started out as Nazis while others incorporated methods and ideologies from both groups into their own organizations. The neo-Nazis and the Klansmen shared their most important belief—White Supremacy—and a list of common enemies. During the 1980's and 1990's, more White Supremacist organizations, such as the Aryan Nations, Aryan Resistance and White Prominence, added members to their causes.

While Blacks, Jews and homosexuals all remain the Klans' primary enemies, some Klan groups now accept American-Indians, Catholics and atheists into their membership. Odd as it may seem, it is not uncommon for different Klan groups to commit acts of violence against each other, in addition to supporting each other and interchanging members. The common denominator for these diverse groups is the desire for the preservation of the White Race. They believe the White race is in jeopardy of extinction because of its "defilement" through miscegenation, the mixing of races.

In all fairness, because of the many reincarnations and factions in the Klan nation, generally referred to as the "Invisible Empire," we can no longer refer to the Ku Klux Klan as one large, cohesive group. Today's Klan is not a single entity, as it is so often presented by the media. One Klan group would not want the credit for an act of violence committed by another Klan group, especially if the act was not condoned by the accredited group. As a result of the splintering, when we now refer to the Klan, we should also indicate the group by its proper name, for example: Invincible Empire Knights of the Ku Klux Klan, Invisible Empire Knights of the Ku Klux Klan, United Klans of America, Christian Knights of the Ku Klux Klan, White Knights of the Ku Klux Klan, Confederate Knights of the Ku Klux Klan,

Daryl Davis

Aryan Knights of the Ku Klux Klan, New Order Knights of the Ku Klux Klan, Dixie Knights of the Klan, National Knights of the Ku Klux Klan and the list goes on and on. With this in mind, when the "Klan" is referred to in this book, it may only be indicative of the particular Klan group being highlighted.

Prologue

I am on a long journey. It's not the kind people take to escape, for a short while, their everyday lives and experiences for one which is exotic or adventurous. No. Though, like them, my travel has covered many miles, a destination is not its ultimate purpose.

Instead, my arduous journey is an odyssey of the mind, heart and spirit, on which, I, a Black man, have set out to meet those who do not know, but hate me—the members of the Ku Klux Klan.

To them, because of the color of my skin, I am the enemy and I must know why. That is the reason I have come to this place and many others like it.

My aim is not to expunge the past of the Ku Klux Klan. Its history of violence and terror are part of me and my race forever. But I believe we must, while never losing sight of the past, move forward. In order to do this, like the Arabs and Israelis, the Protestants and the IRA, the Bosnians and the Serbs, we must first have a cease fire so that we can meet and find a common ground. This is why I began my search. This is the goal of my journey.

PART I

LIVING IN BLACK AND WHITE

1

Growing Up

Though I was born in Chicago and spent a couple of years in the United States, my formative years of growing up occurred overseas, mostly on the continent of Africa. This was a result of my being the son of a United States Diplomat on assignment to foreign lands. I met Presidents of the United States, and Emperors, Kings and other royalties from a variety of nations. My mother taught English to the wife of the president of one African Nation. Ethiopian Emperor Haille Selassie was a friend of my father. I met these people on different occasions, both formal and informal, and in some instances, sat down to dinner with them at their residences. All in all, I grew up in a multi-ethnic, multi-racial environment. My vacations were spent with my parents on the continents of Europe, South America and Asia, rarely returning to the States in my early childhood, except for the first half of second grade and all of the fourth grade.

Words such as "discrimination" and "prejudice" or racial slurs were not common in our playground vocabulary. My earliest recollection of anything of this nature occurred when I was around seven-years-old and my father was on assignment in Ethiopia. My parents were discussing the behavior of an

Daryl Davis

American Diplomat, the parent of one of my White playmates. According to my father, this man would go to extreme measures to avoid shaking hands with a Black person. One afternoon, when he came to a cocktail party at our house, I decided to watch him. Sure enough, just as I moved closer to the diplomat, the Ethiopian official walked over and stretched out his hand to the man. Slowly the diplomat shook it. Then, with me following unnoticed, he surreptitiously walked over to the other side of the room keeping his hand behind his back. As I watched wide-eyed, he wiped his right hand on his pant leg.

In retrospect, I feel it was most undiplomatic behavior for someone on a mission of goodwill from the United States. However, at that time I simply thought it odd that an adult would be playing a game of "cooties"—wiping them off much like we second graders did when touched by a member of the opposite sex.

My second encounter with the phenomenon of discrimination occurred in Massachusetts during my fourth grade year. About one month before we had moved from our house in the city to the White suburb of Belmont, where we rented half a duplex from Marge Peterson, a pleasingly plump White lady, I joined the local Cub Scouts. One day, all the scouting groups were invited to participate in a march to commemorate the famous ride of Paul Revere. I marched right along with my fellow Cub Scouts, totally oblivious to the fact that I was the only Black Scout participating. I even got to carry one of the flags. Suddenly, rocks whizzed by. I was being pelted by rocks and other flying objects. I turned, and to my surprise, saw they came from some of the spectators, even children, along the parade route. In my naiveté, I reasoned that some strange people must not like the Cub Scouts. It wasn't until a Cub Master and my Den Mother ran up beside me and shielded me with their bodies that I realized that I was the only Scout under attack. My parents told me that it was only deranged people who attacked children. Later

4

we heard that the people who attacked me were probably part of a racist group called the KKK who hated people who were Black. It was very hard, at the age of ten, to understand why some people who didn't even know me would inflict pain upon me for no other reason than the color of my skin. It was an incident imprinted on my memory forever.

Not much later, during the afternoon of April 4th, 1968, I sat watching "Bewitched," the popular television show about the adventures of Darren, a human, and his wife Samantha Stevens, a witch. My mother was in Roanoke, Virginia visiting her parents and my father was in the study, typing a report. Part way into the show, the words "SPECIAL REPORT" flashed on the screen and a high pitched beeping sound started. I listened as the announcer reported that Martin Luther King, Jr. had just been assassinated and they would interrupt the regularly scheduled programming as details became available.

I am sorry to say that at the time, given my age and the fact that I had spent so much time overseas, I was not very familiar with Dr. King. I could not understand why this announcement could not wait for the six o'clock news.

Still, the seriousness of the announcement must have made an impression, because I went to the den and told my father what the man on the television program had said. He immediately stopped typing and cried, "Oh, no," as his head fell into his hands. Daddy acted as though he had lost a family member or good friend. Seeing my puzzled reaction and obliviousness to the violence that had just occurred, he proceeded to tell me about Martin Luther King, Jr. "You don't know how proud I am to have marched with this man who dedicated his life to making life better for people of color and promoting racial harmony. That's what he lived for and that's what he died for." Having never had to ride in the back of the bus, use designated restrooms or drink from segregated water fountains, I could not grasp the full impact of my father's impassioned words.

Daryl Davis

Nevertheless, I went back to the television and watched for the rest of the afternoon the reports on shocked and angry people all over Boston and the rest of the country who were gearing up for a difficult night ahead. Already there was footage of scenes of rioting and burning. To alleviate the situation, Boston's Mayor, Kevin White, telephoned the most popular Black singer/performer of the day, James Brown, and asked that he give a concert at Boston Garden to which there would be free admission. His performance was to be televised on the local stations in hope that people would either attend the concert or stay home and watch it on television in lieu of going out in the streets and either causing violence or being the recipients thereof.

My father, concerned for my old friends in our former Black neighborhood of Roxbury in Boston, suggested that I call and invite some of them over to watch the televised concert and spend the night. My father and I picked up all the kids who wanted to come and drove them to our home.

Once we all were settled, we turned on the television to see people lining up at the arena entrance to see the Godfather of Soul. The tension seemed to be subsiding a little bit. Everything was going smoothly, and the rioting, burning and looting in the Boston area diminished. Then it was time for James Brown to appear on stage. The crowd went crazy with excitement. The base of the stage was lined with both Black and White police officers to prevent overzealous fans from jumping on stage to touch their idol.

Despite this, when James did his fancy footwork to the edge of the stage, a young Black boy in the front row took a dive onto the stage in an attempt to touch Brown's shoe. Instinctively, a White police officer reached up and grabbed the boy by the heels, quickly and forcefully dragging him off the stage, but causing his head to fall and strike the floor.

That was it! The concert was over. The air of adulation turned to fury as concertgoers began destroying the hall before taking to the streets to riot. In retrospect, it is the general consensus, as well as my own, that if it had been a Black officer who had pulled the boy off the stage in that manner, it would have surely been frowned upon, but it would not have resulted in a riot. But racial tensions were just too high that night to allow a White law enforcement officer to execute his job in that manner.

Even though, during the next few days, I witnessed the violence around America on television and saw the aftermath in my own former neighborhood, I didn't imagine that the violence would have any bearing on my lifestyle or friendships in my new, all-White neighborhood. Boy, was I in for a surprise.

After that night, things in Belmont changed. Though some new friends and their families treated me as nicely as they had, others took on a different attitude. Those were the former friends who now would not play with me anymore or allow me in their homes. When I asked them what was wrong, most of them didn't know. Their only answer was, "My mom and dad said, 'No.'" Even our nice, old landlady changed. One day when I was out playing on the porch, she came out of her duplex door and told me to stay on my side, as if an invisible line had been drawn down the center of the porch.

"In fact," she said, "you shouldn't be playing on the porch at all, your side or mine."

I couldn't comprehend this sudden change in her attitude toward me. It wasn't until years later that I realized she was fearful that someone might notice she shared a house with a Black family and initiate some type of malicious behavior. I was being introduced to what it was like to be discriminated against.

I wrote a letter to Coretta Scott King, expressing my sympathies the best way a ten-year-old knows how and asked her to please write back to me. At that age I could not have conceived of the millions of letters that she surely must have received as a result of her husband's death. Every day I waited for the postman to come and I checked the mail to see if she sent me a letter. The letter never came. Always full of questions, always seeking answers, many years later I wrote a letter to King's alleged assassin, James Earl Ray, who was in prison, and he wrote back to me.

That same disquieting year was the first time I was ever called a "Nigger." One sunny summer day, I was on the way to my elementary school playground to play kickball with some of my White friends. A girl from our grade walked our way and stood a good distance away from me, but within earshot. I will never forget her name, Jennifer Morgan. There was a television show at that time called "Panorama" which sometimes had a Black co-host. Jennifer began yelling, "Hey, Nigger, you ever watch Niggerama?" I ignored her, and she began repeating those words over and over as she came closer to make sure I heard her. I continued to ignore her until she finally came right up behind me and shouted, "Nigger, my daddy said the Klan's gonna get you!" in my ear. Not only was this the first time in my life I had been called a "Nigger" and only the second time in which I'd heard of the Klan, but it was also the first time I ever lost control of my temper with a girl.

I spun around and jumped in the air, karate style, making an attempt to kick her in the face. Her quick reflexes caused her to reel back, avoiding my foot. Had my foot connected with her face, it would have snapped her neck back and probably broken it. Meanwhile, the momentum of not making contact sent me flying through the air. I fell on my rear-end. Then I scrambled up trying to get Jennifer, who took off like a bolt of lightning, with me in pursuit. Although my adrenaline was pumping, hers must have been pumping more. As much as I hate to say it, she was literally running for her life. There was no telling what I would have done to her had I caught her.

A few of the boys I was playing with circled the block in both directions and trapped her. They dragged her, screaming and fighting to get loose, over to where I was standing. A small crowd of kids gathered around. A few yelled "Slap her!" while she was being held. I am sure that half of the kids who were encouraging me to slap Jennifer just wanted to see a fight and the other half truly believed she deserved it. So did I. At the time, I was leaning up against the chain link fence that went around the perimeter of the playground, my fingers pressed through the holes in the chain links. It is completely impossible to get one's fingers caught in these holes as they are probably nine square inches. I wanted to hit her but, though I tried to free myself, neither hand would release from the fence. I was completely frozen, my whole body immobilized. At that point, Jennifer finally yelled, "I'm sorry."

I called to the boys, "Let her go." However, it was not until she was out of my line of sight that my hands released from the fence and my body relaxed.

After years and years of thinking about my experience with Jennifer and the fence, the only conclusion I can come up with and accept is Divine intervention. I truly feel that God physically restrained me from striking Jennifer. At age ten and never having lived in a racist environment, I had no idea what the consequences would have been for a Black kid and his family had I physically struck a little White girl in an all-White neighborhood in 1968. It wasn't until later I learned of Emmett Till, a thirteen-year-old Black boy who had been beaten, tortured and killed by two Klansmen, J. W. Millam and his half-brother Roy Brandt, for just speaking to a White woman.

The years passed quickly, as childhood often does. At age fifteen, I, like so many teenagers in that era, found self-expression in music. Of all the performers I heard, it was Chuck Berry who I admired the most. Berry had not only made people, regardless of their color, happy through his playing, but I saw his music as a bridge-builder which brought Blacks and Whites together. To me and others, his music did as much for civil rights as others did by protests and marches. Before him, Blacks and Whites were segregated in theaters by ropes. At Berry's concerts, an atmosphere of tolerance permeated. Blacks and Whites danced and intermingled without incident.

Inspired by Berry and Elvis Presley, but having no training, I began to sing and play piano by ear, putting together a small band. Not long after that, my musical ambitions soared when I met another performer who would have a big influence on my career ambitions, Jerry Lee Lewis. "I met" is perhaps stretching the point. When Lewis came to Maryland for a concert, I sneaked backstage carrying a bottle of his favorite whiskey, Jack Daniels. Instead of throwing me out, some of his band members listened to my explanation of having a band of my own and let me stay to meet Jerry. From the start, we hit it off. Afterwards, we became friends and stayed in touch. He has been a big influence on my piano playing.

The spring after I met Lewis, during my tenth grade year in high school, I was in a class called P.O.T.C. (Problems of the Twentieth Century). My teacher invited two members of the American Nazi Party, Matt Koehl and Martin Kerr, to speak to our class. The leader and founder of the party was a man named George Lincoln Rockwell who had been murdered by one of his own members. One of the men who spoke to us, Matt Koehl, replaced Rockwell as leader or furor.

As he made his speech, Koehl scowled, directing his words at me and the only other Black student in the class. "We're going to send you back to Africa," he said. His voice rose ominously as he ended, "Blacks who do not go voluntarily will be forced to leave or be eliminated." It was a frightening message for a teenager. Both Koehl and Kerr saw me alone in the hallway later that day as they were leaving the school. Walking to within inches of me and trying to instill further fear, they sneered as they passed.

As a result of my firsthand encounter with the two racists, I wanted to know more about the subject. Why did people hate me and other people because of the color of our skin? I began collecting material on racism. I purchased books on the Ku Klux Klan, American Nazi Parties and other hate organizations, clipped and saved newspaper and magazine articles pertaining to racist incidents, spent hours in libraries researching the extreme Right-Wing and viewed any films or television programs which dealt with racism. By the time I got to Howard University a few years later, I had a good size library on the subject of racism.

While at Howard, someone who was privy to information told me that the American Nazi Party was going to have a fifteen-minute protest in Washington, D.C. near the White House. This protest was unannounced and unpublished. I drove into D.C. on the date of the protest and waited across the street from their designated protest spot. Soon the Nazis arrived. There were about ten men dressed in business suits who stood on the sidewalk holding placards and signs. They were not wearing swastikas, Gestapo or SS uniforms. However, several of the men had little mustaches and combed their dark hair like Adolf Hitler. A few of the men had blond hair. I still cannot figure out how a White man with dark hair and brown eyes can say that blue-eyed blonds are the Master Race. There were no police officers or any type of visible security present.

I spotted Matt Koehl immediately and approached him. All the Nazis around him fastened their eyes on me and shifted nervously. I shook his hand, introduced myself and asked him if he remembered speaking at my high school. "Of course I do," he nodded politely.

No longer afraid of adults who threatened to "send the Blacks back to Africa," I asked him point blank, "Just who in the hell do you think you are making permanent travel plans for me to go to Africa or anywhere else for that matter?"

He didn't answer, but after this exchange, we got into a civil-toned discussion of White Supremacy, in which he said, "I believe in the superiority of the White Race, but I'm not a racist."

Daryl Davis

When I asked him about some very prominent, highly intelligent Black people, he responded, "They must have some White blood in them."

Koehl went on to say, "Blacks are the pawns of the Jews and I have nothing against the Black race as long as it remains separate from the White race. I strongly believe that Whites are committing genocide through miscegenation and the only way to build the White race strong again is to remove the Blacks. Once the White people are educated and have pride in their White heritage and a desire to keep it pure, they can live side by side with Blacks." As I walked away he added, "I feel Blacks should also wish to keep their race pure."

About a month later, these same Nazis, whose headquarter was in nearby Arlington, Virginia, announced they were having a White Pride Day rally at a high school. Naturally, this drew the press and many anti-Nazi groups. For the event, the Nazis were supplied with police protection.

I went to Arlington and stood as close as police would let me. I watched as the Nazis got off the bus and marched and goose-stepped towards the door leading into the school. There was Matt Koehl in full Nazi uniform complete with a swastika armband leading his Hitler clones dressed in the same attire. Loud shouting of anti-Nazi slogans came from people protesting the rally. Bricks, bottles and eggs were thrown at the White Supremacists. When the men reached the door of the school, they turned and gave the Heil Hitler salute to the angry crowd. The police made some arrests and dispersed the crowd.

It was another scene etched in my memory. One that propelled me forward in my search to understand racism.

That same summer, I drove to the Charleston Racetrack in Charleston, West Virginia, anxious to see my idol, Jerry Lee Lewis, perform there after the horse races. When I arrived at the racetrack that afternoon, the musicians were not there yet. The stage was being set up and the sound system checked. People were beginning to find seats on the bleachers. Besides a Black man, who appeared to be working in the capacity of groundskeeper, I was the only Black there.

As I headed for the bleachers, I noticed some people began putting their sweaters and jackets down in the empty spaces beside them as though they did not want me to sit next to them.

There was music being played through loud speakers before the performance began. Suddenly, blasting from a tower off to the side of the bleachers, I heard what sounded like someone taking a needle off the record and setting it down again. Seconds later a new song was being played. The chorus kept repeating, "Ship those Niggers north, ship those Niggers north." I realized, with shock, this was an official Klan record and it was being played for me. Now everyone in the bleachers was looking at me.

At that exact moment, Jerry Lee's limousine pulled up, and when he got out he saw me. "Hey, Daryl," he called, "come backstage with me and hang out before I perform." As I went through the security rope, Jerry Lee shook my hand and put his arm around my shoulder. I turned and looked back at the people on the bleachers. Their mouths were wide open. Jerry Lee never knew what had transpired prior to his arrival, but his kindness and friendship quite possibly saved me from trouble that day.

Not long afterwards, I turned twenty-one and stopped by a Country Western bar called the Turf Club in Laurel, Maryland, rumored to be the local recruiting ground for the Ku Klux Klan. The marquee advertised live music until 3:00 A.M.

Parking in their lot, I walked in the door of the club and looked around. It was a small room with a bar and some pool tables. As soon as people saw me they stopped playing pool and just stared at me in total disbelief. I knew I wasn't welcome, but I also knew if I ran, I would probably be chased. I decided that I had come to see the band and that's what I was going to do rather than turn around and leave.

Daryl Davis

To the rear of this room were two swinging saloon-type doors. Behind these doors was the room in which the band played and people danced. Slowly, I walked straight back through the doors and stood there among more stares. When the band members saw me, they stopped playing! Everyone's eyes were on me.

On one hand, as they stared, I felt like the most powerful son of a gun that ever set foot in there. My presence commanded attention and caused about one hundred and fifty people to stop what they were doing and focus on me in dead silence. On the other hand, I have never felt so scared in my life. Both emotions were pulling me in opposite directions with such equal force that I could not move. I just stood there motionless.

Then a burly, dark-haired man walked up to me and said in a kind, but firm voice, "Let me buy you a drink."

I politely declined, saying, "Thank you, I don't drink." He responded by repeating himself even more hospitably, but with emphasis on the word "me." I complied and he called a waitress over, raising a hand with a finger that bore a ring with the Ku Klux Klan insignia, and I ordered a coke. When she returned he paid her and everything went back to normal, or as close to it as it could get. Though he never explained nor did I ask, the obvious significance of his buying my drink let everyone in the bar know that if I was alright with him, then I should be alright with them.

These events of both prejudice and tolerance at the hands of White strangers further motivated me to continue my study of racist organizations. I especially wanted to find out more about the kind of people who joined them.

2

The Silver Dollar

After graduating from Howard University with a Bachelor Degree in music, I was formally trained in Jazz and Classical music, and my main instruments were piano, voice and guitar. I wanted to be a full-time musician, but I knew I would have a hard struggle trying to make a living playing Jazz or Classical music, which were my first loves.

However, I also loved the Blues, Rock'n'Roll and Boogie Woogie. With a fellow graduate from Howard who was a drummer, we placed advertisements for other prospective band members in the local newspapers. Once again, I put a band together. At that time, most clubs and bars would only book the same Rock band twice a month and the same Blues band once every other month. That kind of music was taking a backseat to Top 40 and Country Western.

Financially, it made sense to go with the trend. I played Top 40 for a short time, but soon became tired playing these songs without the room to express my own creativity. The movie "Urban Cowboy" had come out and made Country music almost mainstream. I felt Country music allowed room for a little more of one's own personality to be expressed.

So our band began playing Country as well as some

Daryl Davis

Bluegrass and enjoyed a good deal of local success. After a while, my name began to spread in Country circles as most people had never heard of a Black man doing Country other than Charlie Pride. I even made Bluegrass history when I became the first Black to perform at the Annual Hyattsville, Maryland Bluegrass Festival. This yearly festival, a three-day event, draws the top national Bluegrass stars. I was being referred to as, "The Black guy who plays piano like Jerry Lee Lewis." It didn't matter whether some of these people were racists or not, they would pay money to see the "Black Jerry Lee." I was a novelty and good at what I did. Of course, they didn't realize that Jerry Lee Lewis learned that rocking Boogie Woogie style of piano playing from Blacks. Even Jerry Lee admits that.

One of the joints we played was the Silver Dollar Lounge in Maryland. The Silver Dollar Lounge catered mostly to out-of-state truckers who stopped in the almost empty lounge during the day for cold beer and patronized the crowded lounge at night, especially if they were staying at the motel above. The rest of the customers, rough country types, were not adverse to fights. This violence was usually of a racist nature if Black men were present and it is further exacerbated if White women were also present. The attitude that was generally adopted by the alcohol-influenced White bar patrons was that the only reason a Black man was in the bar at all was to pick up White women.

The head barmaid at the club in those days, Kelly Blair, was a strikingly gorgeous auburn-haired woman in her late thirties. She stood about five-feet, eight-inches tall and had a figure most women would envy. Of course, among the male truckers, she was the most popular and sometimes the only lady in the lounge with an upbeat personality to match. Kelly and I became friends, and she would alert me to anything she overheard inside the club that would indicate I was in some kind of danger. However, there were some dangers of which Kelly never knew.

Over time, I was accepted by the White patrons who didn't perceive me as threatening, and I became well-liked mostly because I was a musician. Of course, when they realized I played Country, which they loved, they began requesting Charlie Pride songs. They automatically assumed that any Black musician playing Country would know which songs Charlie Pride played. It just so happened that I did and by this time, I also knew Charlie Pride himself. They liked my music and through it, me.

It even got to the point where some customers became my protectors. On one occasion, a drunk attempted to get on the stage and attack me for no other reason than he didn't like my skin color. Two White truckers grabbed him and beat the daylights out of him right there in front of me on the dance floor. The police were called, and the man who tried to attack me was arrested for being drunk and disorderly. He was handcuffed and placed in the squad car.

The police returned to the club and asked me if I wanted to press charges. I declined because I was not hurt. Moments later, the man walked back into the club in handcuffs and tried to attack me again as the cops were getting details from me as to what had happened. *Had the police officers not properly secured the back door to the squad car which purposely cannot be opened from the inside?* I wondered. Sensitized to the racism of some police officers, I asked myself if that was the case, but it was not. Indeed, the door to the squad car was properly closed and locked. He had kicked out the window and crawled through it in his determination to come back and continue his attack upon me. The police restrained him and this time put leg irons on him. It is my understanding that before he arrived at jail that night, he received a beating, administered by Frederick's finest for his destruction of their property. However, the police were not always as protective of me.

One night, I was performing at the Silver Dollar Lounge.

Daryl Davis

After my performance, I drove across the parking lot to the truck stop restaurant to have a late night breakfast. As I was pulling into the parking space, I saw a woman lying on her back on the sidewalk with a man straddled across her chest, simultaneously banging her head on the concrete and punching her in the face.

Jumping from my car I ran over and before I could intervene, the man jumped up and yelled, "You wanna piece of me Nigger?"

"Yeah, I do. Bring it on," I shouted back at him.

He came at me screaming his racial slurs. I knew this man was out of control, and I would have to fight for my life. Although he was about my height and build, I picked him up and threw him on the ground. He got up and came at me again. This time I let him have it. A sledgehammer fist to his face, delivered with the speed of an express train, took him down. Someone who had apparently seen him having the altercation with the woman had already called the police. By the time they got there, the guy was awakening from unconsciousness and getting up to fight some more.

As the police questioned the man, it appeared to me the officers knew him and were trying to give him a break by telling him to go home. However, he would not settle down and would not leave. Finally, the police arrested him.

On the day of the trial, I drove to the home of Ellie Cassidy, the woman I'd helped that night, and picked her up to go to court. Settling herself in my car, she blurted out, "There's something I have to tell you. I'm the defendant's ex-fiancée." She paused and went on, "He's a member of the Ku Klux Klan." Ellie had left him because he was cheating on her. She wanted nothing more to do with him so his punishment for her was, "If I can't have you, then no one will."

The Klansman showed up in court with his new and pregnant fiancée. I pitied her since she appeared shocked to see a

White woman was a co-claimant. Obviously she thought her beau was only going to court for fighting with a "Nigger." She was equally shocked to hear about the violence perpetrated upon Ellie. Halfway through the trial, the young woman stormed out of the courtroom, angry at her boyfriend. He was found guilty and received a suspended jail sentence, a stiff fine and was ordered to pay restitution.

My experiences with racism and intolerance continued. They ranged from not being allowed to have a drink in some places where I performed to playing in honky tonks where I was invited over to meet those who proclaimed themselves White Supremacists. For instance, in a place called the Silver Moon, a couple of men complimented me on my playing, introduced themselves as Hank and Jim and invited me to have a drink on them. Walking over to their table, I explained "I don't drink, but you can buy me a cranberry juice."

Hank smiled as I sat down. "I've never had a drink with a Black man before," he said. "Neither has Jim." At that, they both pulled out membership cards which bore their names and proclaimed them active members of the KKK. I stopped laughing and stared at them. Their grins widened as they laughed and told me, "You're alright for a Black guy. In fact, you're okay in our book."

That year, I met a pretty brunette, Suzie McClinton at one of my gigs. She was White and eight years older than me. For the next five years, we went together. I had never been more serious about anyone in my life than I was about Suzie.

Some of Suzie's family members disowned her for dating me and some of her co-workers made fun of her. She found out quickly who her friends were. Interestingly enough, some of the people she thought would shun her became her most avid supporters, and some of the ones she thought would rally around her, shunned her. Despite these things which she had never experienced before, Suzie stuck by me. With her I shared my views on racial issues and my interest in learning about the Ku Klux Klan. She would clip and save newspaper articles for me and alert me to any Klan-related news stories on television, radio or in other forms of the media.

By now, I owned or had read every book published on the Klan. One, simply titled, "The Klan," by a courageous lady and fantastic writer named Patsy Sims, had, perhaps, the greatest influence on me. I contacted Ms. Sims that spring. She was kind enough to agree to get together with me and let me pick her brain as soon as our schedules permitted.

Before we could keep that meeting date, another woman in my life, the woman who had the most influence on me and who had taught me to always be kind to others, to strive to be the best I could be and to always treat others as I wanted to be treated, left me. My mother passed away that July after a long bout with cancer.

I put aside my interest in the Klan for a while, and I never did meet my mentor, Patsy Sims. I had assured my skeptical, loving mother, who was always worried about my future, that I would be able to make a living playing music. To fulfill my promise to her, I now focused more and more on my profession and my success grew until I was working around the country with nationally known artists, such as the Muddy Waters' Legendary Blues Band and my idol, Chuck Berry. How I wished she could have been there to see me.

As my musical popularity increased, I began to travel more and spent more time away from Suzie. With the increased popularity came an increase in the attention I received from members of the opposite sex. Although unwarranted, this was a major concern to Suzie, especially when I was traveling alone. I tried to convince her that I loved her and would not forsake her for another. I kept reassuring her we would work things out and soon put aside some quality time to talk about a permanent future together.

However, one night five years into our relationship, something happened that would affect and change our lives forever and bring me back to my quest to explore racism.

3

Under Arrest

On Sunday November 13, 1988, at approximately 1:00
A.M., Suzie and I drove from Potomac to Baltimore, Maryland to
see a friend performing at a local night club. As there were no
available parking spots in the immediate vicinity, I parked my car
on the parking lot of an auto repair establishment. Signs were
posted that parking was for customers of the auto repair establishment, but the repair place was not open at 1:00 A.M. on a
Sunday morning, and we weren't going to be gone more than a
half-hour. I didn't think we'd have a problem.

I've never been more mistaken. When we returned to the car,
I started to unlock the doors when suddenly a tow truck pulled onto
the parking lot near the back of my car. The front of the car was facing a wall. I called out to the driver, "I'm leaving right now." He
ignored me, got out of his vehicle and threw the hooks and chains
onto the ground under the car, but did not attach them. Looking
towards the back of the lot, I saw a police cruiser. Police officers Hal
Roberts and Gayle Hanson walked over to the scene laughing and
introduced themselves. It was apparent that they knew the tow truck
driver. Officer Roberts called out, "What's going on?"

The tow truck driver responded, "Look you know I've got
a job to do, and I'm going to take the car unless the owner pays
$35.00 in cash here and now."

I asked the male officer, "Is there anything you can do?"

Daryl Davis

He gave Suzie and me a sneering look, one we'd seen many times from those who disapproved of interracial relationships and responded, "This is private property and it's not a police matter unless we're summoned by the proprietor, and no one summoned us."

Then the officer turned to me and said, "I suggest you give him $35.00 and get the hell out of here."

Neither Suzie nor I had that amount of money in cash between us at the time. We offered to write a check or use a credit card for the amount so that the tow truck driver would move his truck and let us get on our way. The driver refused to accept either saying, "I want cash."

Roberts gestured toward Suzie and me and whispered something to the female officer. They both laughed. Then he sauntered over to his car and returned, beating his billy club into the palm of his hand while staring at me. Suzie ran to a pay phone, called the number posted on the sign in the parking lot and asked the towing company supervisor to intervene and not have the car towed. He told her that he was not concerned with her dilemma and did not care if she and the man she was with had to spend the night on the street. Then he hung up the phone.

Suzie returned and relayed what was said. Officer Roberts shook his head and said, "That's it, he is taking your car and you either pay him cash or leave the parking lot right now."

I explained to the officer how far away we lived, "Could you give us a ride to a friend's home in Baltimore?"

Roberts first looked at Suzie then at me. Shaking his head he replied, "No, asshole, but I will give you a ride to jail if you don't leave now."

"I'm no asshole but,"—I didn't finish the sentence but I'm sure he knew what I was thinking. I tried to tell him about some valuable contents in my car.

"I warned you motherfucker," snarled Roberts. "Now you're fucked up like all your kind."

He grabbed me, threw me up against my car and hand-cuffed my hands behind my back while the female officer kneed me in the ribs and then called a paddy wagon.

The tow truck driver, looking embarrassed, then told my girlfriend, "Look, if you get the keys to his car, I'll let you take the car for no charge so you can go home or get him out of jail."

When she approached the officers, Hanson said, "Get the hell out of here, White bitch!" Suzie tried to explain what the tow truck driver told her, but Hanson grabbed and handcuffed her as well. When the wagon arrived, officer Dan Donnelly, also White, got out and opened the rear doors.

Roberts yelled, "Get in!" As I stepped up to obey his order, Roberts shoved my leg into the steel bumper causing me to fall in pain. He looked at me lying on the ground and said, "Who's the asshole now motherfucker?"

Suzie and I got in and I said, "You all have no right to treat us like this."

At my words, Officer Donnelly took off his badge and threw it, hitting me in the chest and said, "You think you can do a better job than us, motherfucker? Go ahead, put the badge on!" When I didn't move he added, "I didn't think so."

He shut the doors and drove us downtown. Suzie was dropped off first at the Central Precinct and I was taken to the Southern Precinct. Roberts was already there and continued baiting me, "You feel good now, boy?" He and Donnelly started laughing and began singing the James Brown song, "I Feel Good."

At this point, another officer, Dan Daniels, entered with a person in handcuffs. The officer had blood all over his uniform and his Black arrestee had blood dripping from his head. Roberts addressed the officer, "Did you get hurt or did you do the hurting?"

Daniels replied, "I did the hurting."

Roberts turned to me, smiled and said, "Good, that's what I like to hear."

Next I was fingerprinted, photographed and locked up. I

was never read any rights. For the next twenty-six hours, I was confined to a cell and the guards who were White refused to let me see the commissioner. When I asked to see a doctor about the bruise on my leg and the lump on my head that I had suffered as a result of the violence inflicted upon me by officers Roberts and Hanson, I was refused. The guard, who everyone called "Turnkey," told me, "If you ask one more question, we'll 'lose' your papers and we won't find them for three days."

Finally, I was allowed to see the commissioner, who released me after I told him what happened. I was told that I was not to leave the state and was to call a pre-trial officer once a week until the date of my trial. I suspected that the twenty-six hour wait I'd endured was in hope that my lumps and bruises would have subsided and not be visible to the commissioner when I told him about the beating.

Suzie and I ultimately saw an attorney, and he told us to take a polygraph test administered by a Maryland State Police officer. We both passed with flying colors. Our lawyer then presented these results to the district attorney.

On the day of the trial, Suzie and I went to the district court. A few minutes before the case began, Todd Gordon, the acting prosecutor, offered to "nolle pros" the case and expunge our arrest records if we signed an agreement not to sue the police. Suzie and I told him that we would not agree to the part about not suing the police. So we had to stand trial. We were charged with "Disorderly Conduct" because we had failed to obey an order from the police to leave the parking lot. We both pled "Not Guilty."

The police officers got on the stand, raised their right hands and took the oath to "tell the truth and nothing but the truth so help me God." Needless to say, their versions of the truth conflicted with our very brutal, very real memories of what had actually happened to us.

The Honorable Judge Kenneth Johnson found us "Not Guilty."

Even though our arrest records would be expunged, neither Suzie nor I would ever forget that traumatic night or its consequences. Although she and I will always love one another, this was the final blow to our relationship.

During the five years we were together, Suzie had come as close as a White person could to realizing what it was like to walk in a Black person's shoes. Now she had come even closer. So close that she realized that she didn't want to live this way; that she was not strong enough to live in a world where a large portion of society ostracizes one for his or her skin color or the skin color of the company one keeps. Although the decision pained me greatly, I understood. Though we split up, we remained the best of friends. She has vowed to fight racism however she can from her side of the fence. She has kept her promise.

By 1991, three years after our false arrests on trumped up charges, I was still trying to get the Baltimore police to receive my complaint and conduct an investigation. They still refused.

When I went to get copies of Suzie's and my polygraph tests which proved that we had not lied about the three Baltimore City police officers who had been racially and physically abusive, both tests had mysteriously vanished from the files. For a while, I had been thinking that I would continue my studies of prejudice by travelling to the Deep South where I'd been taught the deepest roots of racism lay. However, my own and Suzie's savage experience at the hands of the police in our home state quickly changed my mind. Bigotry and hate existed everywhere. It was then that I knew this was the time and the place to revive my quest to search out the foundation of prejudice.

4

The Phone Call

It was now the summer of 1991. One night I turned on the television to see a news report on the Ku Klux Klan in Maryland. Grand Dragon Roger Kelly was addressing his group at a Klan rally. Dressed in a conservative suit and tie, he looked like an average businessman, but after listening to his inflammatory remarks, I pictured him dressed in a white robe and hood. I decided he would be the first Klan leader I met with. The question was how to arrange it.

As possible scenarios swirled through my mind, I remembered that in 1983 at the Silver Dollar Lounge, I had met Frank Mara, a 300-pound, likeable, jovial person and became friends with him and his wife, Janet. Although looks-wise and talent-wise he didn't come close, he fancied himself as the next Elvis Presley and would always try to sing "Heartbreak Hotel" and Carl Perkins' "Blue Suede Shoes."

Janet had called me one evening when they had only been married a couple of years. They met each other while attending a World Federation Wrestling event in Largo, Maryland. Watching wrestling was Frank's favorite pastime next to eating and singing. I could tell by the tone of her voice, she was very upset.

"What's wrong?" I asked.

"I don't know how to tell you this. You are not going to believe it. I can't believe it. Frank's joining the Ku Klux Klan."

"What?" I exclaimed. "Put him on the phone."

"He's not here," she said, "He went to the store, but he'll be back soon."

"I'll call him back. No better yet, I'm coming right over. Don't let him go anywhere else when he gets back, and don't tell him I'm coming over," I insisted.

I jumped in my car and sped to where Janet told me she and Frank were temporarily living. Frank wasn't there yet.

"I'm thinking about leaving him," Janet said tearfully. I tried to talk her out of that.

Frank returned and was surprised, but happy to see me. I got right to the point. "Why the hell are you joining the Ku Klux Klan?" I demanded. "I thought you and I were friends."

Frank assured me that we were still friends and was under the impression that the Klan would not have a problem with his maintaining a friendship with me. He wanted to join the Klan for no other reason than a few Black teenagers in the slum where he lived had thrown a glass bottle at Janet when they were walking down the street. They were not injured as the glass exploded a few feet from them. However, he said Janet was pretty shook up. That was when he decided, "I'm gonna join the Klan and get them to come and teach those Blacks a lesson by kicking some ass."

It took me the next three hours to convince Frank that joining an organization that has a problem with an entire race of people, just to get a few asses kicked, was definitely the wrong solution. I volunteered to go with him to these teenagers and talk with them on his behalf, to try and resolve whatever problem they were having and quell Janet's fears. "If it becomes necessary with these teenage hoodlums, I can and will do some ass-kicking myself," I promised.

I finally persuaded him to rethink his Klan idea. He agreed and handed me his application and a Klansman's business card. The name on it was Sam Royer, the Grand Dragon of the State of Maryland.

"Frank, how'd you come to acquire this stuff?" He said that he had met the Grand Dragon, who personally gave him the card and application and was interested in "helping him out."

When I asked Frank when he'd met the Grand Dragon, he replied, "Oh, one night when he was hanging out at my old stomping grounds, the Turf Club in Laurel, Maryland."

About a year or so later, Frank and Janet moved and I lost track of them. Then one day I ran into Ted, a mutual friend who told me he had heard that Frank had joined the Klan. I tried to explain to Ted, that what he had heard occurred years before. "I talked Frank out of it."

Ted shook his head and told me, "Frank joined recently after Janet left him."

Both events were shocking to me. I knew Frank had depended upon, as well as loved Janet. "He must be devastated," I observed.

"Maybe that's what caused him to join," Ted shrugged.

I asked for Frank's phone number. "He doesn't have a phone number, but I can give you the address where he's living."

The next day I went there. There was no answer to my knock on the door. I returned that evening and knocked again. This time Frank was home.

"Daryl! What are you doing here? How did you know where I lived?" He asked not able to hide his surprise.

Ignoring all his questions, I pushed by him and stepped into his apartment. He immediately stuck his head out the door, searching up and down the hallway. I didn't know if he was trying to see if anyone was with me or if anyone saw me enter the apartment. I didn't care.

"What's this I hear that you've joined the Klan?" I demanded to his face.

"How did you hear that?" he asked embarrassed but not denying it.

"So it's true. I also hear Janet left you for somebody else," I said.

"Yeah, she did," he said sadly. "That's over and I've quit the Klan."

"Oh, yeah," I said. "Give me your robe."

"I don't have it. The Klan came and got it. I didn't own it. I was renting the costume."

For some reason, this struck me as funny, and I started laughing. His face turned beet red.

"Well, I didn't have the money to buy one, and didn't you rent tuxedos for formal gigs before you could afford one?"

"Of course I did," I said and felt badly for laughing at him, but renting a Klan robe was still funny.

He went into his bedroom and came back with a Klan belt buckle and lapel pin saying, "Here, you can have these. The only thing I have left from the robe is the mask to the hood. I had misplaced it when they came to get the robe. I can't give it to you," he said showing it to me. "They told me I better find it and give it back or pay for it or I would be in serious trouble."

Frank told me that he had quit the Klan because he did not feel they upheld the Christian principles he now lived by and that they had lied about being a Christian organization.

Later I heard the other side of the story from those Klan members who repossessed Frank's robe. According to the members, Frank had been selected by this particular Klan faction to represent Maryland at the national annual Labor Day rally in Stone Mountain, Georgia. It is one of the biggest gatherings of Klan members from all over the country. Money was taken from the Maryland Klan treasury and given to Frank to fund his weekend trip. When Frank returned from Stone Mountain, he gave a

false report as to what went on at this national Klonvocation—
Klan terminology for "convention." The Klan members discovered that Frank had not gone to Georgia. Instead he spent the
money on going to watch local wrestling. That was, they said,
when they banished Frank and revoked his membership.

At any rate, according to Frank, when he joined the Klan
this time Sam Royer was no longer Grand Dragon for Maryland.
It was Roger Kelly, the man I saw on television; the man I wanted
to meet and talk with.

We sat at the kitchen table, drinking sodas. Frank was
relaxed by now and told me he knew the current Grand Dragon,
Roger Kelly, very well. He boasted, "I've been in his home on
many occasions and attended the meetings every month in
Kelly's basement."

I leaned closer, "I want to meet him."

"Why the hell do you want to do that. Are you crazy? I
won't have no part of it."

I wasn't sure if he was fearful for himself or fearful for me.
But he made it clear, I was on my own. I asked Frank to let me
have the mask and tell me where to find Mr. Kelly and I would
return it for him. Frank declined and looked at me as though I was
nuts. However, he did disclose where the Grand Dragon lived and
where he hung out with the other Klan members.

"In Thurmont, Maryland, not far from Camp David, the
Presidential retreat, there's a restaurant and bar called the Texas
Lunch. It's known as the local Klan bar. You can find Roger and
local Klan members there every Saturday night and most others.
When you first walk in the joint, the first two booths to the left
are reserved for the Klan."

As I said goodnight to Frank, he offered some words of
warning.

"Daryl, don't go there. Kelly will never speak with you,
and if you show up at his house, he will likely shoot you." Frank
added, "He keeps a gun by the front door."

Daryl Davis

Instead of deterring me, Frank's words stimulated my fascination even more. If I was to begin my quest in my home state, I just had to meet Roger Kelly.

At almost the same time as I was trying to find out how to get to Kelly, my musical career was advancing. In addition to working with national music acts, I was concentrating on establishing my own Daryl Davis Band. Luckily, I was achieving a good deal of success. So much so, that I had to hire a personal secretary to handle my bookings, accounting, fan mail list promotions and other things pertaining to the music business.

That night, I played a gig, and afterwards I asked a fan of mine, Mary Barber, a tall, attractive blond-haired woman in her late forties who usually attended my local performances, if she knew someone who might be interested in working for me as a secretary/manager. "I would prefer experience, but I'll train someone without any as long as they'll be dedicated and reliable," I said.

Mary smiled, "I don't know anyone, but I want the job and I'm trainable."

I hired her. She still works for me to this day.

Among her many good qualities is Mary's willingness to take on any task put before her. This was especially meaningful when I explained my long-term mission to find out about the roots of racism through getting to know members of the Ku Klux Klan, and that the first person I needed to talk to was Roger Kelly. Mary readily agreed to help me.

To get to know Roger Kelly's history better, I spent some time the next day checking local newspaper files into his criminal background. Among other things, I found out he had been charged with an insignificant offense, "Obstruction of Traffic" in Martinsburg, West Virginia. He was conducting, at the time, what in Klan terminology is called a "roadblock." His members were standing on public sidewalks and streets, handing out Klan literature. Because they remained in the same place longer than the law deemed prudent, it was considered loitering and obstructing the general flow of sidewalk pedestrian traffic. On another occasion, Roger was charged with illegal cross-burning. The fire marshal claimed he was not notified of the Klan rally at which a cross-lighting ceremony was to be conducted. Roger claims he called the fire department after he received a permit to hold the rally. Interestingly enough, the fire marshal who claimed to know nothing about it was videotaped standing at the rally from the moment it started to when it ended with the cross set ablaze. Also noteworthy, is the fact that when Roger was cited by the fire marshal, the torch in his hand used to light the cross had not yet been lit. Roger was granted probation before judgment by the judge. His offenses seemed rather minor to me, and I felt confident I could handle any problem, so I moved ahead with my plans to meet him.

My Saturday nights were booked with my performances, but I had an occasional Sunday off. I called Mary the Sunday after I had spoken with Frank and suggested that we take a ride to Thurmont and visit the Texas Lunch. "Just maybe, Roger Kelly or some of his Klan members will be there." I explained to her it could be dangerous. "I'm not afraid for myself, but it could be especially dangerous if a Black man walks into a Klan bar with a White woman."

Mary replied, "I want to be part of this. When I signed on with you I told you I wanted to be a part of your Klan mission. I haven't changed my mind."

We arrived at the Texas Lunch in the mostly White town of Thurmont about 9 o'clock that Sunday night. Neither Mary nor I was sure what to expect. The game plan was for me to walk in the door first with Mary right behind me. We would then sit together in whatever seats were available and observe the people who sat in the first two booths to the left. According to Frank, they would surely be Klan members. If they didn't approach me, I decided we would approach them.

Daryl Davis

We stepped through the front door into the dark, dank room. The two booths of red leather to the left were empty. I didn't want to just walk up to someone and say, "Hi, are you in the Klan?" An idea occurred to me. I would sit in the first booth to the left. This would certainly bring a Klan member to me. At least so I thought. I took a seat. Nothing happened.

"How about the bar," Mary said. So we got up and sat there.

On the wall was a Confederate Rebel flag and an article with Roger Kelly's picture. I was definitely in the right place . . . or the wrong one, depending on how you want to look at it.

The bartender politely waited on us and the weathered-looking man sitting on the barstool next to me said hello. I took my time drinking my Coke and Mary did the same with her beer. We left about an hour later with no incidents to report. "The Klan must take Sunday nights off," I whispered to her as we walked out the door.

By Monday morning when Mary arrived for work, I'd decided to take the direct approach. I asked her to phone Roger Kelly for me and request an interview. A few minutes later, she was back.

"I called him. He didn't ask and I didn't tell him that you're Black." He had granted her request and even invited me to his house.

PART II

TALES OF THE DRAGONS

5

Roger Kelly, Grand Dragon

I wanted to go to Roger Kelly's house on the day agreed upon, but a conflict came up when I had to go to a meeting to set up a future musical performance. In the interest of saving time, I asked Mary to call the Grand Dragon to relocate the meeting to a place between his house and my own. Again, Kelly was agreeable. Our chosen meeting spot was none other then the motel above the Silver Dollar Lounge, in whose parking lot some years prior, I had my altercation with another Klansman.

Feeling a bit nervous, Mary and I checked into the motel room about a half hour early. I had brought some cans of soda for my guest, and Mary went down the hall to fill a container with ice.

At precisely the appointed time, there was a knock on the door. The rooms in this particular motel are situated so that one cannot view the room from the hallway door, but must enter and turn a corner to see the inside. Mary let them in.

A young man dressed in military camouflage fatigues with the Ku Klux Klan insignia, a white cross in a red circle with a red blood drop in the center, on one side of his chest and the initials "KKK" on the other side, entered the room. This was the Grand Knighthawk, bodyguard to the Grand Dragon. Upon seeing me, he stopped short, causing the Grand Dragon, following behind him, to almost bump into his back. I noticed the apprehension in their faces as their eyes quickly scanned the room and darted back to me. I rose from my seat with an extended right hand, walked over to the head of the Ku Klux Klan in Maryland and said, "I'm Daryl Davis, come on in."

He shook my hand and replied, "Roger Kelly."

Walking into the room, he sat down, his Knighthawk standing rigidly on his right.

"Could you show me some form of identification?" he asked me. I showed him my driver's license and presented him with my business card.

Seated across the table from me, dressed in a suit and tie as he had been in the television report I'd seen, Roger Kelly appeared to be a professional businessman. It was hard to conceive that he headed a leading chapter of an organization known throughout history to display a profound hatred for Blacks, Jews and other minorities—an organization known to perpetuate violence through lynchings, murders, bombings, floggings and other atrocities for no other reason than the victim's sexual preference or racial, ethnic or religious background. The only visible sign of his Klansmanship was the cross and blood drop insignia ring on his finger.

I wanted to find out about Kelly's early childhood experiences with the Klan. He spoke of those days readily.

"I became interested in the Ku Klux Klan as a school child. When I watched the rituals, robes and cross burnings, they were extremely fascinating to me."

Like many others in the organization, Roger had a family member who was a Kluxer. In this instance, it was his grandfather who had been a hero to him. He had grown up in the all-White town of Rocky Ridge, Maryland.

While Roger and I sat at the table and talked, the body-guard, whom I later came to know as "Shakey," remained at attention on full alert for anything that might create a danger for his leader. Every time I reached into my bag to pull out a blank cassette or other item I needed, Shakey brought his hand to rest on his gun. Mary and I watched him as closely as he watched us.

Kelly soon began explaining that he was a White Separatist as opposed to a White Supremacist. The Grand Dragon instructed me in the difference between the two. I tried to remain silent and maintain a neutrality as best I could.

"White Supremacy means they think they're better than a certain race. A White Separatist means that he wants to be separate from different races. The only way the different races can show their true potential is apart. The Bible preaches separation of the races. The Bible is the most segregated book in the world. I don't feel that any race is better than another. If I had to say one was better, then I would say the Chinese are the superior race."

With Shakey fingering his gun, I quickly reached into my bag, produced my Bible and asked him to point out where this philosophy could be found. The Grand Dragon paged through the Book and began quoting from Isaiah 13:14: "And it should be as a chased roe, and as a sheep that no man taketh up: they shall every man turn to his own people, and flee every one into his own land."

It appeared to me that Roger Kelly interpreted the last three words of this passage to mean that different people had different lands and they should not traverse into another land. If they do, they must return or "flee" back to their land of origination.

"Somehow this only applies to the Blacks and other minorities, not to the Whites who came here from Europe," I said and he nodded.

The conversation then turned to another topic: the Klan's militant opinions about homosexuality. When I asked Roger what he thought of the homosexual's place in today's society, his words were more but the response was the same one I eventually got from all the members I talked to from various Klans scattered throughout the country.

"They belong under a rock," Roger proclaimed. "I believe that the Bible plainly states that it is God's purpose that the men and women are to be fruitful and multiply. This cannot be accomplished by two men or two women."

This prompted me to ask Roger if he had any children.

"No, I don't," he replied.

"Well," I asked, "Let's say you did have children and your son or daughter turned out to be gay or lesbian, what would you do?"

"I'd disown them!" Roger emotionally avowed, almost before I completed my question. "It all depends on their upbringing, too. It can be in their society, like in New York City. If you want to find a bunch of gays, you go to New York City because the values there are deteriorating a whole lot faster." Then he added, "You know it starts in the inner cities."

As he went on, it was obvious to see that he believed homosexuality, sexual perversion and deviations all began in the inner city where most of the residents are Black. At his implication of the origin of sexual perversion, the thought entered my mind that I have heard about the practice of having sex with sheep being performed on rural country farms where most of the resident farmers are White. *Does this mean that bestiality is a "White thing?"* I wondered, but I didn't convey my question. I held it for later as the time was not right yet.

Roger continued, "I wouldn't go along with gay-bashing, but, I would go along with being harder on gays than I would be on Blacks. I don't believe you bought your skin, but I believe that a gay went out and produced what he is today. You didn't have a say if you were going to be Black or White, but a gay, I believe he could change if he wanted to. It's like being born a racist; everybody says that you're not born a racist, it's bred into you, so how can you be born a homosexual?"

Kelly went on to express his vehement opinions about how society now advocates the promotion of homosexuality into the mainstream.

"It also has to do with our learning pattern. Our government is saying it's okay for a homosexual to come out of the closet. But once you say it's okay to do this, it's like throwing gas on a fire. But, if we were to denounce it and stood up to our children and say, 'Denounce homosexuality,' then our children would learn that. Instead, we put a fag like Pee Wee Herman on the air and our children all look up to him."

As our talk went on and I allowed Roger to freely vent his opinions, his bodyguard eased up on his nervousness and no longer reacted by fingering his gun whenever I placed my hand in the case I'd brought with my notes and other materials.

"Tell me about your feelings on the racial issue," I said, meeting Roger's eyes.

Roger's voice rose, "I feel that the morals and values of society are deteriorating severely."

His opinion seemed similarly strident to those he expressed about homosexuality. The bulk of the blame he believes is the fault of miscegenation.

"I diametrically oppose any form of interracial marriage or race-mixing."

He expressed great concern that the children produced from an interracial union would be mistreated while going through school because they looked different from other "normal" kids.

"So, do you believe the bulk of the problem an interracial child may suffer is the humiliation, taunts and teasing?" I asked. "Or do you think that a child has actually become inferior because his or her race has been defiled one way or the other?"

He scanned my face. "A true Black African-American is even a lot darker than you are. When races mix, skin color changes and this produces a mongrel race. It doesn't matter if it's a woman or a man, they're going to have trouble. The Whites are going to denounce them and the Blacks are going to denounce them. You see that happening today."

Roger leaned towards me. His tone was sober. "In today's society, we're just letting kids run too wild as far as saying it's okay for fourteen or fifteen-year-olds to go out on dates. We're letting them date Blacks. Black people are letting them date Whites, and they're letting them do drugs."

I nodded. "As a musician," I said, "I am exposed to and have never indulged in or advocated the use of drugs. Some of my fans, interestingly enough, mostly those that are White, have tried to bestow everything from alcohol and marijuana to LSD and cocaine, as well as various other barbiturates and narcotics upon me."

Both the Grand Dragon and I are very much opposed to the recreational use of drugs. It was another area on which we could agree. I suggested to him, "Since the drug problem in our country affects all races, would you consider engaging in a joint effort with Blacks and other White non-Klansmembers to try to wipe out this problem that is so common to us all?"

Roger replied, "The United States government could put a stop to illegal drugs if they wanted to by bombing the poppy fields in Asia and South America."

He told me that he had approached the head of the local chapter of the National Association for the Advancement of Colored People about having a parade in which the Klan and the NAACP would march together in an anti-drug crusade through the streets of the local low-income projects to denounce drugs. He said his suggestion was flatly turned down by the NAACP leader. This, according to him, is one of the things that has caused Roger to disrespect the NAACP.

"The NAACP leader would rather sit back and bitch to the government that we need this and that for minorities, but around here, the deterioration of the Black race is being made in those low income projects," Roger complained. "There are three, four, five shootings and arrests there every night. Shootings and drugs. If he really wants to help, send the NAACP in to help advance the colored people. There's little kids in there dealing drugs and stuff, because they can't get caught. Now if he wants to advance his race, the Black race, he ought to be in there with them. I had meetings with another Black activist and a separatist named Robert Brock and the NAACP denounced Brock for doing that and said, 'We shouldn't have any part of the Klan.' A lot of the things they believe in are the same things that I believe in. I am for equal justice in the courtroom for Blacks, Whites and Asians. I believe in hiring people based on their qualifications regardless of their skin color."

In an interesting aside, Kelly told me he was a member of the NAACP for one year during which time his dual role as a Klansman was discovered. The NAACP refused to renew his membership when his term expired. When asked why he joined, Kelly told a *Washington Post* reporter, "I joined them so I could know the enemy." Interestingly, his words mirrored my own early motivation for meeting him and other KKK members.

A couple of years later, the NAACP would also denounce one of their own Black attorneys, Anthony Griffin, who had chosen to represent a Texas Klansman in a Civil Rights case. The Klansman had gone to the American Civil Liberties Union for representation and was shocked when the Black NAACP lawyer, who also worked for the ACLU, accepted the case. While the attorney and his client were at opposite ends of the spectrum regarding their moral beliefs, they were in agreement that the Klansman's rights had been violated.

Roger considers a racist to be a person who is proud of his or her race. He is in agreement with Louis Farrakhan inasmuch as Farrakhan also preaches separation of the races. "I wouldn't call him a racist. I would call him a man who's proud of his race."

He does consider Farrakhan to be prejudiced because he makes no secret of his belief that, "The White man is the Devil."

I told Roger, "It is one thing to be proud of your race and another thing to try to oust another race from this country."

He responded, "If that's the definition of being racist, then the Jews would have to be considered racists for ousting the Palestinians." Being very much opposed to the Jews, he believes that the United States is run by what is referred to as ZOG, Zionist Occupied Government.

Roger claimed that his particular Klan group, The Invincible Empire, advocates separation of the races but not hate and violence like some other Klan groups. He did indicate that he would resort to violence in the event he needed to defend himself in an attack.

Although we disagreed on many topics, everything was now going smoothly and the apprehension we had both felt earlier seemed to be alleviated. Suddenly, a loud clattering noise filled the room! We all jumped. Roger and Shakey cast suspicious stares at me and I returned accusing looks at them. Each of us was wondering what the other party was trying to pull.

Seconds later, Mary discovered the culprit. Some of the ice cubes in the bucket containing the sodas had melted, causing a mini avalanche. Once Mary pointed out what had happened, we all began genuinely laughing at our distrust of each other over nothing. After that, our conversation became increasingly more informal and candid.

I felt that now that Roger had been able to express his views fully, I could slowly begin to reveal my own.

I asked him, "Why do you want to be associated with a name like the "Ku Klux Klan" when it has been responsible for an infinite number of murders, beatings, bombings, burnings and other violent atrocities committed against Blacks and other minorities?"

He stressed, "No matter what name my organization could choose, the Klan stigma would always be attached, much like the

Klan stigma which haunts David Duke in all of his political endeavors."

It continually bothered him, he said, that organizations geared toward the promotion of Blacks, such as the Black Miss America Pageant, the Black Coalition of State Troopers and others, are allowed to exist unharassed. He argued that if there were a White Miss America Pageant or a White Coalition of State Troopers, there would be a stream of protests and allegations of racism.

I pointed out to him that had Black women been treated fairly in the first place, they would not need their own pageant.

Roger responded by saying, "There has now been more than one Miss America who was Black, starting with Vanessa Williams." I asked him whether or not he thought Ms. Williams was selected the winner because she is Black or because she is pretty or for other assets.

"I don't know. I can't really be honest with somebody and look at somebody that's Black and say, 'Oh, they're beautiful.' But a Black person could," said Roger.

In discussing affirmative action, Roger said he resented being forced to hire a Black or an Asian and cited the fact that one does not find Chinese people being forced to hire an American to work in the kitchen of a Chinese restaurant and that the Chinese prefer it that way.

I said, "If I chose to eat in a Chinese restaurant, I would hope that an American would not be doing the cooking because I would want authentic Chinese food prepared as close to the Chinese way as possible."

Roger replied smiling, "If these are your feelings, you are, therefore, a segregationist."

Chuckling, I replied, "I never really thought about it that way nor have I ever considered myself to be a segregationist. However, I guess to a degree there is some merit in what you say. It would be similar to the thought that a Black person cannot do

Daryl Davis

an authentic job playing Country and Western music, nor could a White person duplicate the feel of the Blues. As a musician, I can assure you that those notions are not true at all. While they may be few and far between, there are a number of Blacks who can perform Country and a number of Whites who can play the Blues. There are quite a few White singers who cannot sing Country and not every Black singer can sing the Blues. Stereotyping people in my estimation doesn't do justice to our capabilities to stretch beyond narrow limits into the self we could be."

Then we began to speak of another subject which I find puzzling. "After the resurrection of the Klan in 1915, only White Anglo-Saxon Protestants were accepted as members. In addition to persecuting the Blacks, this new Klan now persecuted Jews and Catholics. The Jews were frowned upon by the Klan for not believing in Jesus Christ, but I don't understand why Catholics were no longer accepted until the late Sixties."

Roger explained to me his view of this part of Klan history. "Catholics, back then, would have to confess their sins and everything they've done at nighttime to the priest, and there was no lying. There probably was night-riding back then in the Twenties and Thirties and things like that. But it wasn't only on Blacks. It was on child-molesters, wife-beaters and anybody that was against society itself. It wasn't just anti-Black like the press leads you to believe. Catholics didn't want to do something like that and then confess their sins to the priest the next day. It just wasn't kosher, you know?"

"Funny you should use that term." I smiled, but he didn't get the irony that he had appropriated a Jewish term. Then I asked, "Why are American-Indians accepted in some Klan groups today?"

It is a well known fact that Catholics and Jews were members of the original Ku Klux Klan in the latter 1800's. It is a very little known fact that today many Klan groups now accept Native American-Indians as Klanmembers. I never would have believed that members of a race of people whose culture was all but destroyed by White men who murdered them, stole their land and forced them to live on reservations, would ever join the Ku Klux Klan. I have now seen some Native American-Indian Klanmembers with my own eyes.

"We're allowing that because they're Americans," said Roger with a ring to his voice. "When the White man came here, he set the cornerstone and formed a government. He made what the United States is today. He has a Constitution, he has a Bill of Rights, he has a system that works.

"The Indians came here or migrated down from the Eskimos, that's how they got here. Not to run the Indians down or anything, because we do have Indians in the Klan, but there was no cornerstone for a government, there was no Bill of Rights, there was no Constitution, there was no government whatsoever. In other words, they had their tribe set up and that was it."

After that, the Grand Dragon went on to explain to me why he believes Blacks did not reap the benefit of these "great things" the White man shared, however unequally, with the Native American-Indians.

"When the Blacks came here, they didn't come here through Ellis Island, they came here as slaves to do a job and that job's been finished for over fifty years now."

I wanted to tell him that I sometimes wonder about that— some people in this country still treat minorities as though they were slaves—but I remained quiet, letting him continue.

"If I brought you as a slave into my house and then the government says I can't have slaves anymore and I open my door up, would you leave or would you stick around for a little longer? Chances are, if it were me and you opened the door, I'd get out. I wouldn't hang around and say, 'I like it here, I'm going to stay here a little longer.'"

"But Roger," I asserted, "slavery went on in this country for several hundred years. So, the homeland is detached. After generations, the only thing Blacks knew as home, regardless of their treatment, was this country. Why would they just get up and leave?"

"Say Africa is my homeland, that's where I would go. That's my culture. Those are my roots. I would want to bring my kids up in the African race and stuff like that."

Although I disagreed with things Roger had previously said, this was the first time I stopped him while he was speaking to debate a point rather than let him go on unchallenged. "Your forefathers came over here from Europe because of their being persecuted by the king. They were not allowed to worship the way they wanted or to have free enterprise. Most of their money went towards paying the king. So they came over here to this land of free enterprise and opportunity and freedom of religion. Yet, once they got here, they persecuted the people who were already here, like the Indians. Then, they persecuted the Blacks, Orientals, Hispanics and other minorities. Your last name is Kelly. Are you Irish?"

"Yes, I am," he proclaimed proudly, "but I'm curious as to what you are driving at."

"Since all of these different races are here, and there are not a lot of Blacks in Ireland, why don't you pack up and go back to Ireland?" I attacked using his rationale.

"But, see, I didn't come over here as a slave to do a job," he countered.

"Have you forgotten how badly the Irish were treated in this country at a time when they were used to build railroads? At that time, they were being called indentured servants. In fact, they were only a low cut above slaves, sometimes called serfs."

Roger continually gave me examples of how different people naturally segregate themselves. He noted how motorcycle bikers, young people, old people, hippies, rich and poor, all tend to hang with 'their own kind.'

However, he did not mention that, while this may often be the case, the reason these groups may hang around together is because they share the same interests, financial status or other commonalties. I personally do not believe that race is always the overriding factor that determines with which groups people will affiliate themselves. In my estimation, people of different colors or backgrounds sometimes associate with one another because of their shared common interests and economic class. This may result in groups that are integrated.

I had asked Mary to have Roger bring a particular tee shirt for me which he'd mentioned in the broadcast on which I'd heard him speak. He produced the tee shirt from a briefcase that also contained his robe and hood. The shirt depicts a rifle target with the bull's eye centered on the forehead of Martin Luther King, Jr. The caption reads, "Our dream came true!"

"The only size I have is 3–X. Will that fit you?" asked Roger, seeming genuinely concerned whether he had brought the right size for me. "Oh, I doubt that you will wear it," he quickly added, realizing that he had momentarily forgotten that he was speaking with a Black man.

"No, I'm not going to wear it. It's just for my research," I said, while memories of the day Dr. King died flooded my mind, and I watched him closely. "To me, that's a violent tee shirt." I tried to keep my voice calm so that I could continue to learn his feelings.

"What's violent about it?" he demanded. "We consider him a Communist, and the United States sent millions of people overseas to kill Communists, but we have Communists in our own society. We actually believe he was a Communist whether he was Black or White. We're not saying because he's Black he's a Communist."

"What did he do that was Communistic?" I prodded. "Communists advocate a dictatorship in which people have been known to be executed if they do not agree with and abide by their government's policies. Reverend Martin Luther King, Jr. never preached that kind of thing."

Roger retorted, "I believe that a man who has never really had a job—and you might even say, like Jesse Jackson—you have to wonder about a man like that. He's worth millions of dollars. Where's he getting that money if he ain't dealing drugs or isn't a Communist? I think Martin Luther King was paid by the Communists to disrupt the United States from within."

Anger smoldered beneath the surface as he continued. "When I was a kid, I remember coming home and watching the race riots and they were always attributed to Martin Luther King. They say he gave a speech in Selma, Alabama, and it wasn't long after that a riot broke out. He came to Cambridge, Massachusetts, and there was a riot. It just seemed uprisings followed him."

I shot back, "What about when the Imperial Wizard Virgil Griffin of the Christian Knights of the KKK came to Washington, D.C., in 1990, and back in 1982 when Imperial Wizard Don Black of the National Knights of the KKK came and riots broke out? Cars got turned over, people got hurt and the National Guard had to be called in."

"Yeah, but I didn't see robes turning cars over or throwing rocks through the windshields," the Grand Dragon defended his views. "If one is going to decry violence, I believe one cannot perpetrate it." His face clouded.

"The anti-Klan crowd was made up of mostly Blacks and some Whites. Many of these protestors resorted to violence directed at the Klan, the police protecting them and any governmental property, including cars and buildings."

Roger took a deep breath and continued, "It seems to me, a lot of these Blacks today want equal rights, but they want them for themselves."

I still would not let the Klan off the hook. Making sure he acknowledged their violence, I asked, "How about the Freedom Riders back in the Sixties? The Klan was in collusion with the police department. When the bus pulled into the Birmingham, Alabama bus station, the Klansmen were allowed fifteen minutes by the chief of police to knock heads and commit violence."

"It's like in the Twenties, there were some cops in the Klan and there are some today," said Roger.

Though I tried to probe, Roger did not exactly address the issue of whether he considered this to be violence on the part of the Klansmen or "robes" as he sometimes refers to them. He did, however, admit that Klansmen have committed acts of violence against Blacks, but in the same sentence he stressed that his particular organization does not advocate violence against anyone of any race unless it is provoked and his Klansmen are forced to defend themselves.

"Roger, do you see the different races being able to get along with one another in the future and co-existing without any strife?"

"There are a lot of different ways that can be done," he said slowly. "Richard Butler of the Aryan Nations wants five different states out there for Whites," Roger told me, referring to the notion of dividing up the United States and designating certain states for Blacks, certain states for Whites and certain states for other races. The Grand Dragon offered his own solution.

"We could have a three-tier society: a Black school, a White school and a mixed school. If a guy owns a liquor store and he's Black and he says, 'No Whites in here,' he should have that prerogative. If I owned a liquor store and I didn't want Blacks or Asians coming in, I should have the same prerogative. But, we're being forced, and you can't force people to do something and we're being forced to do this thing."

Our talk was winding down, and I thanked Roger Kelly for his time. Then I asked if he would don his hood and robe and pose for some pictures. He agreed.

While Mary got the camera out, I watched Roger put on his robe and hood. He stood proudly in front of the mirror while his bodyguard made sure that his cape, belt and pointed headpiece were adjusted straight. I could not help feeling an array of emotions as I witnessed this ceremony.

Daryl Davis

These emotions were anger, bitterness, hurt and sympathy. I felt angry about all the violent atrocities that have been committed against my forefathers, family and race by people who wore similar robes. I wondered if Roger, who I found to be genuine, knew how bitter and hurt I felt that he, a person I was beginning to like, would associate himself with an organization that had perpetuated such dastardly behavior. I felt sorry that he never had the opportunity to experience as many different cultures as I have, thus learning of their wide variety of attributes and allowing me to accept them unconditionally as I would a member of my own race whose intentions were not detrimental to me.

The realization came to me that in view of my strong feelings and race, many people would find it hard to believe that I was calmly discussing racism with, not only a Klansman, but a Grand Dragon. After explaining this to Roger and telling him I hoped the fact that we had been able to share our ideas was a good omen for the future, I asked, "Would you mind if we posed for some pictures together?"

"Okay, but we don't have to stand with our arms around each other, do we?" he asked half-jokingly and half-concerned. I assured him that we did not have to do the arm thing.

We had our pictures taken, agreed to keep in touch and shook hands. Shakey, the Grand Knighthawk, who was wearing gloves the entire time removed the glove on his right hand and extended his hand to shake mine. For some reason, I remembered the diplomat I'd met as a child who hadn't liked shaking a Black man's hand, but I did not see them wipe their hands off and so I put aside the thought.

Then I accompanied them to the door. Afterward, I went back and sat in my chair to reflect upon what had just taken place. A Black man with a White woman meeting with the Grand Dragon of the Ku Klux Klan and his bodyguard in a truck stop motel room for two hours seemed inconceivable based on what I had heard and personally knew about the Klan. I went looking for a violent man who hates people for no other reason than the difference of skin color. This quest failed. Roger Kelly does not hate, nor is he a violent man. Roger Kelly is a very opinionated man. Expecting to find that Roger Kelly and I had absolutely nothing in common, we found ourselves having some of the same concerns and sharing some of the same opinions. We disagreed on many things and saw humor in others, causing us both to laugh, thus proving that a Black man and a Klansman can stand on common ground, if only momentarily.

After our meeting, I called several of my friends who had been genuinely concerned about my safety to assure them that I was fine and had not been lynched or attacked by the Grand Dragon of the Klan, as some had thought I might be. When I woke up the next morning, no cross had been burned on my lawn. A couple of weeks later, I stopped by Frank's home and told him that I had met with his former leader. He looked at me as though I was joking until I produced the photograph of Roger and me together. Then he said nervously, "You didn't mention my name, did you?" After reassuring him of our confidentiality, I asked him if Roger had ever done or said anything of a violent nature that would cause Frank to be fearful of his safety.

"I can't think of anything," Frank said, "except to say that if Roger was cornered he would most likely fight with whatever weapon was available."

"That would be no different from the reaction that I would have if I was cornered," I said, adding, "depending upon the extent of personal danger I perceived." Saying it, I was struck by the similarity of our views on physically defending oneself. It gave me pause for even greater reflection.

A short time later, I sent Roger several articles to read on a North Carolina Klansman who had quit the organization. I wanted to see if they would have any influence on him. He phoned me to let me know he had received the articles and had read them. "In fact, I already had one of them."

When I questioned him about what he thought about this man's transformation, I was not prepared for his answer. Roger said that the man had joined the Klan for the wrong reason, that he had joined out of hatred. "Anyone who hates has no business being in the Klan." In the light of history, it was a difficult premise to accept.

I questioned incidents of Klan atrocities stemming from the hatred of members of the Klan. He reminded me that not all Klans agree with each other and that there is good and bad in any and every group of people regardless of their color or beliefs. Roger professed not to be a hater of other races, but a lover of his own and said that the Klan should want to keep the White race pure through separation of the races not through the destruction of other races.

Shortly after our talk, Roger was voted the Imperial Wizard for the Invincible Empire Knights of the Ku Klux Klan.

6

Searching for the Stereotype

After my discussions with Roger Kelly, the current Imperial Wizard of one of the largest KKK factions, my motivation to seek out other Klan leaders was renewed. I wanted to learn more of the Grand Dragons who reigned during the racially turbulent Sixties and Seventies and whose members showed violent opposition to the Civil Rights movement. To do this, I located one. His name was Vernon Naimaster, former Grand Dragon of the United Klans of America under the Imperial Wizard, Bobby Shelton. In the Civil Rights era, members of his organizations, according to the news media I reviewed, had been charged and imprisoned for, among other things, cross burnings on the lawns of Blacks, the attempted bombings of the Baltimore NAACP office, the attempted bombing of a local Jewish synagogue, the making of death threats to Coretta Scott King, widow of Martin Luther King, Jr. and the attempted murder of two Black men.

During his tenure in the Klan, Vernon once addressed a Klan rally saying, "Before the Blacks take over this country, there's going to be an awful lot of bloodshed. I hope to God this won't happen. But, I'm gonna keep fighting. The only thing that is gonna stop me is a bullet."

Once again, my secretary Mary made the call and there was no mention of my skin color. Like Roger Kelly, Naimaster was affable to accommodating me and invited me to his home.

As Mary and I approached the house, a White boy, maybe sixteen-years-old, was leaving. He appeared to either live there or was a family member. We passed each other at the gate separating the front yard from the sidewalk. He never gave me a second look. Didn't he think it odd that a Black man was coming to this place? I wondered if I was at the right house; the house of a man who was a Klan leader during some racially troubled times. Indeed, I was at the right house and Vernon, who answered the door making no mention of my race, invited Mary and me into his living room.

We sat on the couch and began to talk.

Unlike many Klanmembers, Vernon did not have any family members to his knowledge who were already in the KKK prior to his joining nor did he have any children who joined. He joined the United Klans of America under Imperial Wizard Robert Shelton in the Sixties.

"I joined because of the various things that I had read and heard about it," he explained. "These were things which I agreed with. Of course, after I joined, I found that a lot of people just wanted to get in there just to go out and do as they pleased, which wasn't really a part of the policies of the organization. But, nevertheless, you still got them. It's like anything else, the police department and government. You got people in there that are not worthy of their positions.

"It seemed to me that the whole country was going to the dogs, instead of building itself and keep its morals and standards the way it worked and made it as great as it was. The government kept passing policies that weren't sound or sensible, changing one way of life to another way of life, forcing people to accept things that weren't constitutional. It seemed to me that the Klan was the only organization that was really working to overcome some of those problems that were around at that time."

When it was discovered that Vernon was the Grand Dragon for the Maryland Chapter of the UKA, the NAACP brought pressure on the company which employed him as a Baltimore city bus driver. Naimaster was fired from his job for being a Klansman. Surprisingly, while many Blacks protested his being employed by the Baltimore bus company, many Black co-workers supported him and protested his firing.

"Your tenure in the Klan was during the height of the Civil Rights movement. These were some very turbulent times. Did you participate in and advocate night-riding?"

"Oh, no. I never advocated that kind of business," Vernon claimed. "The Klan was more or less a political thing, to take a stand—the different laws they was passing, the different Liberal candidates that was going out and changing the American Freedom ways to the Communistic or Socialistic ways as they called it at that time, which was just another name for Communism as far as I'm concerned. That's my opinion. The world today is far different than it was sixty or eighty years ago. There's no comparison."

I leaned towards him, but kept my tone friendly. "You advocate changing things politically like what David Duke is doing by running for office?" I asked.

He nodded. "That's exactly right. During my time, Governor George Wallace was pretty famous, and naturally all the Right-Wing Conservative organizations were pretty strong for Wallace," he told me.

"Was Wallace a Klansman, a secret Klansman or just a Klan supporter?" I asked, noting that during that time many government officials were silent members.

He pondered my question silently for several seconds before answering. "Well, I can't say one way or the other, but I know he wasn't that much against them. Then again, all the people liked him in that state, both Blacks and Whites. In fact, they loved him and they loved his wife. I don't know for a fact that he was, but if I was to take a bet, I would probably bet that he was a member."

Curious as to what makes a Klansman leave the organization, I asked him why he quit. Although he is no longer active in the KKK, he does not denounce it and claims that in his heart he still believes in the basic principles of Klankraft.

"I got out in 1972. I got tired of all the hassles and all the controversial problems being created within the organization. Too many people were getting in there with their own ideas. You get this one starting a chapter over here and that one starting a chapter over there. They bring in people you don't know and they verify that they are great people, and they are not. You find out that they go out and do cruel and damaging things that will bring the blood down on your hands.

"So, I just got tired of that and said the heck with it, I won't have any more to do with it. Not that I disagree with the basic foundation of the Klan, because I do agree with it, working politically to solve problems. Not that you can solve them all, but you can work politically to try. Like I say, I don't have any disagreements with what it stands for. I have disagreements with some of the things taking place, some of the violent acts."

I asked Vernon if he knew his successor, Tony LaRicci, which he said he did. "Do you think Tony LaRicci and his group handled things properly?"

"No, they were rabble rousers, too. That's why it went the direction it went. That was another reason I decided to leave because I didn't agree with what they wanted to do, and I wouldn't let them do it. Then, of course, you know how things go. They start undermining you and they work behind your back and you don't know. Before long you've got more problems than you want to handle or that you care to handle. So the best thing to do is leave them go in their direction, you go in yours and everything's solved.

"In my mind, the Klan will always be. The only thing the law and its representatives are doing is keeping it underground. It might not be as wealthy today as it was twenty years ago, but it will become wealthy if the country keeps going in the direction it's going now. This trend that the country is in now may last twenty-five years, but you see the problem with people is, once they get a foothold, that's not enough. Instead of carrying the thing on an even keel, they want to keep going and taking and grabbing. It's greed, and the next thing you know they got people in a corner and that's when things will start changing again."

I wondered, out loud, had the Freedom Rides and sit-ins of the Sixties not taken place, would Vernon think that today? In the Nineties, would Blacks be able to ride in the front of the bus or eat in all-White restaurants? Vernon had some definite opinions about these subjects.

"That was a legit complaint, but the Civil Rights activists didn't stop there. They're out now to take control of the country. Also, I never agreed back then and I don't agree today that certain people have to ride in the back of the bus, or something of that nature, whereby others could ride in the front. To me, if you pay your fare, get on there, mind your own business and do what you're supposed to. I don't care if you're black, green, yellow, purple or whatever. It doesn't make any difference to me."

Vernon tried to convince me that the main focus of the Klan during his tenure was stopping forced integration. He felt strongly that his rights, one by one, were being taken away from him by the government. He also felt strongly that restaurateurs and homeowners should be able to serve and sell or rent to whomever they chose. Vernon went on to tell me how, in his opinion, without pressure or force, he grew up accepting and playing with Black children. Problems did not occur until he was forced to associate with them.

"All my life we lived and played together, me and the

black kids. Their house was ten feet from my house. We played together, we fought together, called each other names and there was nothing to it. We went to their house, we slept in their house, they slept in ours and we ate at each other's table. They were decent people. But when you get these trashy Whites and trashy Blacks—and that's what they are in my mind—and they're out there tearing up things, destroying things, you throw them in a pen somewhere and keep them out of society. They're not worthy. You don't mind the decent ones coming into your area and associating with them. But you don't have that choice. The decent ones will not come into an area such as this. It's only the rabble rousers and the ones who want to live like animals. I'm not talking strictly Blacks, but Whites also.

"It seems to me that there are certain people right now that are trying to live an animal way of life instead of a human way of life in the things they do. The high-class Blacks will not move into areas like this. They will move into some highfalutin' area. Naturally, they want to be as good as you are, or better, and there is no problem with that. But, when you are forced to live among trash that you don't want to live among, then there is a problem. If you are forced to sell your house to a bunch of trash that you know is going to cause problems in a neighborhood, then there is a problem and it is going to continue to be a problem."

I wanted to retrace our verbal steps and return to the subject of the Civil Rights years to understand his perspective of that era. "Do I understand you to say that back in the Sixties when you were a Klan leader, integration was the issue. However, it wasn't that you were so much against integration as you were against the way it was being forced upon you?"

"That's right, that's exactly right," Vernon reiterated. "Back then everybody had a right to be free and do as he seen fit and be responsible for his own actions as long as he stayed within the boundary of the decent laws. That freedom was all taken away. Today, there is no freedom. You hear all this hugaballoo on television and newspapers about America's freedom? Tell me something that is free! You can't name one thing that's free. The air is about the only thing you can name me that's free in this country.

"Anything you do, you got to get a permit or permission to do it. Even if you want to put a new window in your house you got to get a permission slip from the zoning board or something to put that window in there. Nothing you can do, nothing, is free in this country. I'll go so far to say that in the next twenty years, they'll put a meter on you and put something in your mouth to monitor the amount of air you breathe, then charge or tax you for that.

"Let's face it, when I was a kid there was freedom. If you wanted to go hunting, then you just went hunting. If you wanted to go fishing, you went fishing. You didn't have to worry about all these restrictions and all these licenses and taxations. If you bought a car you only paid tax on it once. You want to sell it, just sell it. You put up a shanty or chicken house in your yard, you could do it. Try it today and see what they do. If you wanted fifteen dogs then you could have fifteen dogs. Man, that was freedom. Today they tell you where you can and where you can't smoke. These non-smokers can force their way upon you. How would they feel if we smokers forced them to smoke?" he asked as he puffed away on his pipe.

Wanting to test whether or not Vernon practiced what he preached in respect to his past association with Blacks by his own choosing and not being forced by the government, I questioned him, "Do you think thirty years ago I would have been able to sit here in your house and talk to you like we are talking now?"

"I know fifty years ago you could sit in my house! In fact, you could have ate at our dinner table if you'd have wanted to! There wouldn't have been a damn thing said about it. I've got people all over this state that are very acceptable and agreeable with me. Again, I have friends that disagree on some things but that's human life. I mean that everything you agree with, I may not. Everything you disagree with, I may not. That's what makes life interesting and keeps the thing rolling."

I asked Vernon if he had his way, how would he have approached the integration/segregation issue.

"Like I say, you've got to politically fight things in a decent, understandable way. You can't just go out there and say, 'If you don't do this, we're going to destroy you.' You don't do that kind of business or threaten people, that's not the proper way to do it. That's not the human way of life. The human way of life is to work politically or sensibly toward things. Now, there are times when you may have to defend yourself and if you have to get violent to defend yourself, then you get violent. But, only when it's necessary, is the way I look at it. If I walk out of this house and someone hits me in the mouth, I'm going to hit him back. That's just as plain as it can be. Again, if someone comes on my property and starts messing up my stuff, I don't have the right, but I'm going to bust him upside the head anyhow, whether I have that right or not because he ain't got no business being here. Then they'll haul me off to jail and lock me up and probably let him go, but I'm going to do it anyhow. That's why I couldn't accept it being shoved down my throat. If I didn't want you here, I'd say, 'No' and if you tried to force your way here, then we're going to have a problem. The same thing with you, if I asked to come to your place and you said, 'No, I don't want you here,' and I try to force my way in, then you'd have a problem. We'd both have a problem again."

I nodded. "I understand, but have your views changed over the last thirty years, and if so, in what direction?"

Vernon took a couple of drags from his pipe, pausing before answering. "I would say they may have changed…a little…damn little. The little I'm talking about is, there has been some good coming in from the other side, this Liberalism thing.

Many things have come up. For instance, there have been programs that have been started because of the force of the liberalization of things that is helpful to people, including me, if I wish to use them. The prisons are one, for example.

"When I was a kid, the authorities would take you in the prison and beat the hell out of you for no reason at all and then they'd say that you attacked them. These liberalized programs have brought up policies and laws that allow you to write your complaint and call a lawyer. Prisoners' rights."

Having read about the incident in which the NAACP had caused Vernon to be fired from his job as a Baltimore city bus driver when it was found out that he was a Klan leader, I asked him to tell me the story from his perspective.

"The basis was that the NAACP didn't like the idea of me being in the Klan. That was not the case with the Blacks working with me or the ones I was working with. They were all in favor of me working. There was one of the biggest Black rallies to support me that Maryland has ever seen. You didn't see that on the news either, incidentally.

"Today, I see Blacks and talk to them and they can't believe that just because I joined the Klan I was fired and had to jeopardize my job because of it. It was the politicians that were pushing this thing. Not all of the politicians, but enough of them were behind the NAACP and they just put the fear of God into the transit administration."

"So, after that happened, what did you do for work?" I inquired.

"Well, I was blackballed for a while. Everywhere I'd go, the NAACP would jump right in there saying, 'Oh, you can't let this guy work there,' and things like that. I overcame that by going out and doing work I hadn't done before. It was hard labor, but they didn't care who you were, and as long as you did the job, they kept you working. So I did that for some time and eventually I worked myself back into the category of work I was used to doing."

Daryl Davis

Having already been given a reason by Roger Kelly, I wanted to see if Vernon's reason coincided on the issue of why Catholics, at one time, were not accepted in the Klan and so I asked him about it.

"They wouldn't accept a Protestant oath that the Klan had. The Catholics have their own Catholic oath. It would be like the Jews coming over to accept a Protestant sort of faith. The Catholics would have to denounce their religion to come over and accept a Protestant oath.

"Tony LaRicci was a strict Catholic up until he joined, but he disagreed with what the Catholics were doing at the time. They were allowing yippies and hippies to come in and play music at the churches and having all kinds of bungo music going on in the churches."

Having been a musician for sometime, I wanted to know his definition of this term and asked, "What is bungo music?"

His face poker straight, he replied, "It's a bunch of wild hippies out there beating on the drums and the music so loud it rattled the inside of your brain," he replied soberly.

The way he said it caused me to break out laughing. His description reminded me of what my grandfather would sometimes say when he had the misfortune of visiting my house during band rehearsal. Trying to regain my composure, I changed to a more serious subject. "You mentioned Jews. How do you feel about Jewish people?"

"I have nothing against Jewish people as long as they don't try to force their way of life on me. If they were to come up to me and tell me that I had to become a Jew, I would tell them outright, they could go to hell. That's the same with the Black situation. As long as they live their life and don't force me to mix with them, I have no problem, I'll help them."

"Let's say your son or daughter…"

"Oh, no!" Vernon interrupted me, raising his arms to cut off the topic, perceiving with horror what my next question was going to be. "I don't want them mixing, that's out! God didn't intend that. The law won't allow it if you got a pedigree dog and let it get mixed up with a mongrel dog. See if they give you papers on it." His arms fell to his sides.

"On what do you base your beliefs," I asked, "the Bible, your own personal feelings or what?"

An edge crept into his voice. "Pride and God. God didn't create people to mingle together. He created them to stay within themselves and their own groups. He didn't create us to go out and act like animals. That's what it's boiled down to, acting like animals. They go out here and marry a queer and they want as much rights as the decent people. If it looks like it will satisfy them, they'll marry it. What the hell, it makes no difference to them, they don't care." He shook his head.

"If I was Black," he continued, "I certainly wouldn't want to go out here and marry a White woman. I'd look for a Black woman. I see a lot of pretty Black women, and they are beautiful. In fact, there are some very gorgeous Black women as far as I'm concerned."

As Vernon was attesting to the beauty of Black women, I couldn't help thinking back to Roger Kelly who would not concede to them the slightest degree of beauty.

"But I'm not going out there to marry a Black. That's destroying a race of people," Vernon vehemently declared.

I challenged the Grand Giant on his animal analogy. "About the dog example you gave me. I don't know where they get police dogs, but they are mixed. They do not use one hundred percent pedigrees. Instead, they use mongrels. It has been proven that mixed breed dogs are smarter than pure breeds. In order to keep the breed pure, it will eventually get to the point of incest, which in dogs, like humans, can cause deficiencies and retardation."

"Well, I can't equate a human being with an animal to start with. That was just an example I was using about how the human race is trying to destroy itself within, but yet they won't even let dogs go out and do their business and destroy their pedigrees."

His strident ideas on the purity of races brought another question to my mind. "What's your opinion as to the intellectual quality of Blacks?"

He responded, "I think there's just as many intelligent Black people as there are White people. The fact is there is something the Black people have followed through all their life or it's bred into them. For every one decent Black upstanding citizen you find, you will find ten of them who don't give a hoot for nothing and five of them is out there ready to knock somebody in the head and steal from him. They're ready to sell dope, ready to shoot, ready to throw big drunk alcohol parties, ready to rape, ready to do every damn thing they want to do. Then they wonder why all the prisons are filled up with the Blacks.

"I don't know what makes them do it. If I knew I'd be a wealthy man because I could help get them straightened out and on the right road, I'd do it, but I just don't know. I don't know whether it's chemicals in their systems or what. I just don't understand what makes them do it."

I'd been leaning back on my chair listening with my eyes half-closed when I sat up with a start. "Are you saying that there aren't any White drug dealers?" I asked, wondering if he really thought the drug problem was something that was indigenous to the Black race.

"No, no, no, no," he assured me. "The White ones are doing the same thing, but there is a greater percentage of Blacks that would rather steal. When I was a kid, you never heard of a Black stealing. They'd help you and you'd help them. Today, in eighty percent of everything that happens, there's a Black involved. The other twenty percent is the trashy Whites and its list is growing. So, in the next twenty years if things don't change, you'll have fifty-fifty."

There was a long pause and then our discussion turned to the issue of homosexuals and then to the Klan's idea that Martin Luther King, Jr. was a Communist. The relaxed mood prevailing earlier vanished. Like Roger Kelly and most of the Klanmembers I would meet, Vernon was homophobic.

"Homosexuals," he said, "are the lowest form of life."

He also maintained that he'd seen pictures furnished by the FBI in which Dr. King had been photographed with some people known to be sympathetic to the Communist ideology. "If he was not a Communist, he was definitely a supporter of that philosophy."

I found the Klan's beliefs about Dr. King to be largely influenced by so-called FBI data, which in view of the FBI's stance on the Klan was most interesting. The FBI in the 1960's devised a top secret counter-intelligence program which they named "COINTELPRO." Information was gathered by informers on the groups that were under surveillance. Then, through dissemination of misinformation, internal strife was created within the power structure and rank and file of an organization.

The idea that J. Edgar Hoover was a racist was widely rumored then and has been articulated now. Although the murders of Blacks that fell under the Federal jurisdiction often went uninvestigated, he detested the Ku Klux Klan.

Thus the Klan became a target of COINTELPRO. The FBI paid informers to gather information. Later, letters were sent anonymously to the employers of Klansmen telling of their affiliations, costing many of them their jobs. The fact that they were Klansmen was usually only known to their fellow members who had sworn an oath of secrecy not to reveal their identities. The plan was that Klansmen would think that someone within their organization had betrayed them, creating an air of doubt and causing everyone to be suspicious of each other.

Letters were also written under female aliases to the wives of Klansmen, detailing, and sometimes fabricating, sexual, adulterous adventures of their husbands. By breaking down the family structure, causing Klansmen to lose their jobs and dissolving their marriages, distrust was generated amongst the membership.

Daryl Davis

It has amazed me that while Klansmen know where Hoover stood in regard to them, they still insist that Dr. King was a Communist because they assert J. Edgar Hoover and the FBI said so. For whatever reason, although they also state Hoover made up lies about the Klan, they refuse to believe that Hoover could have lied about Martin Luther King.

Sadly, the subject of Martin Luther King was not one on which Vernon and I, nor many other Klan leaders with whom I talked, found any common ground. Despite this, the Grand Giant had been most cooperative and forthcoming with me and would have gladly talked much more, but I needed to get to a performance. I thought him a decent man, who had a set of standards for his family and at one time advocated these standards for all White families. He has since given up that struggle and now tolerates other families "race-mixing" as long as it does not happen in his own.

As I was leaving, I could not resist asking, "Do you have any regrets about joining the Klan and would you rejoin?"

"No, I don't have regrets and no, I wouldn't join now. And I have nothing to say against them. I wouldn't join the NAACP either. The problem is now I'm getting to an age where one foot is in the grave and the other one's on a banana peel. I'm retired. I finally gave it up and quit fighting the problem.

"It's becoming too much of a hassle with all these damn laws they're passing. You turn your head and look at this person over there and he could sue you and take you to court because you looked at him the wrong way. Or, you get out there and say to some woman, 'You're beautiful,' and you're accused of sexually harassing her and she's taking you to court. That's crazy, these are downright stupid laws. If you have to live your life according to the laws they've passed, you're gonna be awfully bored. You won't be able to cut a joke nowheres because someone will get offended and you'll wind up before the judge trying to explain it or you'll wind up paying for it the rest of your life. That's no way to live.

"Your generation grew up thinking, 'This is the greatest generation of all.' The generation that you bring up will be different from the way you are living and naturally they'll think that theirs is the greatest generation of all. The one I grew up under, as far as I'm concerned, was the greatest one of them all, and, each year it's been going down hill."

I had to smile.

He nodded. "You younger folks have accepted this way of life because this is the only thing you know. Now, your next generation of people will adopt a way of life you will probably be against. It's gone so far now that there is nothing I could do myself to change it. It's going down the road to nowhere and it's almost at the end now. It'll get to the point where you'll have to put a side arm on just to protect your own life when you walk out your front door. It's getting that bad. If you don't think so, go to New York, Cleveland, Detroit or even Baltimore. If you look like you got ten cents on you, you're going to get busted in the head."

I could not argue against the fact that street crime in most large cities was worsening. It was the cause of this condition that I saw differently, but I told myself once again, I was not looking for the many areas on which we disagreed, but for the ones on which we could find common ground.

Though their racial ideologies drastically differed, Vernon Naimaster reminded me in his last remarks of my own grandfathers, sitting comfortably in their favorite chairs, smoking their favorite pipes and recalling the "Good ol' days." One of the only differences being, in my grandfathers' cases, the "Good ol' days" weren't so good. They have both passed on now and I know that they have gone to a better place far from Roanoke and Salem, Virginia, where they will enjoy themselves eternally in harmony with all.

As I sat there letting Vernon reminisce for a while, I remembered a story one of my grandfathers, a porter for the railway, told me about the Klan.

Daryl Davis

Granddaddy had gotten off the train for a short period somewhere in North Carolina. Somehow, the train pulled out without him. As he tried to decide what to do next, he was approached by several White men who told him they were Klansmen and began shoving him around. They informed my grandfather that if he was not on the next train out of there that afternoon, he would be swinging from a tree that evening. He informed them that if they would let him go, he would catch the train that just left! *What would my grandfather think*, I wondered, *if he could see me sitting here calmly discussing views on racism with Vernon Naimaster, who, had he lived in another time and place, might have been one of those Klansmen?* Knowing my grandfather believed there was good in all people, I somehow knew he would have approved.

7

Tony LaRicci, Former Grand Dragon

Anthony LaRicci was born in Norfolk, Virginia, but spent most of his childhood living in New Jersey. During his tenth year, the future Klan leader moved with his parents and siblings to Baltimore, Maryland. In 1965, he joined the Maryland Chapter, led by Vernon Naimaster, of Robert Shelton's United Klans of America, headquartered in Tuscaloosa, Alabama. LaRicci later replaced Naimaster as Imperial Representative for the state of Maryland.

Following a disagreement with Shelton, LaRicci left UKA and helped form the Maryland Knights of the Ku Klux Klan, which became a division of the Confederation of Independent Orders Knights of the Ku Klux Klan. Within three years, Tony had become Grand Dragon of this Klan faction. During his reign he organized a paramilitary group called the Klan Beret and a Klan Youth Group for children. Tony had much support from the Baltimore City Police in the way of silent members and supporters, but at times, found himself on the wrong side of some law enforcement officers who did not share his racist philosophy. One of his arrests included the charge of kidnapping.

Daryl Davis

In an effort to curb the illegal drug movement, Tony and four members of his group apprehended a man, whom they thought to be a drug addict and pusher. They turned the man over to the police. The media quickly and falsely put forth a story of the Klansmen kidnapping a police officer who was working undercover as a drug pusher. The truth of the matter was that the man who was apprehended was not an undercover police officer, but an informer who, in actuality, was a drug pusher and an addict working out a deal with the police. Tony, while making an effort to do what he thought was right in effecting a citizen's arrest, ended up being charged with kidnapping because he held a person and took him to the police station against his will.

It was drizzling the day Mary and I went to meet with LaRicci, Grand Giant (former Grand Dragon) of the Ku Klux Klan. We pulled our car up to LaRicci's house and as we walked to his door, I could see him staring through the window with a puzzled look on his face.

I knocked on the door and he immediately opened it. Extending my hand, I identified myself. He shook it and invited us in.

"This is Mary, my secretary, the lady with whom you spoke over the phone." He immediately asked her, but not in an angry or violent way, why she did not tell him that I was Black. He seemed somewhat confused and probably felt deceived about not having foreknowledge of this fact. Nonetheless, he was very cordial and hospitable, leading to some comfortable chairs and inviting us to sit down.

A few minutes later, a lovely woman whom Tony introduced as his wife, Frances, joined us. Frances offered us coffee. Mary and Tony accepted and I politely declined.

Tony insisted, "I would be honored if you were to have a cup of coffee with us. It will be the first time in my life that I have had a Black man in my house and drank coffee together."

Again, I politely refused, not realizing that Tony was taking my refusal personally. Mary quickly picked up on his feelings and explained that I did not care much for coffee. Frances offered me a glass of orange juice which I gladly accepted. Everyone felt better and that set a more convivial atmosphere for us to begin to talk of more serious matters.

Tony told me that he was the first Klansman of an Italian Catholic background to become a Grand Dragon. He renounced his Catholicism in order to join the Klan. In his opinion, he explained, "Catholics, by holding allegiance to the Pope, are therefore holding allegiance to Italy since the Pope is in Rome. In order to be in the Klan, a Klansmember must give his allegiance only to the United States of America."

Tony continued, his voice pitched low and serious, "The liberal politicians! That's what's wrong with out country today. That's why I joined the Klan and we still have the same situation today. People do not want to be forced to accept something. You, as a Black man, cannot truly say that you've been accepted by the White man if he was forced to accept you. You can speak to a lot of White people and they'll pat you on the back, but what's in the back of their minds?"

I had to admire Tony's candor, if not his philosophy. He told it just the way he saw it and pulled no punches.

Tony made sure that I knew he was a White Supremacist. He insisted that everything received and accomplished by Blacks was because the White man gave it to them. Throughout our conversation, he apologized to me if he hurt my feelings but he reminded me that I came for the truth as he saw it. I assured him that while I did not agree with many things he had to say, I would not take them as a personal attack on me.

A silence filled the room as he scrutinized me. Then he loftily declared, "I believe in White Supremacy. Our country, our nation was founded by the White man and it was fought for by the White man. Sure, years later the Black man was involved in it, but still, I'm firmly entrenched in White Supremacy."

He pointed a finger at me. "Take your education system today. No matter how many times people say that schools are doing great, it keeps coming out on national television that our educational system is failing. Now, you did not have this back in the early 1900's up until this here Civil Rights movement. History will prove this. This is my opinion from what I know from my sixty-three years on this earth."

I had come to his house in order to understand his views and though at times that was difficult in view of mine, I chose my next words calmly and carefully so that they would not inflame the atmosphere.

"Do you believe that the advances that other races have made were only because the White race allowed it?" I asked.

"Of course, of course! Now, there were some Black people that did advance on their own, and those people I'll give credit to, but not those that were handed everything on a silver platter at the expense of the White man.

"Our nation back before the Sixties—before your so-called Civil Rights movement—was the greatest nation on Earth and the most powerful and the smartest. I think history will prove this. Now, you look at our nation today compared with it back then. Integration would have come along if they would have let the people accept it on their own and not be forced, because even I, myself feel that whether you are Black or White, I wouldn't want to see you mistreated."

An almost inaudible sigh escaped my lips. Wondering if he felt that forced desegregation was the sole reason for the existence of the KKK, I asked, "Do you feel that, back then, if integration was never forced, there would have been a need for the Klan?"

His voice slammed back. "Yes, there is a need for the Klan because they are the only opposition, and this is the only way to get it across to the people. I'm not saying there weren't any violent acts committed, but nothing like the violence down in Washington, D.C. today and those being committed by Black people. If myself and the Klan and every other Right-Wing group disappeared, we would have nothing but liberalization. They dominate the whole country now because there is no opposition."

I asked quietly, "Vernon Naimaster told me about some liberal policies of which he approved. Will you tell me some liberal policies of which you disapprove?"

"I don't approve of the positions that women are taking today." LaRicci looked troubled. "I think they are anti-American and anti-Christian. I think that women lowered their standards when they joined the Civil Rights movement. They joined the Civil Rights movement to try to bring themselves up to a man's position; they should be in a woman's position. Which is a nice housewife, a mother, a teacher—anything that pertains to a woman's position; not what they are doing today—policewomen, firewomen, soldiers, this is ridiculous. They are not women in my eyes. I don't feel that they are ladies like they were back prior to the Civil Rights movement. They are destroying their own gender."

"What about the economic factor where today we need two incomes to raise a family? Back in the Sixties, a man could earn enough money to support a housewife and a family," I argued.

"I can dispute that. Women were doing jobs that were not expected of them in World Wars I and II, not because they had to, but for their country. They were called to come into our defense plants and help while the men were over there fighting. Now the war is over, and the men came back, we don't need them in there working."

His deep, rumbling voice continued. "I raised six kids and started at forty dollars a week. We didn't have to have our women working, and our women didn't work then. All this came up after the Civil Rights movement. Once again, you can blame the

Daryl Davis

Liberal politicians for that. I don't even think the Black people are as well off today as they were then."

I looked searchingly at him. "Do you think that thirty years ago, back in the Sixties, I could have been sitting here in your living room talking to you?" I asked somewhat surprised by his last statement.

"Yeah, maybe with me you could," the Klansman answered, taking exception with me. "I think more of some Black people than I do of some White men."

As I did with Roger Kelly and Vernon Naimaster, I brought up the subject of Dr. Martin Luther King, Jr.

Echoing Kelly's and Naimaster's vehement sentiments, if not the exact words, LaRicci spat out, "It's been proven that he went to a Communist school. We got photographs and everything, and they could not be distributed unless he did," asserted Tony.

"Making Martin Luther King Day a holiday is a disgrace in my eyes," he went on.

I opened my mouth and then closed it.

"I know a lot greater men than him who have not been made martyrs. Now, maybe you feel that he should be a martyr, but not to me, and not to a lot of other White people."

I kept quiet, feeling that disputing this point would be useless. Instead I changed the subject. "What about homosexuality?" I asked. "Do you feel that gays are born that way, or do you feel they adopt their lifestyle later in life?"

"No sir, they were not born that way," he assured me curtly. "If they were born that way, there would not have been any bitterness or arguments or anything against them. None of them were born that way. No, not from what I know of them."

He looked at me sardonically. "We had gay people in our days, but they stayed under the rock, that's where they belong. I don't believe in gay people or lesbians. That's not a normal living. It's not raising a family, it's not American and it's not

Christian. Let's take that trash and put it back in the closet. That's one way to straighten out this country today."

"Would you feel that way if one of your children were gay?" I prodded.

He shuddered involuntarily. "If one of my children were gay, I would have nothing to do with him, no more than I would have anything to do with one of my children if they married into the Black race. Yes, sir. If the Good Lord wanted a mongrelized race," he stared directly at me and I stiffened but said nothing, "He wouldn't have put all the different races here on earth and segregated it. If He had wanted a mongrelized race, He would have put a Black man with a White woman or a White man with a Black woman here on earth for Adam and Eve."

At this point in our conversation my own feelings were bubbling under the surface. It was much harder to remember my objectives than it had been with Kelly or Naimaster. I began firing off questions, deposition style and resounding to his queries in a like manner.

"Do you think Adam and Eve were White?" I asked.

"I definitely do." he replied, "Just as I believe that Jesus Christ is White. Do you?"

I took a deep breath and let it out. "Not necessarily."

"Why?"

"I don't necessarily believe that He is Black either."

"Fine, but, once again, it's through your being raised in this liberal domination process we have here today. Had you been raised thirty years prior to that, when the country believed in God, worshipped God, you would not feel that way today."

"I'm a Christian and a deacon in my church and I believe in Jesus Christ," I shot back.

"But you don't believe that He is White! And you're a deacon? Yet you have nothing in this world throughout history to give you a reason to doubt it when everything stated has proven that Jesus Christ is a White Jew. You call yourself a deacon, but don't believe He's White. You won't paint another color on Him, but you won't give Him the color He's got. Where do you stand?"

Before I could choose a more reflexive phrasing, my words burst out. "I will tell you where I stand. If you believe the Bible, God created man in His own image."

He nodded. "That's right."

I wasn't about to stop. I did not conceal my anger. Even though I had schooled myself to stay calm, he had hit a nerve and my emotions got the better of me.

"I am as much a man as you are. Do you agree?"

"That is right."

"Some people consider me to be a monkey, not a man, because I am Black."

"I did not say that," he snapped.

"I know you didn't. If you believe that I, like yourself, am a man, that God created both of us in His own image as it says so in the Bible, then His image must be made up of Black, White, Oriental, Hispanic, Indian and whatever else. So, why wouldn't His son, Jesus Christ, have all these characteristics and colors as well?"

Tony frowned as he answered. "I believe, especially if you say you are a deacon, and I know I'm right, it says in the Bible and I can't quote you exactly where right now, but it explains why God created a Black man. I believe it was punishment. Now you can correct me if you believe I'm wrong through whatever faith you have, I don't know. If you go through the Bible you will find that God created Adam and Eve, who were White, and down the line someone was killed and God had to punish him and turned him Black. That's how the Black race came about."

I moved to keep his face in view and felt my own tighten.

"Now wait a minute. The story to which you are referring, is that of Cain and Abel. If I recall correctly, one brother killed the other in a fit of jealously stemming from one brother's sacrifice being accepted by God and the other's sacrifice being rejected. Because Cain murdered his brother Abel, God punished him by marking him. This would designate to all of society that he was an outcast. Nowhere in the Bible was it said that God turned him Black, put a black mark on him, or put an X on his forehead, or anything else. It just said he was 'marked.'"

"Have you read anywhere in there where it says the mark wasn't black?"

"No."

"Well, then, you and I can argue this point until doomsday and neither one of us will come out more than the other." He leaned back and smiled as if he had won a round in a fight.

I decided to bring down the fervid tone of our conversation. "Back to my original statement and question. If we both are men and created in the image of our Lord and I believe in Jesus Christ, why can't we sit side by side in the same church and worship the same Man?"

"Now you're getting off the subject," he said with a slight smile. "Who said we couldn't sit side by side in church? All my life I've been raised Catholic and then later I changed to Presbyterian. I don't ever remember even as a kid when I had to go to church that there were no Black people in there. You see, what you are doing is only because of what you know from what you've heard or what you've read. I lived in New Jersey until I was eleven-years-old. I walked three miles to church every Sunday. There were colored people in Sunday school. How could you sit here and say that you were not allowed to worship in the same church with the White man? You cannot make that statement. You can only make a statement on what you know or have heard, but you can't base it on fact because I could dispute it." His features rigid, he looked off in the distance.

I twisted my body in the chair so as to force our eyes to meet. "I can't go and worship Christ in the Aryan Nation's church or the Church of Jesus Christ Identity."

"Fine, we can't go and worship in Louis Farrakhan's church either," he shot back.

Daryl Davis

"He may not believe in the same faith in which you believe."

"He don't believe in anything but Black Supremacy."

"I don't believe in that. I don't believe in anybody's supremacy."

"Fine. I don't agree with it either. The man is interested in his race. He doesn't go for interracial marriages."

I ignored the bait and told him, "I believe in Black Pride, the same way I believe in White Pride. Be proud of what you are, but I don't believe that one race is superior to another. To me, that's what supremacy is. That's not pride, it's being supreme. One is inferior and one is superior, but White Pride and Black Pride, to me, are acceptable."

Tony countered, "Once again, this proves a fact about what God has done. If man would have followed His laws, we wouldn't have this today. That's why you have Africa. Pride, Black man, my country. Fine, what do you have today? You bring them out of Africa; you bring them out of Japan. Why did He segregate the races if He wanted them mixed? You are a deacon and you can't answer that."

I tried to curb my rising indignation, but couldn't quite do it. "Why are you out of Italy?"

"Sir?"

Obviously my words touched a nerve. "Why did you leave Italy?"

"Same reason. There is no difference between Italy, America and England. In fact, in your Aryan nations, Italy is part of them. I didn't know if you knew that or not."

"How do you feel about South Africa, then? If you say that's our country, the Black man's country, then why are the Dutch over there taking over?"

"I'm not saying they are right for doing that, no more than I'm saying we were right in conquering this country and getting rid of the American-Indians. I hate to see it happen. Africa is the

Black man's home and you don't take it away from them."

I dug my heels in metaphorically. "We've been here for 200 years. This is our home. So, it doesn't do any good to tell us to go back to Africa."

He gave a slight smile. "I agree with you. I don't question that with you at all. But you said, 'What am I doing here from Italy?' My grandparents came here to make themselves a better life. How did you get here?"

"We were brought here as slaves."

"Okay, right. So, that right off the bat, answers your question. White people came here to help build this country."

I wasn't about to let that go unchallenged. "So did we, except we were forced."

"No, you were forced to work in cotton fields. You didn't build this country. When I say, 'build the country,' I'm talking about building the bridges, the buildings and the government and making America the greatest nation on earth, the most respected nation on earth and the richest. The White man did this. In what respect can you say that you helped build the country?"

I struck strong and clear. "Blacks and American-Indians were used most of the time on high buildings and bridges because the White man was afraid of heights. You should check into who built the upper tiers of the Empire State Building. As far as working the cotton fields goes, the clothes that the White man wore while he was, as you say, 'building this country,' were 100 percent cotton, picked by the slaves on the cotton fields. We didn't have polyester back then."

I realized my own feelings were getting in the way; the conversation was deteriorating. I had not come so far to trade wisecracks. I took another tact.

"What, in your opinion, can we, as Black people do to advance our race?"

"You need people to stop believing those Liberals like the Kennedys. Sure they gave you what you got today, but the Blacks are saying they don't have that much today. Well, President JFK sure gave a hell of a lot for you not to have that much today. So, if you don't have it today and you didn't have it back then, there's still something wrong with our system. So, let's get rid of this system that we've had and let's get rid of the Liberals. Let's have a little bit of common sense. If you don't want to put Conservatives in there, then get Moderates in there. Sit on the fence. Let's play it that way. Any change we make has got to be better than what we have. I believe it can be worked out.

"I believe that the Black man will be more accepted by the White men, those that you claim don't accept you, than those that are patting you on the shoulder and saying, 'This damn Nigger,' behind your back. How many of those Democrats sat on that bench who were saying that about them witnesses?" He was referring to the alleged sexual harassment scandal involving Judge Clarence Thomas and Anita Hill during the Supreme Court confirmation hearings. This was airing on his television in his living room at the time. "They were talking and treating them like they were White people. They acted like they respected them and they didn't have a bit of respect for them. I'm not anti-Negro. It doesn't matter to me which way the vote goes. I think it's a disgrace what Senator Metzenbaum did to that Black man.

I held his eyes for a full ten seconds on this point. There was silence and then he continued his rationale.

"I am not anti-Negro. I don't hate you because you're Black. I just don't invite you to my home, and I don't want you marrying my children, but there's nothing wrong with a friendship with you. I'm not against that. I believe this is what the Klan is for."

Again, I changed the subject, searching once more for those on which we could fruitfully exchange ideas. "Do you believe in the Holocaust?"

"I have my doubts. I know a lot were killed, but until I get some more proof, other than what the Liberals have shown us, I don't believe that millions and millions of Jews were killed just because they were Jews. This is because we have lost many of our own people that were not Jews, but Americans and allies."

"Tony, I hate to cut you off, but that about does it for me." I looked at him; it was a soulful look that I hoped conveyed a long lasting trail of pain. Then I asked, "Would you pose for some pictures for me?"

"I would be glad to."

Tony went into a back bedroom, emerged with his robe and began putting it on. Unlike Grand Dragon Roger Kelly's white robe with green stripes, Tony LaRicci's was all green. The color green signifies Grand Dragon. He explained to me that most of the different organizations use the same colors, but in different ways. He allowed me to take as many pictures of him in his robe as I wanted. He would not permit me to pose with him while he had the robe on.

"Some people," he said, "would feel that it's degrading to the Klan to pose with a Black man while wearing the robe."

I said nothing.

"You sort of made me feel good putting this robe back on. I haven't had it on for so long, I forgot what it feels like. I don't mind talking to you. I hope you're satisfied with the answers I've given you. I think we've had a pretty good conversation here. I don't think I've held any punches back. But, on the other hand, I think I've proved that I'm not a bigot. However, if being a bigot means being a believer in God, country and home and self preservation, then I'm a bigot. I believe in everything I spoke for and stood up for in twenty-one years. I did not put anyone down strictly on race. From our conversation, you take it for what it's worth. I hope you will keep in contact with me. Drive carefully, the roads are probably slippery."

As I drove back home, I thought a lot about Tony LaRicci. After meeting him, one is not likely to forget him. In my opinion, it is no wonder that he, at one time, had one of the biggest and most powerful Klan factions. Tony is strong, candid and intractable. Moreover, he is unlikely to change and is very adamant about his opinions. But, he was very hospitable and courteous to me when I expressed my opposing viewpoints.

LaRicci was much more a Klan icon than Naimaster or Kelly, but I knew there were others even more relentless in their beliefs and actions. My goal was to meet them too.

8

Private Investigation

According to the media, one man who most fit that description was Tony LaRicci's successor, Robert White, Grand Dragon for the Confederation of Independent Orders. However, though Tony LaRicci and I had many points of disagreement, there was one thing we did share the same feelings about. This was the fact that the media sometimes has the propensity to get information screwed up, be it for sensationalism or be it an honest mistake. I decided to find out about Bob White myself. I started by looking into a well publicized incident involving Grand Dragon White and two Black men. The incident took place not very far from where I live.

The news media reported that two Black men had entered a bar to purchase carryout beer. Already in the bar were two White men, who had been in there for some time drinking. They began hurling racial epithets at the two Black men and telling them to leave because their kind was not welcome. The bartender intervened telling the White men that the Black men were indeed welcome there and that the White men would have to leave. The two White men went outside and waited for the two Black men to purchase their beer and come out.

When the two Blacks walked out into the street, they were jumped by the two Whites. The two White men began losing the fight. One of them went to his pickup truck and returned with a shotgun. He fired at the Black men and missed. Police arrived at the scene. They arrested the White men and charged them with assault. It was not until the police searched the men's pickup truck that they found Klan literature and determined that the two White men, one of whom was Bob White, were Klansmen. One of the articles on the incident mentioned that Robert White had been a police officer.

Immediately I thought about Sheriff Lawrence Rainey, Deputy Cecil Price and "Trigger" Nash, all police officers, who were also Klansmen, who had murdered Black people. The last one acquired his nickname because he had proudly claimed to have killed thirteen Blacks "in the line of duty." All of those mentioned and others were feted at Klan rallies and besieged by autograph-seeking Klansmen and Klanswomen.

Having digested the media's version of the incident involving Bob White, I drove to Baltimore and went to the courthouse to review the case files in order to get the official version.

I found they differed. Some media reports said that Mr. White was charged with "Attempted Murder." In fact the court records showed he was charged with "Assault with Intent to Murder." It is my understanding that "intent" means that the idea is present in one's mind, whereby "attempt" is defined as actually trying to execute the intent. The media had presented more incorrect information. According to the files, White had fired the gun, but not at either of the Black men. Robert White was in a federal penitentiary serving three years for his conviction on this charge. The prison was not named, but judging from the time he went in, he still had a couple of months left before he was to be released.

I made notes of the names and addresses of the two Black men, the witnesses and Michael Monaghan, the other Klansman who was by this time free. He was charged only with "Assault" and "Property Damage." One of the Black men had a prosthesis on his leg. Mr. Monaghan beat him with a bar stool and destroyed the prosthesis. I went to each of the Black men's last known addresses, only to find their mother and grandmother respectively. I was told at both houses that they did not live there anymore, but would get messages that I would like to speak with them. I left my card with these maternal ladies and drove to Monaghan's house. He did live there, but was not home at the time. I left my card with a young man who said that he would see that Michael got it.

I never heard from Michael Monaghan or the two Black men, but the lawyer representing the two Blacks called me asking what I wanted from his clients. When I told him that I was investigating the Klan and would like to talk with his clients about what had happened, he agreed to help me. He arranged a day for his clients to meet with me in his office. I arrived at the time agreed upon and waited and waited and waited. The lawyer was there, but his clients never showed. He apologized to me and said that he would try to set a meeting for another time, but I never heard anymore and did not further pursue it since the men did not seem to want to tell their story even after their lawyer okayed it.

My next move was to see about locating the witnesses. At the time of the incident, they were all working at the bar in which the Klansmen had been drinking. I drove through a town strange to me, wondering if they would still be working there three years after the fact and whether I had taken the right direction. Within a mile of the place, I passed an overpass that had the letters "KKK" spray painted on it. I obviously knew I was in the right neighborhood and glad I wasn't lost in the wrong one!

When I arrived at the bar and went in, I was in luck. I

found out they all still lived and worked in the community. According to the court files, only one of the witnesses had actually seen Mr. White fire the gun. The others could only testify to the fact that the two White men were in the bar drinking and were asked to leave for reasons of racial harassment.

It just so happened that the witness who testified that he saw Mr. White fire the gun was there working that night. He was an amicable fellow who did not seem to have any particular fondness for the Klan and was willing to talk to me. He spoke slowly and pensively to make sure he was giving me an accurate account of what he had seen.

"After all," he explained, "it's been three years."

I nodded.

"I was upstairs in the building when shouting outside drew my attention to the window. When I looked out, I saw Mr. Monaghan on the ground fighting with the two Black men."

He then observed Mr. White walk calmly and casually over to a truck and remove what he said looked like a shotgun. The witness then left the window for a moment. When he looked back outside, he observed Mr. White fire the gun into the ground. I asked if White pointed the gun at anyone, and the witness said he did not.

"It seemed as though he only wanted to scare the guys."

He then added that the shot fired by Bob White came closer to hitting his own foot than anything else. I thought it apropos.

9

Visiting My Prison Pen Pal

Though I now had some insights into Bob White, I still had not achieved my objective to meet him. I acquired a phone number for tracking federal prisoners. Dialing it, I supplied the necessary information the official required on the prisoner I was trying to locate. When they gave me Robert White's prison ID number and mailing address, I wrote him a letter telling him about my investigation into his crime and asked him if he would be interested in talking with me.

A few days later, White replied, agreeing to get together with me. I wrote him back, thanked him for his letter and promptness in responding. Again, he quickly sent a letter back to me. This time, he wrote, "You have written to me twice and in neither letter did you tell me that you were Black. Why?" He went on to say that just because he was in prison, it did not mean he was cut off from the outside world when it came to getting information. He added that he hoped I was sincere, as he wanted to get together with me and that he hoped I was not trying to trick him into anything. Immediately, I fired off a telegram to him so that he would have it the next day, or at least as soon as the prison gives the inmates their mail. I reassured him that my intentions were sincere and the omission of my skin color was not to deceive him. We continued corresponding.

Not long afterward, he wrote and told me that he was being transferred from Petersburg, Virginia, to the state prison diagnostic center in Baltimore, Maryland, while they decided in which state prison he would serve out his remaining time for the state, since his federal time was up. He said he would phone me as soon as he was out and had taken care of the things he needed to do upon re-entering society.

True to his word, Grand Dragon White phoned me about a week after he was released. Everything he ever had was gone. His marriage, his job, his home and most of his belongings were all part of the past. His old life had been decimated in the three years he was in prison. I wondered if this would alter his old values for the better or worse.

He asked me if it would be possible to wait another week before our getting together so he could complete the procedure of replanting his roots. He explained, "I have to get my driver's license renewed, gather up my things that I had to leave scattered around three years ago and find a place to live." He was currently staying with friends and relatives. A different night, a different place. I told him to do what he had to do and call me; we would meet as soon as he was able to do so.

About a week and a half later, Bob White phoned me again and said he was ready to get together. He suggested a time and a surprising place—the bar where the incident that landed him in prison had taken place. He also told me that the gun—which was never found—used in the incident should still be where he hid it near the scene three years earlier.

"I wanted you to be there when I go to check on it."

He would then contact the police and have their laboratory technicians, through scientific procedures, verify that the gun had been sitting there for that long. According to the media reports, the gun was a shotgun. According to Robert White, it was a broken Daisy air pellet rifle. He felt that this new evidence might help him in the civil cases being brought against him by the two Black men involved in the incident and overturn his conviction of "Assault with Intent to Murder." In compliance with his request, I went alone and unarmed to our meeting.

Driving to Finnagan's Bar on the outskirts of Baltimore, I parked my car. I had arrived a few minutes early but went in anyway. The bar was dark and dingy, but was doing a good lunchtime business. The clientele was mostly blue-collar types.

Taking a seat at the counter, I ordered a soda and looked around. No one seemed to take notice of me. I wondered if the Grand Dragon was already in there observing me. Scrutinizing each face, I also watched anyone entering the door. I felt a disadvantage in that I did not know what Robert White looked like, but he could pick me out instantly, as I was the only Black in the place.

A few minutes later, a well-built man with dark, thinning hair and an attractive woman walked in. The man seemed to be looking around for somebody. When he saw me, he smiled and walked over—the Grand Dragon had arrived. We shook hands and he introduced me to his companion.

We seated ourselves at a table and Bob ordered some cold drinks. Bob told me disappointedly, "I have already gone by the location where I had hidden the gun just to make sure it was there before we went and contacted the police." He paused. "It wasn't," he added dryly.

As we sat there, Bob looked around. "This is the first time since the incident three years ago that I've set foot in Finnagan's," he said, swirling the ice in his glass with a mixer. A few people recognized him and came by the table to say hello. As I said, I did not get any stares when I entered the bar, but now some people were looking inquisitively at me. I knew what they were thinking—a Black man was sitting at a table socializing with a Grand

Daryl Davis

Dragon of the Ku Klux Klan who had been charged with and convicted of assault with intent to murder two other Black men. Was the man crazy?

In a way it felt as strange to me as to them, but I wanted to get to know Bob White and, perhaps through him, others of his group. We continued making small talk for a while, getting to know each other and feeling each other out. I judged that, unlike some others, his years in prison had mellowed him somewhat and though he seemed committed to his beliefs, he was receptive to change. I looked forward to getting together with him many more times and learning a great deal. Upon our departure from the bar, we agreed to meet again the following week.

The days passed slowly. The appointed day for us to meet again finally arrived. We each arrived at the designated parking lot on time and I insisted on buying him lunch. I watched as he hesitated and then agreed. He told me to park my car and ride with him. We ended up at a Chinese-American restaurant and our conversation began naturally enough as he told me what it was like growing up and what the influences were that led to his joining the Ku Klux Klan Confederation of Independent Orders. It was a story he seemed to want to tell me.

"Well, I was born in Walbrook which was a predominantly Black neighborhood. I grew up with Blacks. We played together, we did alright. Then when I was about twelve, we moved to Baltimore County, which, at that time, was predominantly White. That was a complete turnaround from what I was used to. As I grew older and began spreading out with my territory, I began observing how Whites were being assaulted by Blacks. My first job was at an amusement park, which at the time was segregated. Blacks were starting to try to get the park integrated. Their way of going about it was through breaking windows and tearing the park apart. The owners of the park were three brothers. Their father originally owned it. They inherited the park through his death. He always said that if there ever came a time at which point the park was to be integrated, he wanted it closed down. So, the brothers kept it segregated. White people were taking their kids there and getting assaulted and robbed, so they went along with their father's wishes and closed the park down.

As I grew older, I went through several other jobs. When I turned twenty-one, I put in an application for the Baltimore City Police Department. I worked for them for seven and a half years in predominantly Black neighborhoods. Granted, down there in the Black neighborhoods there is a lot of Black on Black crime. I will go along with that, but it seems that if there was a choice, the White people would bear the brunt of violence, assaults and robberies, you know. It was like they were being preyed on."

Because of my horrendous experience with the Maryland Police Force, I was especially interested in the days he had been a police officer.

"As a police officer, you would have to go in and investigate these crimes. What did you find the motivation of these Black people to be? Why were they assaulting each other? Why did they want to assault White people? Was it economic depression? Were they just hoodlums, or what?"

His eyes narrowed. "They were basically hoodlums. My post was ninety-nine percent Black. The only Whites around there were store owners. Believe it or not, I was well liked by the Blacks around my post. They would give me a lot of information on other ones. There were some winos who would sit out in back of the bars in the alley and drink their booze. The other police would run them out of there. I went in the alley and caught them. Instead of locking them up, I told them I wanted them to keep the alley clean, not to throw bottles in the alley and break them, but to throw them in the trash can. Surprisingly enough, I got along pretty good with them. They gave me information I needed, and I let them sit there and drink their bottles back there in the alley."

"Were they compliant about throwing their trash in the trash can?"

Daryl Davis

He shrugged. "Oh, yeah, they kept the place clean. We worked with each other. I watched several neighborhoods change from White to Black. The attitude with the Blacks was, 'If you don't like it in our neighborhood, why don't you move out?' They don't stop to think that it was our neighborhood at one time."

"When did you join the Baltimore City Police Department?"

"I joined back in the Sixties and was with them into the Seventies. I went through the riots of 1968 with the police department. I discontinued with the police department in '72 and started collecting money for installment houses. By that time I had already joined the Klan. I didn't join particularly because it was anti-Black, I joined basically because it was pro-White. Let's face it, Blacks had their organizations, also."

"You told me once before," I said leaning toward him, "that you had an incident on the police force and they decided that you were anti-Black."

He nodded. "They had put me working in the most violent neighborhoods in Baltimore City. The Western District. It has always been the worst district in Baltimore City. I put six years in down there in that district. I got commendations to prove it. I got ribbons and all other kinds of commendations for the cases I worked on. When you work in an all-Black neighborhood, naturally the only complaints that are going to be on you are going to be from Blacks. I had some problems when I was on medication one night. A lieutenant caught me sleeping on duty and got me fired. I went and saw someone who got me re-instated and switched me to the Northern District.

"I was up there working and made two arrests. This particular night there were remarks exchanged and the two Black men in custody started running their mouths and they just pulled my right string and I went off on 'em. I didn't hurt 'em, all I did was back hand them."

I wondered if he was being as candid as he'd been about other matters, but decided not to pursue it. He seemed to know what I was thinking and said, "There's a long story behind it, but they never did prove it was me that did it. Rather than lock 'em up, I just run 'em off and told them to stay off the street. My sergeant and my lieutenant were always hollering about seeing them hanging on the street corners. People were afraid to walk the streets and go in the stores, this and that and the other. I had my job to do and these guys didn't want to go along with it so one thing led to another. I wound up locking 'em up after they threw some bottles at me. I ran 'em down and had them in the back of the car and was on my way into the station. They were going on with their remarks about what they were going to do to my mother and wished my wife was there and all these filthy little remarks and it pulled my right strings. Instead of taking them in the station, I went on up the road with 'em and took them out of the car one at a time and just back handed 'em and told them to get the hell off the street. They never did pick me out of a lineup or pictures or anything. They never could figure out who did it. My captain figured it was me so he put in the report in my folder that he thought I was anti-Negro and he felt that I should be moved to a White neighborhood."

His tone changed and his voice clouded. "So, they put me out in the White area feeding the squirrels. Wasn't a damn thing happening out there. I remember a Black policeman named Larry, who worked the Western District when I was there. I won't forget him. He used to beat the shit out of those Black people. I will tell you straight out. Those Black police down there in the Western District beat those Black people more so than the White police. Those Black people were glad to get locked up by White police." I grimaced as memories of racism, as well as White police brutality surged through my mind.

For a few minutes, silence filled the room. Then, gathering my thoughts together, I continued. "You say you joined the Klan not to hang people, but to be in a pro-White fraternal organization. When most people think of the Klan, they think of hate and violence. Why don't you call your organization something else besides a Klan group?"

White stared straight at me and spoke clearly. "Let me put it to you this way. When most people say, 'Negro,' they think hate and violence. Should I ask you to change your color?"

I returned his gaze and answered, "I don't think hate and violence when I hear the word 'Negro.' Even if I did, I can't change my color."

"We can't either. It would still be the Klan." White's eyes brightened as a good comparison suddenly came to him. "Look at David Duke. Who recognizes him? They keep bringing it up that he was a Klansman. I am a Klansman in my heart and to the bone. If I change the name of my organization, then I am an imposter. Duke's post office box for the National Association for the Advancement of White People is the same as the Klan's."

Later I did check that out, and Bob White was right about David Duke's post office box.

He picked up his glass to take a drink. "Why deceive people?" Bob went on. "Why make people think they're giving money to one organization while it's being funneled into another organization that they oppose? That's deception.

"There is one thing people don't realize. A Klansman is not punched out of a standard cookie cutter. You have all walks of life coming into here for all various reasons. Some of them basically just hate Jews. A lot of them just hate Negroes. Some of them hate both. Some of them don't like Orientals and that's why they joined. It depends on what part of the country you're from as to what your problems are."

I wondered, as I gazed at the man before me, if he realized the full meaning of his words—that people who joined the Klan had problems and that perhaps the most significant similarity between them was the feeling of hate.

This was borne out the next time that Bob and I got together when he showed me a large stack of applications. They had been filled out by people who wanted membership in the Klan. One of the questions was to state one's reason for wanting to join the organization. Shielding the peoples' names, Bob allowed me to read these reasons. Most were, "I hate Niggers," "I hate Jews," or "I hate Niggers and Jews."

To be sure I was correct in my determination, I tested him. "Like in Florida, it's the Cubans, in Mississippi, it's the Blacks, in New York, it's the Jews and in Texas, it's the Vietnamese fishermen?"

White leaned closer towards me, "It's whoever happens to be a pain in your ass at the time, depending on what part of the country you're from."

"Why does the Klan keep changing its qualifications to join? Before it wouldn't accept Catholics. Now it accepts them and American-Indians, too. Do you think somewhere down the line Orientals will be accepted or even Blacks will be accepted in the Klan?" I asked grimacing.

White scoffed at my question. "Not our Klan. Like I said, you have to go by our main constitution. There is nothing said in there that is detrimental to Catholics. We go by the constitution and its bylaws dating back to the Twenties. They got accepted as time went on. I am not really familiar with why they were not accepted in the first place."

"How many Klan groups do you think are out there now that uphold the traditional constitution and bylaws of the original Ku Klux Klan?"

"UKA was one," Bob quickly offered.

"Are you talking about Robert Shelton?" I asked.

"Yeah," he cleared his throat, "Shelton's out of business now, thanks to Morris Dees."

I smiled and watched him even more intently at the mention of Morris Dees, the powerful Civil Rights attorney who has devoted his life to successfully fighting and suing Klansmen, as well as others, who have violated the rights of minorities. Not too long before this meeting, Morris Dees had bankrupted the UKA.

"Is there any current effort to try to unify the different Klan groups? It seems to me the disorganization and rivalry among the different organizations weakens its strength in numbers. Whenever an incident occurs involving a particular faction, the media simply refers to it as 'The Klan' without deference to any specific Klan group. Thus, if one Klan group does something that is frowned upon, it makes it more difficult for another Klan group that was not involved with that particular incident."

The corners of White's mouth raised slightly but his eyes were stern and his words conveyed his strong prejudices. "The media has a funny way of operating. Anything detrimental, they'll smear everybody. If it's anything worthwhile, they won't print it. The media is run by Jews and their main objective is to do away with the Klan. The only way then can do away with it is denunciation. The Confederation of Independent Orders was the largest group in the state. If they happen to be involved in a situation that hits the newspapers, the media will list all the other Klans operating in the state of Maryland and say that the Confederation is the smallest one or a splinter group. We weren't the splinter group, we were the original group."

"Everyone else in Maryland splintered off of your group?" I interrupted.

"Right, but they put down that we were the splinter group. When new members we have read that in the newspapers, they'll think, *Damn, I'm not in the real Klan.* Some of them will lose interest and drop out before they even ask. We'll have some that will come up and ask, but a lot of them will say, 'Damn, I've been taken.' This is the media's little way of tearing up an organization. Police agencies do the same thing."

"The creation of internal strife to create self-destruction," I offered to clarify White's point.

"That's right. Divide and conquer," said Bob, making a chopping motion and leveling sweep with his hand.

"Every time I hear of David Duke, he's involved in something different; the Klan, the Nazi Party, the NAAWP (National Association for the Advancement of White People), the Governorship, the Presidential nomination."

"When David Duke gets finished with his search, he's liable to find himself," White sarcastically replied.

"You don't support him?" I asked surprised.

"To an extent I do, to an extent I don't. He changes hats too much depending on whatever situation will suit his purpose."

I uncomfortably shifted my weight around in my seat. "Why have many of the Klan groups today aligned themselves with White Power Skinheads, Nazi movements and other White Supremacist and Right-Wing Groups? Twenty years ago, most Klans would not do that. Today, some of them hold joint rallies and march together and recruit each other."

"The need of support," White shrugged. "It's smaller and like you said, there is strength in numbers. Back in the Seventies we used to have rallies in Gamber, Maryland. We invited the Nazis. We didn't allow them to distribute their literature, but we did let them speak. The Posse Comitatus was invited onto our rally grounds, not to distribute literature or recruit, but they could speak."

"Did you know J.B. Stoner and Connie Lynch?" I asked.

J.B. Stoner is a Klansman and co-founder of the National States Rights Party. He was responsible for numerous church bombings in the Fifties and Sixties and other heinous crimes against Blacks and Jews. Today, he still parades around saying, "Praise God for AIDS. It helps us rid ourselves of Niggers." In 1945, he organized the Stoner Anti-Jewish Party advocating legislation which would make being Jewish a crime, punishable by death. As an attorney, Stoner was once scheduled to represent James Earl Ray in the assassination of Martin Luther King, Jr.

Daryl Davis

Connie Lynch was a violent Klansman, originally from California, but who traveled the country inciting race riots and racial murders with his partner in crime, J.B. Stoner. His, "Kill all Niggers," speech in Baltimore in 1966 caused a riot for which he was arrested. He had a Black attorney who managed to get him acquitted based on freedom of speech. He later murdered two people in a shootout in Kentucky but was never brought to trial. Connie Lynch died in 1972.

White folded his arms on the table and leaned towards me. "Yeah, I knew J.B. Stoner. I met him several times. I met Connie Lynch once or twice."

"What is the agenda of the Klan for now, as of the 90's?" I asked, changing the direction of our conservation. Bob hesitated for just a moment.

"Well, Daryl, I've been away for a little while and I really wouldn't want to comment on that right now because I'm not really so sure myself. It appears though that the times are right. There's a lot of interest in joining the Klan now. The latest example would be what happened in California."

Bob was referring to the riot resulting after four White Los Angeles police officers were acquitted after being seen on video tape savagely beating Black motorist Rodney King.

"That leads up to something I was going to ask you," I interjected. "Being a former police offer, how do you feel about what you saw on the videotape of the Rodney King beating?"

White looked at me intently and began speaking. "I saw the videotape, but I didn't see what led up to it. What I saw on the tape looked bad. There was more than one-on-one and King was actually subdued. He was on the ground. I mean he was done. All they had to do was handcuff him and take him to jail. They didn't have to do what they did. They can call it what they want to call

aryl Davis' fourth grade class.

aryl attends a dinner party for his father
osted by famous Nazi hunter Simon
Veisenthal in Vienna, Austria.

mperial Wizard Roger Kelly's home at
hristmas.

PHOTO: © BOB ROLLER

KKK Imperial Wizard Roger Kelly and
Daryl Davis are brought together by
Davis' music.

Grand Giant
Vernon Naimaster
of United Klans of
America.

Visiting with Grand Giant Tony LaRicci in his
home.

Grand Giant Tony LaRicci,
Confederation of
Independent Orders,
Maryland Knights of the KKK.

Grand Giant Bob White, Confederation of
Independent Orders Knights of the KKK.

Klan marching through Germantown, Maryland.

lan members arrive for a march and rally.

Klansmen and women in their multicolored robes begin their march.

A black family on bicycles stops to watch as the Klan passes by. The police are close, ready for action.

Imperial Wizard Virgil Griffin and Grand Dragon Horace King of the Christian Knights of the KKK.

An unidentified klansman poses in his house.

A Klan roadblock used to distribute literature.

When Daryl Davis asked the klansman to pose with him, he agreed, then kissed Daryl!

A young klan member stops to pose with Daryl Davis at a march.

Another klansman poses with his hood on.

Daryl with three klansmen.

Daryl Davis attending a Klan march and rally.

Imperial Wizard Roger Kelly gives a speech in front of the Maryland Governor's Mansion

Roger Kelly holds a rally in a park.

With the Klan yelling "White Power," on one side of the Maryland Governor's Mansion, these protestors painted themselves green and stood on the other side with their signs which read, "Green Power."

A Klan gravestone at a cemetery. Notice the "KKK" under the cross. The deceased was a member of the first klan in Maryland formed in 1922.

ms from Daryl Davis' Klan memorabilia collection.

Chester Doles,
Leader of the
Territorial Klans of
America.

Chester Doles and his Klan arriving on the boardwalk in Ocean City, Maryland.

At the boardwalk in Ocean City: Daryl Davis in the foreground, Chester Doles in the background.

call it, but they were wrong...as far as I was concerned."

"So do you feel that there was a use of excessive force?"

"Oh, definitely!" White exclaimed as he unfolded his arms and leaned back in his seat. "They're going to try to tell you that they didn't hit him, some of them missed him. What the hell, they were trying to hit him. That was obvious. They surely weren't trying to scare him. As far as what everybody did in California, setting that city off like that, that was wrong. Stuff like that is going to lead to a race riot in this country one of these days and there's going to be a lot of innocent people killed for no reason at all. The police were wrong as far as I'm concerned. No matter how wrong this Rodney King was, these police were wrong for beating him like they did." Bob was very adamant and sincere in his disapproval of the action of the Los Angeles police officers.

"But," he continued, "that gave no excuse for the riots that took place, and especially pulling a truck driver out of his truck. That truck driver wasn't a policeman. Why didn't they go around and grab all the police and knock the hell out of them if that's what they wanted to do? Don't grab a man that's out there trying to earn a living and just knock the hell out of him because he happens to be a White guy," Bob said, slamming his hand down on the table top for emphasis.

"Were you surprised at the verdict?" I asked.

"Yeah, I was surprised!" White responded in a petulant voice.

I nodded and couldn't help the edge in my own voice as I commented, "You obviously understand the negative reaction of the Blacks in Los Angeles and all over the country, and that negative reaction was shared by many Whites. How would you say these people were supposed to react when they have tried to do the right thing? They have gone to the court, they have tried to work it out though legal means within the confines of the law. But then they find out that the law is crooked, as demonstrated by that verdict in Los Angeles. How should the public have reacted?" I asked, tilting my head to one side.

"Daryl, your ancestors wore chains. How did they get out of them? Not through violence. People are a lot smarter today. A riot to me signifies an excuse to tear a town up and steal what you need. A color television, a ten-speed bike, groceries, jewelry. The boy Rodney King was beaten out there in Los Angeles, so that signified an excuse to steal, rob and loot. The bottom line is, half of those people that they were stealing and looting could have cared less if the police had lifted his head up and shook his brains out all over the street, because they're shooting each other. I'll bet two of them get killed today right here in Baltimore City as a result of Black on Black crime. The riot was an excuse to get their new television sets. I was in the riots in 1968 while I was on the police force. They said they were hungry, that's why they were looting, but I saw them hauling ten-speed bikes down the street. You can't eat a ten-speed bike. Let's face it."

"So what should have been done?" I asked, raising both my hands in the air.

"Any case can be appealed." He raised a finger for each alternative he rattled off. "There's appellate courts, there's community relations committees. Violence is not the answer."

"When people saw how the first court was so corrupted in rendering a verdict that was so blatantly biased, they have very little faith in going to the next court," I argued.

He shook his head. "They don't want the next court. They wouldn't be able to get their color television sets and their ten-speed bicycles. What tickles me is, the damn fools tear their own neighborhoods up and now they have to stand in line in another neighborhood to buy groceries."

Bob frowned, "History has proven that when a major injustice occurs against a Black person, there is rioting, burning and looting. When Martin Luther King, Jr. was shot and killed in

Memphis, the Blacks rioted, burned and looted. When a White police officer killed a Black teenager by shooting him in the back in Miami, Florida, they rioted, they burned and they looted."

"When Don Black brought his Klan to Washington, D.C. in 1982, people White and Black rioted, burned and looted. When Virgil Griffin came to D.C. with his Klan and marched down Pennsylvania Avenue, they rioted, burned and looted," I argued.

Now it was White's turn to ask the questions. "How many times have the Black people marched and the Klan got out and rioted, burned and looted?"

I shot back, "I have seen the Klan riot, and I know they have burned down and bombed Black churches."

"When did you see a Klan riot?" Bob's eyes widened.

"Decatur, Alabama, 1979," I immediately answered. It was another indelible memory.

"The Klan rioted?" he asked somewhat surprised.

"Bill Wilkinson's Invisible Empire Knights of the Ku Klux Klan rioted," I matter-of-factly answered.

"How did they riot, Daryl?" he asked, looking engrossed.

My tone was bitter, though I spoke quite calmly. "They rioted with their batons, baseball bats, chains, and some wore crash helmets. They attacked the marchers who were coming down the street, and one Klansman got shot."

"Did they burn and loot or was this a personal confrontation?"

"No, they didn't burn and loot." I looked at Bob curiously.

"Then they didn't riot." He sat back with a slight smile on his face.

He defined, in his opinion, what a riot is. "A riot affects the general public. This was one group versus another group."

"Are you implying that it's similar to a gang war?"

"Yeah," he nodded, "like a gang war. You said the Blacks react this way with the rioting, burning and looting. Tell me, where did these killer bees come from that we have coming into the country?"

"South America, as far as I know," I said, not knowing where this was going.

"But where were they originally?" he prodded.

"Are you trying to say they originated in Africa?"

"A lot of wild things come out of Africa," Bob replied laughing.

I dismissed that comment and continued. "We have nowhere else to go. When we look for justice, we have to look to the White man. It's the White man who administers justice. He's the one who makes the laws. Look at the Supreme Court. Out of all the Justices, there is one Black and two females. Therefore, Blacks and females are expected to abide by whatever laws the majority of White men on the Supreme Court bench create."

"Based on the percentage of Blacks to Whites in this country, I think they have a fair representation in the Supreme Court," White countered.

"Regardless of the fact that Blacks make up a small percentage of the population of this country, they or any other minority should be entitled to the same justice the Whites who make up the majority receive," I stated forcibly.

He settled back in his chair. "I'm not saying that at all, Daryl. Let's get off on a slight tangent here to explain what I mean. Half of your political and community Black leadership in this country do have a decent head on their shoulders. The other half don't and are racist. They get on television and denounce Black on Black crime. Isn't that a form of discrimination in a certain round about way? I read it to say, 'If you need to go out and steal a pocketbook, go out and steal a White lady's pocketbook. Don't steal a Black lady's pocketbook. If you have to go out and rob and shoot somebody, rob and shoot a White person. Don't rob and shoot a Black person.' They are telling the Black people to go out and get the 'honkies.' They are instilling this in the Black people's heads. How many White people go out and assault and rob Blacks?"

I looked straight into White's eyes. "It happens. In fact, a few months ago, right in my neighborhood, two White guys assaulted two Black women and tried to set one of them on fire."

"It happens, but that was a few months ago. When was the incident before that?" he asked, surprised that I was able to come up with one.

"I don't recall specific times and incidents, but I can get that information for you," I assured him.

"Well, let's not pick sides. Let's just take an unbiased point of view. Let's turn on a police scanner and listen to descriptions coming over the air. Blacks cannot sit in prisons occupying ninety percent of the prisons and say they're being picked on."

I raised my eyebrows. "Do you really feel that Blacks who have committed the same crimes as Whites receive equal punishment?"

White nodded, "Well, I'm about as White as you can get Daryl, and I couldn't even get a trial."

"You are a public figure. You are a leader of a Klan. Society at large has a negative image of the Klan," I shot back.

"I'm a Klansman to the bone, but that's not my problem. That's their problem. I was forced to suffer for it," he said with a smirk.

Feeling my stomach churn, I gritted my teeth and then went on. "If an ordinary White person hits someone on the head and takes their wallet and an ordinary Black guy does the same thing, would there be a balance of justice?" I queried.

"In this state, I believe there would be," White said sincerely.

"Would you say that there was a time. . . "

He broke in. "I would say there was a time in the Sixties when you would be right about what you are hitting on," said Bob, picking up on what I was going to ask.

Daryl Davis

"You are saying that has changed?" I leaned forward.

"Sure, it's changed. Do you remember a long time ago I talked to you about attitudes and if it wasn't for the attitudes, our people could live together better?"

"Yes, I remember," I affirmed, shaking my head.

"I say a lot of wrong has been done and should not be forgotten, but let's not dwell on it beyond the point necessary to ensure that it does not happen again. Let's acknowledge that it was wrong and move forward and try to get along and make this a better place in which to live," he said, using his hands to get his point across.

Continuing, White vehemently argued the point. "During the generations of slavery, these slaves surely discussed among themselves how it was living back in Africa. So why was it that when they were freed so many of them didn't want to go back to Africa? The slave owners over here treated these people good compared to how they would have been, living over in Africa, had they still been there. They were given their own land to grow crops on. A lot of the slave owners even took them over to the Dominican and Haiti trying to establish them over there to get them more or less in their own environment or habitat. President Lincoln wanted to take them down to Panama and establish them there where they would have some shipping docks and ports with ships coming in. They could do their own trading and everything else. It's not like they just totally walked away and abandoned them. At that particular time, as slaves, they were considered no more than farm animals, but doesn't a good farmer take good care of his farm animals? He tries to keep them healthy and he tries to keep them content."

"Those Black slaves who had been here for generations did not know much about life in their homeland," I disputed. "They were born and raised here. They helped build this country. This is what they knew."

"Being accepted is very easily done if you have the right attitude. I have accepted you," White said looking straight at me.

"You are an exception among Klansmen," I said returning his gaze.

"No, I am not an exception. You are an exception because you're not the typical Black. You…"

"Wait a minute," I interrupted. "What is the typical Black?" I asked him taking slight offense.

"The typical Black has an air of arrogance about him that everybody owes him his next loaf of bread because his great, great-grandfather worked the cotton field. You didn't come on to me that way. You came on to me like a man, and I will come back on to you like a man. Me and you can communicate."

I picked up my glass and took a sip of the cold drink before responding. "I agree with you Bob, that a change in attitudes towards one another would help solve a lot of differences and people would get along better. But it has to be a change in attitude on both sides, White and Black. There are a lot of Blacks who are not exposed to Whites and there are a lot of Whites who never come in contact with Blacks."

"Sincerely," he agreed readily.

I leaned towards Bob and continued. "I think the media has played upon people's perceptions. For example, the bad guy in the old western movies usually wore black and the good guys wore white. He wore a white hat and rode a white horse."

Bob started laughing. I was referring to "The Lone Ranger," but he may have been thinking about the Klan symbol of the Knight in a white robe with a white hood on his head rearing back on a white horse. Many of the early Klansmen even put white sheets on their horses.

"Subliminally," I went on, "it plays on your mind. White is good and black is bad. Even in cartoons like 'Mighty Mouse.' All the mice in 'Mighty Mouse' were white. Even Mighty Mouse himself was white. Who were the bad guys? The big black cats."

"Mighty Mouse wasn't white!" said Bob, looking at me incredulously.

"He was so!" I insisted.

"No, he wasn't!" Bob countered.

"Look at his face," I demanded. "He's white."

"Look at the rest of him, he's black!" Bob said not giving up.

"Are we going to argue about Mighty Mouse?" I threw up my hands. We both started laughing hysterically.

I wasn't ready to quit yet. I quickly ticked off many more examples. "And then you have Tarzan who is supposed to be king of Africa. And he's a White man! There are terms like blackmail, blacklist, blackball and if a black cat crosses your path, you'll have bad luck. The term black is almost always associated with something negative. This becomes ingrained in peoples' minds subliminally. So, naturally when they see a Black person, they think negatively."

Bob drew in his breath before calmly responding. "The discrimination has nothing to do with the color. It has to do with fear. When I lived in Randallstown, Maryland, I had a Black man named Bill move in next door to me. He worked and his wife was a school teacher. We were great friends. We used to sit out in the backyard and drink beer together and everything. As far as nice people, you couldn't ask for better people. The fact is, Bill was one of the few neighbors around there that I even fooled with and socialized with. But I couldn't help thinking the whole time, this was the start of 'there goes the neighborhood.' I know it wasn't a year later that I had 250 pigeons stolen out of my pigeon loft in my own backyard, ten feet from my house. I found them a block and a half away.

"A Black kid moved in the neighborhood. He wasn't a kid, he was eighteen but he was like six-foot-three. He cleaned me out three or four times and he just kept coming back and coming back. The neighborhood went to hell after that."

"But Bill wasn't a participant in that," I pointed out.

White shook his head in agreement. "Bill used to get out on the sidewalk and run them out from in front of his house. They'd come back with this motherfucker this and motherfucker that stuff, and he was raising little girls and I had girls. One day my daughter come home from school and she's seven or eight-years-old and she asked her mother what a 'motherfucker' was. My wife looked at her and asked her, 'Where did you hear that?' It turned out it came from one of the kids in school. My kids never heard this. Like I said, it was a start. I couldn't help but think to myself what a nice guy Bill is, but it's a start. It seems like when the first Black moves in the neighborhood, the 'For Sale' signs just fly up. They call it White flight. But why, why does it happen? You can tell they're coming from blocks away. Stores that have been there for fifty years start putting bars over the windows and grills over the doors. Why is this?"

"Because they fear something?" I offered as an explanation.

"Right!" Bob said pointing his finger at me.

"But do they take the time to explore this fear and see if it can be alleviated?"

He leaned back in his chair. "The Blacks here simply turn their heads if they see Blacks coming to break in the stores. They don't call the police. At least ninety percent of them won't. They'll just think it's one of the bros doing good. He's snakin' a score," Bob said in a loud voice.

"Aren't there Whites who break into stores and rob people?" I said defensively.

"We have statistics and percentages and let them speak for themselves. Sure, there was a little Jew that broke into my house. His own sister told me he did it. If you call Jews White. I don't think they're White."

"Well, let's talk about Whites. Are there not any White criminals who do this type of thing?"

"You're damn right there is. But percentage wise, how many Whites are there that go in and prey on Blacks? How many Blacks prey on Whites? That's why we don't want them around us." White waved his arms in the air to make his point.

Daryl Davis

I shifted around again in my chair. "Speaking of percentages, you must know that there are more Whites on welfare in this country than Blacks. Are you going to tell me it's because there are more Whites in this country than Blacks?"

"That's right," White nodded.

"What do you think about Black organizations like the NAACP, CORE and others? Let me point out that these organizations also have White members."

Bob looked around the room before he responded. "I think they're trying to profiteer one way or another."

"If things were fair to begin with," I argued, "there wouldn't be a need for organizations geared towards the benefit of Blacks, such as the Black State Troopers Association, the Black Coalition for this, that and the other thing or the Black Miss America Pageant."

He immediately had a comeback to my statement. "What do you think would happen if they had a White Miss America Pageant or a White State Trooper Association?"

"People would be up in arms," I said with no doubt in my mind.

"Why should White people apologize for being White?"

"They don't have to," I shook my head.

"But in a roundabout way they are," White spoke in an even voice.

"Thirty years ago, you and I probably would not be sitting together in a restaurant talking. I probably would not be allowed in or I would have to get my food out the back door of the kitchen or something," I said, pointing to the back area of the restaurant.

White shook his head in frustration. "That was thirty years ago. Now, you don't have that problem. How many stores did you burn to get this?"

"I didn't burn any," I said quietly, but my stomach was churning again at his stereotyped insinuation. "I think that while some things have come a long way in a certain regard, the media and the powers that be are doing a lot of things to keep us separated and keep us fighting. Personally, I don't think the government cares whether you're Black or White. The only color they are interested in is green. Money. As long as they can do things to keep us preoccupied with fighting each other down here on this level, they can do the sneaky things they do at the top level to make the money without us interfering. Violence generates money, wars generate money, drugs generate money. You know, we could work together and solve the drug problem in this country."

"Sure," he shrugged, "we could definitely solve it."

I didn't try to match his composure. "Now don't start saying, 'Get rid of all the Blacks,'" I said determined.

"No. I'm saying anybody you see handing drugs to somebody else, blow their damn brains out."

I had no doubt from the agitated hostility in his face and eyes that he would be willing to execute such an order and draw the first blood.

"That eliminates the courts and everything else," he continued. "I mean they are out there shooting each other anyway, so you might as well shoot them for something worthwhile," he held up both his hands.

I thought this was an interesting insight into Bob White's subconscious feelings because moments ago he was saying violence was not the answer and now he was advocating blowing someone's brains out.

I posed another question to the man sitting in front of me. "What do you think Blacks and Whites can do together to solve some of the problems that we both commonly face? I am not necessarily talking about the racial problems but, for example, the drug problem which does not discriminate by color. We all are affected by this. I am talking about the Klan and some Black people working together to solve a problem that we both have in common, problems that are both Black and White."

"Daryl," he rubbed his chin as he replied, "there are people from all walks of life who join the Klan and they are not really interested in hooking up with other races to accomplish their goal. You are going to find that hard to do with the Klan or with the Skinheads or Nazis or whatever. Now, with these neighborhood groups who don't belong to the Klan or other organizations like that, sure they will get together to expose these drug people. As far as the Klan helping to picket a house . . . it's easier to burn," he said laughing. "Why waste all day on a three-minute job? You know what I mean?"

I smiled but was jarred not only by his words but at his candor. "Bob, there has to be something we can do jointly where we can stand on a common ground, even if it's just a small piece of common ground. Once this is accomplished, the fears are alleviated and the common ground widens."

Once again, White had an immediate response. "The first thing that has to be done is people have to stop preying on each other. Stop the violence. The only way the violence is going to stop is Blacks turning Blacks in for it instead of them turning their heads. That's why I moved all the way the hell out here to get away from it. I keep moving from one place to another to get away from it. Just keep on running. Where's everybody going to go when they're all standing on the state line? You'll be able to look down from a helicopter and tell where the state line is by all the White faces. Everybody's moving out. Let's face it. As a rule, Whites do not assault and rob Blacks. Whites do not go into a Black neighborhood and burglarize their homes."

"We may not have anything in our homes that they want to steal," I replied laughing.

White answered in a serious tone, ignoring my little joke.

"Come on, Daryl. Now, we're two people who just met. I'd like to take you for a walk through my house and then take a stroll through your house. I don't know what you have, but, I guarantee you, it's more than what I have."

"Well, according to you, what I have in my house, I got from your house," I said and we both started laughing.

"If you can stop that, then people would be comfortable around each other and they can start mixing it up then. But until then, until all that fear is erased, that problem will continue. It's not a fear of dying. It's a fear of somebody taking your stuff away from you. While you are out working, somebody else is in your house cleaning you out. Why work?"

"So, let's march together to say we don't approve of violence," I said leaning forward.

"Everybody knows already that we don't approve of violence. We also know that every morning the sun comes up, so why should we march to prove that?"

"I don't know that the Klan doesn't approve of violence," I said looking him straight in the eye.

He returned my gaze. "The thing to do is for your people to start realizing that whatever this purse-snatcher or burglar is doing, it is going to affect my kids and their kids and generations to come. It's not going to get better while that purse-snatcher is standing on that corner. Now, I know for a fact from being in the police department that everyone in that neighborhood block knows who the purse-snatcher is but they won't tell. If nothing else, they could take a Polaroid picture of the person and turn that in anonymously. That's the greatest thing I ever thought of when I was on the police force. Everybody in every block, they know who these purse-snatchers are. All they have to do is take a Polaroid picture of the person and write down on the back what his name is and where he lives. Say a lady gets her purse snatched, the police can give her a stack of pictures and let her thumb through them and pick out who did it. That eliminates all this crap."

"Yeah, but people can't spend their whole day walking around with Polaroid cameras taking pictures all day," I argued.

"People don't realize it," White said adamantly. "They think he's such a nice kid and he needs the money. To the people ten blocks away, he's nothing but a common sewer rat that's prey-ing on them by going around breaking old ladies' hips and legs so he can get two or three dollars out of their purses for his bad dope problem. That's not a nice kid. Tomorrow somebody else's nice kid will be over there breaking some other lady's arms and legs for her two or three dollars. You all have to get together on this and get it all solved."

"I agree with you. I have no problem with Blacks turning in Blacks for crimes committed. Most of it boils down to drugs these days. But what about the Whites who are responsible for being the masterminds behind bringing these drugs into the coun-try? They are the ones who are financing it and are at the top level paying off law officers and judges who will cooperate and elimi-nating those who don't. I am sure at the highest level of any drug ring in this country, you will find a White person, not a Black. You may find the dealers on the street corners but they are not the ones who have the small propeller planes or the private Lear jets and own shipping companies that transport these illegal drugs into the country. Those are the White people you never hear about or never suspect or if they do get nailed, they can afford the best lawyers to work out the best deal for them."

White shook his head. "I'm not excusing the Whites for this. The feds know who they are. It's just a matter of catching them."

"Some of the feds are being paid off," I told him. I wanted him to know the problem is bigger than just 'a matter of catching them.' I went on explaining, "Just a couple of months ago the story came out about a Drug Enforcement Administration officer who got busted for accepting bribes and hindering the bureau's war on drugs. I don't believe that our government is doing all it can to win the war on drugs. I may catch a lot of flack from some people for saying that, but that's the way I feel."

"Daryl, it's the same with me for talking to you. Some people that don't know me will call me a Nigger-lover. They will say that I'm trying to make a Nigger rich. They will call me a race-traitor. The people who do know me know that I have bigger and more far-reaching objectives than separatism. Separatism is not going to happen. We have multitudes of races and mixed races operating and living in this country. I don't believe in mixing the races. I believe the White race should stay White and the Black race should stay Black and the Yellow race should remain Yellow. But socially, there has to be a change or there's going to be a lot of race riots and race wars.

"Our offspring is going to get hurt by it. So, we might as well start getting things together now. It's not like we're uncivilized. If we don't set an example now of living together... let's face it, what we got now, we inherited from our ancestors. Our great-grandchildren are going to inherit a world from us. Don't hand them a bomb. Give them something they can take care of and enjoy their life with. It's got to start somewhere, so why not with us?" he said resting his hands in front of him.

It was a sentiment I didn't argue with. After all, it was mine too.

10

One Version of
the Truth

Although Bob White and I had spoken of many things, I still had not asked him about the incident involving the two Black men which had resulted in his being sent to jail for three years. I had been waiting for the time to be right. Now I felt it had come and at our next meeting a week later, I came straight to the point. "I have heard it from the media, and people I've talked to," I said. "Now I want to hear it from you; the story about what led to your last prison incarceration." I leaned forward, not wanting to miss a word.

White lowered his voice and began telling his story. "Well, once a month, we normally had a state board meeting. It was usually on the first Sunday of every month. The heads of the various units around the state came to the meetings and took back literature and whatever pertained to their particular unit; information, mail, applications for membership, whatever. At the end of the meeting we had a few beers at one bar and Mike Monaghan wanted to walk across the street to another bar."

Daryl Davis

Michael Monaghan was a member of Bob White's Klan group and was listed in the newspapers as an officer in the Klan and a full-time fireman for Baltimore County.

He continued his story. "So we walked across the street and we had a couple of beers in there. His truck was parked right outside there and mine was directly across the street at the first bar. I was sitting to his left and he was talking to two men on his right while I got into a conversation with the men who were on my left. We drank a few beers and the next thing I know, it was time to go home. He turned around and said, 'Are you ready to go?' I said, 'Yeah,' as I was finishing up my beer. Out the door we went. We stopped at the corner of the bar to tell some members, 'See you later, see you next month.' We were there for just a few seconds. I started across the street to my truck and I hear Mike hollering. I turned around and looked and there were two Black guys on him. One was on him and the other one was standing there hitting him with a stick and kicking at him. I had a pellet rifle that needed repair in the back of my truck. I was supposed to take it down to a Baltimore gunsmith and get it repaired that week. I was going to give it to a friend of mine for his kid. I continued on across the street to my truck. I pulled the pellet rifle out of my truck. It was the pump up kind, you know. It holds air but the tube was missing out of the front. So I hollered across the street for them to stop and apparently they didn't hear me. I hollered a little more and I pumped it up real quick and then I popped it." He made the motions in the air to demonstrate how he popped the gun.
"Where did you pop it?"
White pointed to the ceiling. "I popped it up in the air."
"Did you also pop one into the ground?" I questioned.
White stopped to think for a moment. "I might have popped one into the ground when I was pumping the gun. It lost so much air from it seeping out that you almost had to pull the trigger as soon as you got it pumped up. Well, they got off Mike

and took off running. One ran over the embankment into the woods at the back of the parking lot. I went to the edge of the embankment and stayed there for a couple of minutes to make sure he wasn't coming back, then I turned around to go back and look for Mike. I couldn't find him so I went into the bar and he wasn't in there. As soon as I came out the door, Mike came running up and said, 'Let's get the hell outta here. I just messed up one of them pretty bad.' He had chased the other one into the other bar and knocked the hell out of him."

Other sources say that this particular Black man had a prosthesis and Michael Monaghan beat him so severely that his artificial leg detached.

Bob scratched his face and continued, "Anyhow, we took off running. I took the pellet rifle and threw it up on this ledge up under this bridge so it wouldn't get lost. All the police in town showed up. It looked like a Christmas tree down there," he said referring to the emergency lights flashing on the police vehicles.

"Mike was bleeding all up behind his ear and said that he was going to walk up to a buddy's house. So I figured I would go inside the other bar and get me a beer while I waited for the cops to leave. I looked out the window and there was my truck up on a flatbed tow truck and they were getting ready to haul it away. So I walked over there to the police and said, 'Is that truck parked illegally officer?' He said, 'Why, are you driving it?' I says, 'Yeah.' That police officer got on me and said, 'Get over the hood!' So I put my hands over the hood of his car and he patted me down and handcuffed me and threw me in the back of the police car. He got my keys and searched all over my truck and took my attaché cases and unlocked them and saw the Klan literature in there. I asked him what he was looking for and he said, 'Shut up hillbilly.' That's all he kept saying to me. When his sergeant came up and looked in the back of the cruiser, the policeman told him 'He's a goddamned Klansman. The fucking Klan.'" White's voice grew louder as he told this part of the incident.

"Was the sergeant White or Black?" I asked curiously.

"Black. They kept staring at me like they had caught a polar bear in the back of the car. I tried to tell them a couple of times that if it was a gun they were looking for, that it was right down the street. They refused to go get it," White said as an angry look spread across his face.

"Anyhow, when they booked me and the White desk sergeant said, 'You are being charged with shooting,' I told him I wanted a paraffin test and a lie detector test right then. The paraffin test shows whether you just recently shot a gun. He said that it wouldn't be necessary and they put me in the cell. I figured I'd be out of there, but they held me till the next morning. Come to find out I was being charged with "Assault with Intent to Murder" against two people and "Assault with Intent to Murder" against the same two because of the color of skin. Now, how many times can you attempt to murder somebody? What, to kill them one time on general principle and then kill them again because of the color of their skin? They also charged me with carrying a firearm openly, carrying it concealed and discharging it. All because of the Klan literature he found, he was trying to make a racial incident out of it and it really wasn't a racial incident."

Bob leaned back and finished his beer. "After all was said and done, I found out later that Mike had seen the two Black guys come in the bar on the side he was facing while we were sitting there. I was facing the other way having a conversation with a couple of people. The Black men had come in the carryout to get a package of beer to go and Mike began making remarks at them."

"What kind of remarks?" I queried.

"Something like, 'We don't serve Niggers in here,' and this, that and the other."

"Why did Mike initiate this?" I wanted to know.

White shrugged his shoulders. "That's the kind of guy he is. So they approached him about it when they came out and all hell broke loose. They nailed him and down he went."

I motioned for the waitress to come to our table before asking my next question.

"Why didn't anybody stop the fight when Mike went back into the bar after the Black guy with the artificial leg?"

"I don't know. When I had gone back in there, everything was calm and there was no signs of a scuffle, and nobody said anything about it," explained White. "I later heard that Michael Monaghan ran into the bar screaming, 'That Nigger just raped a White woman!' and the patrons moved the furniture out of the way so Monaghan could beat him up.

"They put me in jail and the judge put a $200,000 bond on me. I sat in the Baltimore City Jail for seven months waiting for my trial." White's face started to turn red.

"What happened with Monaghan?" I asked.

"Well, he turned around and snitched on the whole works. They asked him if he had ever seen me in possession of any guns and he told them that I had guns up at my house. The feds went up to my house and took all my guns and everything. They just broke him because he was scared to go to jail so he just turned on me, to keep himself out of prison."

"Then you went to prison?"

"Yeah, for three years. First I went to Lewisburg Penitentiary in Lewisburg, Pennsylvania. Then I went to Terre Haute in Terre Haute, Indiana. Then I got transferred to Petersburg in Petersburg, Virginia, and from there I went to Hagerstown in Hagerstown, Maryland."

"When you finally came out, everything you had was gone. Your house, your possessions, your wife, everything was gone and you had to start all over." When I first met Bob, he showed me his divorce papers to prove to me how dedicated he was to the Klan. Apparently his wife had given him the ultimatum: the Klan or her. He chose the Klan.

"Yeah," he admitted, "I had to start all over from scratch."

"Do you feel that your marriage crumbled because of the Klan?" I asked as I reached across the table for my drink.

"Well, I had done time before because of the Klan. The state police set us up. I did four years then."

I raised my eyebrows. "This was for the attempted bombing of the synagogue?"

"Yes," he replied, blinking several times.

"Tell me about that."

"Well, there was a fellow in the organization named Bill Aitcheson. He was charged with hate bombing and sending threatening letters to Coretta Scott King which caused the state police to come into the organization, undercover."

"Are you still in contact with Aitcheson?" I asked.

White shook his head. "I haven't heard from Aitcheson in years."

William Aitcheson was a student at the University of Maryland while a member of the Maryland Knights of the Ku Klux Klan under Grand Dragon Tony LaRicci. He later became an Exalted Cyclops in a group that splintered off of the Maryland Knights. He was arrested for sending death threats to Coretta Scott King, who was to appear on the university campus. In addition, he was charged with possession of weapons and explosives and numerous crossburnings. He was also suspected of plotting to blow up the local NAACP office and the communication facilities at Ft. Mead, Maryland.

I tracked down his parents' home and had my secretary try to contact him there. His father said that he no longer lived there and doubted that his son would be interested in meeting with me. He said that was in the past, and he is no longer involved, but he would take my number and pass it on to his son. However, he doubted Bill would call me. Bill Aitcheson never called.

Bob shifted around in his chair before continuing. "The police said they had infiltrated the organization. They didn't infiltrate. They just came on the rally grounds and got sworn in. The news media, or the 'Jews media' as I call it, made a hero out of Detective Sergeant John Cooke. I didn't know it, but he was involved with a young fellow in the organization named Gerald Allen. John Cooke was having Gerry make him these little pipe bombs and little explosive devices. LaRicci was Grand Dragon and I was Grand Klaliff. One day after a state board meeting, I had gone outside and this other guy, who turned out to be an informant, called me over to John Cooke's car. It was a raggedy old car, and Cooke was standing there. Anyhow, we lifted up the blanket and he showed me all these blasting caps on the back seat. He was trying to set up his program then. I looked at them and said, 'They're cute,' and went on about my business. Meanwhile, he was keeping Gerry making these little bombs for him.

"Then one day on the weekend, we were all out shooting pool and having a couple of drinks together. Somehow it was set up that somebody saw a sign in front of a synagogue that said, 'Save Soviet Jewry.' They misread it to read, 'Save Soviet Jewelry.' They thought communist jewelry was being sold out of the synagogue. Gerry and a couple of other ones wanted to blow the synagogue up. I didn't really pay that much attention to them. It didn't mean that much to me. If they wanted to blow it, let 'em blow it. Detective Sergeant Cooke and Gerry were going to blow this synagogue up the following weekend. I was home watching television. I couldn't have cared less what they were going to do. So, John Cooke came up to my house and knocked on the door. He said, 'Gerry can't make it. Can you come with me?' I smelled a rat all over this guy, but I'm wondering if he has the balls to do this. So, I say, 'Let's go.' We stopped and got a twelve-pack of beer. We were drinking these and he says, 'Which way to the synagogue?' I'm pointing the directions out to him and I say, 'Make a left here,' and he says, 'Oh, make a left here on Eugene Avenue?'"

Bob sat straight up in his chair.

"You were being recorded," I interrupted.

"Oh, yeah, I knew right off the bat. So, we passed the synagogue and parked up on the next corner. Finally he reaches in the back and hands me this bag. So I look in it and it's got the pipe bomb in it. It wasn't the real one. He done switched it. I cut off a piece of the fuse and lit it and threw it out the window. I wiped my fingerprints off and handed the bomb back to him. He says, 'You ready?' I said, 'Let's go!' So, he takes the bomb and he's carrying it. I didn't carry it. So we walk alongside the synagogue—this is at night time. I saw a light on in the back so I said, 'Lay it up under that bush for the time being.' This was on the side of the synagogue. So, he laid it under the bush and we walked around the back and looked to see if anybody was in there. Now, at the time we were around the back, the car he was calling out the streets to, pulls in the driveway alongside the synagogue. There was a house sitting there and two driveways. He pulls into the one next to the house. One guy gets out of the car on the passenger side and goes around and leans in the driver side and is talking to the driver. I told Cooke, 'Let's get the hell outta here. I ain't getting locked up for no punk shit like this.' Now, I called it off and I said, 'Go down and get that bag,' and he went down and got the bag and came back. We got in his car and left. That was in Baltimore County. We drive out to Howard County. We stopped in a bar out there and he goes and gets on the telephone. He said he had to call his girlfriend, but I knew what he was up to. We had a beer then we went further into Howard County. Then he makes another telephone call. I know damn right and well what he was doing. He kept saying, 'You gonna blow it up, you gonna blow it up?' I wouldn't answer him. We get down to Ellicott City and he gets on the phone again. I said, 'Well let's get on home. I've got to open up my store in the morning.'"

White took a long drink from his glass and then went on with the story. "John Cooke said, 'Before we go home, let's ride out by the Holiday Inn. I've got to see some guy about some stolen jewelry.' I said, 'I don't want to get involved in no stolen jewelry. You take me home and then you can go back and meet the guy.' He said, 'It's right on the way. Come on, ride over there with me.' So, I rode over there with him. We get in the parking lot and he starts sliding out the door on his side. As he does, he hands me a little plastic baggy and says, 'Here, Bob, read this.' I knew what it was as soon as I saw it. It was his badge. Meanwhile, the other undercover agents are opening the door on my side saying, 'Get out! You're under arrest!' They said it was for conspiring to blow up a synagogue. Cooke also had me down for Parren Mitchell being on my death list, starting a strike force in the Klan and all kinds of stuff."

"What is this about Parren Mitchell?" I asked curiously about the Black Maryland Congressman.

Bob paused before explaining, "Well, we went past Parren Mitchell's house one time just to see where he lived at. We went down the alley and checked everything out."

"What was the purpose of checking him out?"

"In case we ever needed him," Bob answered laughing.

I raised my eyebrows at that last comment. "What had Parren Mitchell done to get on your bad side?"

"I guess you could call him a racist, an arrogant big mouth racist. He had told the news media that he was on the Klan's death list. He wasn't on our death list. Then a big thing blew up in the paper that I was organizing a strike force against the Black political leaders and Jews."

"How did they find out that you were checking out his house?" I pried.

White picked up his napkin and started shredding the corners. "Cooke was with us. Then one night something was said about burning a cross in Mitchell's yard. Cooke called down to Baltimore City Police Department Intelligence to notify them. One of my members worked in there and he called me up and said, 'Stay the hell away from Mitchell's house. That place is loaded with police all over the place.' So, when I called it off, Cooke couldn't figure out how we knew."

"Why didn't your Klansmen in police intelligence tell you about Cooke?"

"They didn't know him. When you have two different police agencies investigating something like that and being undercover, they don't even know who each other are. We had a crazy nut who we threw out of the organization named Richard Savina. He went and founded his own group called the Bloody Knights of the Ku Klux Klan. He said he had a thousand members but he really only had five, and all five were undercover police from different agencies who didn't know each other was undercover. He was ninety-cents short on a dollar. They locked him up. He was going to firebomb a NAACP leader's house," White chuckled.

I had read a similar story about Richard Lee Savina who was arrested in 1981 for conspiracy to bomb the NAACP headquarters in Baltimore, Maryland.

Again, I turned the topic to White's time in prison. "Tell me about your relationship with the member of the Black Panthers while you were both in jail."

"We worked on a lot of cases together at the City Jail for these fellows who came in and weren't familiar with the law."

"Were these things you were doing for the prisoners' rights for both Black and White prisoners?" I interjected.

"Oh, yeah," Bob nodded. "He was a Black Panther and I was a Ku Klux Klansman, and we were working side by side down there for everybody."

"Did it seem odd to people there?" A picture of the two men working came to my mind and I couldn't suppress a slight chuckle.

Bob smiled in response. "Yeah, it seemed odd to people who saw us getting along pretty good together. I liked him. He had a lot of balls. He is out now, living here in Baltimore. He gave me his address. His name is Henry."

I shook my head. "A Black Panther and a Klansman working together side by side. You found a common ground to stand on," I marveled.

"Certainly, and we became pretty good friends."

I tilted my head and asked another question I'd been wondering about. "Do you feel for the most part that your experiences in the Klan have been positive and you have done some good for other people?"

"We've done a lot of good as far as I'm concerned. We've donated to the Cancer Society and the Red Cross. We've taken up Christmas donations for the poor and needy. It was never publicized."

"All needy people, Black and White?" I wanted to be sure.

He shook his head no. "Poor White people. Poor Blacks have enough help. We got to help our own. We used to play charity baseball games for the March of Dimes. Of course, that was never publicized either. Every other team got recognition, but we never got it. We were on all the mailing lists for all of these organization and charities. They would always send us things asking for donations, but they never gave us any recognition. It's that stigma of being the Klan."

"The Klan has promoted so many inequalities when it comes to Blacks," I protested. "We could not stay in the same hotels or ride in the front of the bus, just to name two."

"Preferably, I'd rather ride in the back of the bus myself," said Bob. "I always sit with my back to the wall if you notice, so I can see what's going on up front."

Daryl Davis

I wondered if prison had anything to do with his assuming the position of keeping his back to the wall. I kept my thoughts to myself and let Bob continued explaining his views. "A lot of Blacks were perfectly satisfied with their way of life, had no problem living in those conditions and got along fine with White people. These Blacks resented people trying to change them. That's when the trouble started."

I stopped for a moment to think about what Bob said, then slowly replied, "There may have been a few who were content because they didn't know better. I think there were many more who were afraid to speak out and now there are more than that who want a change and are willing to speak out about it."

An incident that occurred when I was on the road with The Legendary Blues Band, the late, great Blues singer Muddy Waters' backup band, flashed through my mind.

We were in Atlanta, Georgia for a performance. On the same day, members of a Georgia Klan group attacked Black Civil Rights marchers in nearby Forsyth County. Earlier that afternoon, the guitar player, Louis Meyers, one of the truly great Blues guitarists who has influenced countless guitar players, and I were driving around town in the band van. It was rush hour and I was behind the wheel in the left lane. A White woman in the right lane suddenly decided to make a left turn at the break in the median right in front of me. I was forced to slam on the brakes to avoid broadsiding her. Cars in the oncoming lanes were forced to stop for the same reason.

Now she had two lanes of traffic travelling in opposite directions at a standstill. She looked at me and even though the windows to the van were rolled up, I could hear her yell, "Why don't you pull around me you stupid Nigger!"

I rolled my window down, looked down at her and answered, "Why don't you go to hell you stupid bitch!"

Louis, who was fifty-eight-years-old at the time and sitting in the passenger seat next to me, quickly climbed over all the seats and hid on the floor in the rear of the van and kept saying, "Let's get out of here!" He then began cursing me out, "You jackass, don't you know where you are!? You don't talk to White people like that! Go on back to Washington D.C. and talk that shit to the White people there, you'll get us killed down here! She's probably married to the Grand Dragon of the Ku Klux Klan."

At first I laughed at Louis for his overreaction to a situation that happens everyday, in every town, in every rush hour, whether or not racial slurs enter into the dialogue between agitated motorists. He agreed that it happened all the time, but said a Black man should never curse a White woman even if she is in the wrong. He continued berating me and swore that the Grand Dragon would show up at our gig that evening and possibly kill the whole band. He was considering not even appearing in the club that night.

That night Louis stood on stage the whole time facing the entrance to the club. Every time the door would open, beads of sweat would poor down his face and his whole body would shake. His guitar playing that night was the worst I'd ever heard from him. I realized he was not putting me on and I was horrified that I had at first been amused by his phobia.

Louis told me that he had moved from a small town in Mississippi to Chicago back in the Forties. As a child, he had witnessed the Klan come to his Black neighbor's home and tie the man to the back of their vehicle and drag him down the street. This memory was still very much alive in his mind. Although he had gotten out of that town, he still subscribed to the White belief that, "Blacks have their place and they had better stay in it."

Louis Meyers passed away a year ago. As I looked at the man sitting across from me, I wished he were still alive to witness a Black man and a Klansman having dinner together.

Daryl Davis

I refocused on the present. Bob and I had long since finished our dinner and we were about the only ones left in the restaurant.

He leaned towards me and said, "Well, Daryl, the key to our races ever getting along is one seven-letter word, R-E-S-P-E-C-T. First you have segregation then you have integration and then you have saturation. Unless we respect each other there will always be a race problem."

Nodding, I smiled at the Grand Dragon of the Ku Klux Klan. "Well, Bob, I hope you've found this as interesting as I have. Thank you very much for your time. Let's keep in touch."

He smiled back at me and said, "I'd like that. Thanks for dinner. I am sure we will get together again.."

Driving home, I reflected on Bob White's life. There was no doubt he was still a Klansman in his heart and to the bone, as he had said, although he had mellowed a bit. He seemed to have come full circle in some ways. In the past, he used to arrest people and put them in the "cesspool of the world," or the "innermost circle of hell." Now he has spent a portion of his own life there. It is more than ironic that he has been discriminated against on the basis of his being a Klansman the same way too many Blacks have been discriminated against on the basis of their skin color.

PART III

CROSSING THE LINES OF RACISM

11

A Cross-Burning

Despite the fact that a kind of friendship was growing between Roger Kelly and me, he was nonetheless a Klan leader advancing his cause. He and his group had a public rally, complete with a cross-lighting in a small Maryland town a few miles below the Pennsylvania state line. A couple of days after the rally there was a cross-burning on the lawn of an elderly Black couple in that town. This Black couple lived in an all-White community and had been on good terms with all of their neighbors.

Roger was very upset by the incident. He told me—and I believed him—that he had not sanctioned this cross-burning. While he thought that his rally was probably a catalyst for the perpetrator or perpetrators, he did not believe that any of his members had anything to do with it, but alluded to the possibility that it could have been a member gone bad. At any rate, Roger wanted to see the perpetrator caught and prosecuted. He said that if he ever found out that any of his members had done something like that, he would turn them over to the police himself. I can attest that he has done this in the past.

He phoned the police and the fire marshal handling the incident and asked to view the remains of the burned cross. "The Klan has a certain way of wrapping and burning a cross," he explained. "There may be a chance that if a Klansperson had committed this act, he or she would have used this method."

At first the police were receptive to the idea of Roger's scrutiny of the cross, but later rescinded before he had a chance to look at it. The authorities apparently changed their minds because it was later concluded that it was not a Klan-related incident, but had probably been committed by some kids, so the incident was dropped. This is in contrast to the police who years ago would let the incident slide for other reasons. In those days, many officers of the law were, in my opinion, participants in such acts, as they were silent members of the Klan. Some still are today. I do not want to suggest that I am anti-police; I know many police officers who are honorable, diligent, law-abiding people, but I have also come across many who are not.

Anyway, Roger expressed concern to me about how this elderly Black couple must have felt, knowing that they probably could recall times when the Klan did do some pretty terrible things to Blacks for no other reason than the color of their skins. The burning of the cross in their yard would be a reminder of those times. Roger also conceded that some Klans still do such things, "but I don't advocate that in my group."

"If you're genuinely concerned," I suggested, "why not go to the couple's home, identify yourself, express your concerns and your desire to be of any assistance."

He said, "Daryl, I would like to do that, but don't you think they might be intimidated when I tell them who I am?"

I agreed that possibility distinctly existed. "However," I suggested, "I would go to their home with you." I'd go in first, explain why he wanted to see them and lay the groundwork for his introduction. He found it surprising that I would do that for him.

"You've done some surprising things with me," I said using the opportunity to express my mission. "It only goes to show, if people do not get so hung up on skin color and have

136

mutual respect for each other and act like the human beings that we are supposed to be, it should come as no surprise when one wants to help the other."

We found a mutually convenient day and I met Roger by himself at the usual place. We took my car and drove about an hour and a quarter, almost to the state of Pennsylvania. The couple's name was not published in the newspaper, but they did name the street. We went there. It was located in a White neighborhood. We began looking for someone working in their yard or walking around so we could ask at which house had the cross been burned.

Seeing no one, I decided that I would start knocking on doors to ascertain where the couple resided. I knocked on several, but no one was home. Then, a weak male voice from within a house told me to come in after I had knocked. I pushed open the door but didn't see anyone. I called out and the voice said, "Come on back here." I walked through the house to the back bedroom and there was a rather large, aged White man laying on his bed. He had obviously been napping. He did not seem the least bit surprised to see a large Black man, who was a total stranger, standing in his bedroom looking at him. "Can I help you," he asked.

"Do you know the house at which the cross burning incident occurred?"

He said, "The one directly across the street. I know the couple very well and have nothing but good things to say about them."

I thanked him and left.

On my way out, I couldn't help but think how wonderful it must be to live in a neighborhood in which you do not have to lock your doors and strangers of any color are welcome. I live in a big city in a predominantly White neighborhood and you don't ever tell someone to come in your house without looking out the peephole if you are not expecting someone. I know some neighborhoods where people, if they answer their door at all, do so with a gun in their hands.

Daryl Davis

I pulled my car into the Black couple's driveway. I realized the irony in our mission. "Roger," I suggested to him, "why don't you remain in the car while I find out whether they're willing to see the Imperial Wizard of the local Ku Klux Klan. If it appears that they won't be receptive, I won't mention that you're sitting in their driveway in my car."

I knocked on the door and an elderly Black lady with a friendly smile opened it. I identified myself and asked if I could talk about the cross-burning incident with her and her husband. "Come in," she said. "My husband won't be home until this evening, but I'll be glad to discuss it with you."

I explained my mission and my association with Roger Kelly. "Would you be willing to meet the Imperial Wizard?" She looked at me closely as if establishing a sense of trust. Then she nodded. I told her he was sitting in my car out in the driveway.

"In your car!?" was her response. She then looked me up and down again and, after a moment, sensed there was no need to have any fear or reservations even though she did not know me. With her doubts allayed, she told me to invite him in.

Roger sat down in the living room. She offered both of us some soft drinks. After he expressed his regrets to her, she and Roger talked for about forty-five minutes about the incident and her childhood when the Klan was thriving and these types of incidents were commonplace.

She said, "I don't believe it was the Klan that placed the flaming cross in my yard, but possibly some young punks just outside of my neighborhood."

I asked why she thought that. She replied that several months earlier, she had found some racist literature with swastikas on her lawn. She also said that every now and then a group of these young punks would drive through her street, and if she or her husband were outside, they would yell racist epithets. From her description of them, they appeared to be Skinheads.

138

She added, "One of them had been in a lot of trouble before with his parents and the law." Then she turned to Roger, fastening her eyes on his face. "In the many years my husband and I have lived here, we've never once had any problems with the neighbors. We're all friends, who visit each other's homes regularly." She was, however, disappointed that the police did not show much interest in the vandalous, terroristic incidents. She also mentioned that her young son had been murdered in Baltimore while sitting on his porch. This tragic loss touched Roger and me deeply. I could see the compassion Roger felt for her loss as if relating it to his losing one of his family members.

Roger and I thanked her for her time and hospitality and I told her I would keep in touch. Roger told her to let him know if there was anything at all he could do. We all shook hands and Roger and I departed. We stopped in a small diner on Main Street and had lunch before returning to our original meeting place where Roger had parked his vehicle.

After dropping Roger off in the parking lot, I drove home thinking that it was very decent of Roger to try to right a wrong. I believe he did this from his heart. I knew and he must have known that some of the Klansmen would severely criticize him or worse when they found out. In addition, I wondered what the combination of our deepening friendship and this reaching out to decry a racial incident would have on Roger's role in the Klan. Perhaps some members would be sorry that the Klan had not been the perpetrators of terror against an old Black couple.

12

The Enigmatic Klansman

While Klan leader Roger Kelly was on vacation, I heard on the news that there had been another cross-burning. Someone had burned a ten-foot cross on the roadside about thirty miles from where I lived. Sometimes, as in the case of the old Black couple we'd visited, this type of terrorism is not the doing of the Klan, but of kids, pranksters or other radicals. This time, however, the cross-burner was arrested and was identified as a young Klansman in his twenties.

The radio report identified the Klansman as David Black and later that night when I read his address in the papers, I decided to meet him. The next morning I called the detention center at which he was being held, to find out he had been released on bail. His phone number was unlisted, so Mary and I drove to his address about 9:00 P.M. the next night.

The unlit street was dark and deserted, but we finally found the address number on a mailbox by the side of the road. The driveway led into the woods. We drove onto the property despite the "NO TRESPASSING" signs and parked. Getting out of the car, we approached a large, well maintained double trailer. An attractive older woman came out, "Can I help you?" she asked pleasantly.

"Are you David Black's mother?"

"Yes, I am."

I explained that I was gathering information on the Klan and that I would like very much to talk with her son about the cross-burning.

"My son doesn't want to talk about the incident."

I handed her my card, "Please give it to David in the event he changes his mind."

She accepted the card, but commented, "I doubt my son will call you." After thanking her, Mary and I left.

I phoned Roger Kelly at his parents' vacation home in Florida to see if he knew about the cross-burning and to find out if David Black belonged to his Invincible Empire. He confirmed that Mr. Black did belong to his group, but was stunned when I told him of the incident. He kept asking me if I was sure the media said David Black. I read the address to Roger.

"That's David, but I can't imagine what possessed him to go out and burn a cross without proper sanctioning by the State Office for the Invincible Empire." The irony did not escape me.

A couple of days later, I received a telephone call from David Black. His mother had given him the card I'd left, and he said he would be glad to talk to me. We made an appointment to meet a few days later.

David Black, well dressed and very well spoken, came to our meeting accompanied by his fiancée and his father. I took them all out for lunch to allow him to get to know me on a social basis so he would feel more at ease. Before going, David's father, who worked for the court system, wanted his son to meet his boss and asked me to accompany them.

To my surprise, as I suppose they both anticipated, the senior Mr. Black's boss was a very attractive Black woman. I invited her to accompany us to lunch, but she had a prior engagement and insisted that we give her a raincheck.

At lunch, I began to ask non-threatening questions about David Black's background. At this first meeting I wanted to make him feel comfortable in expressing himself so that in future meetings I could delve more deeply into his ideas and psyche. We had an enjoyable lunch and agreed to get together again.

For our next meeting, I went out to his home by myself and spent a good hour and a half with David and his father. His mother was out working. She is a professional clown who has performed for everyone from common citizens and children to the First Lady at the White House. After seeing a picture of Mrs. Black with the First Lady, I could not help but think to myself, *What makes one family member put on a costume that brings joy and laughter to many people, and another family member put on a costume that brings fear and terror to many people?*

Prior to joining a Klan group, David was a Skinhead. He had been involved with both the non-racist and the White Power Skinheads. Originally from Alabama, he was a descendant of Supreme Court Justice Hugo Black, who at one time was also a Klansman. David's great-grandfather had fought alongside his good friend General Nathan Bedford Forrest on the side of the Confederacy during the Civil War. Prior to the war and to becoming a general, Forrest was a slave trader. After the war, he became the first leader of the original Ku Klux Klan. Ironically, hours after the incident when David was arrested, he was wearing a Nathan Bedford Forrest tee shirt.

I learned that David had been in the military but was discharged for trying to recruit members for the Klan. He had been a member of several different Klans, including some in the southern states. Of all the Klanspeople I talked with, David has more knowledge than most in respect to the organization's history and his knowledge on the workings of various Klan groups with whom he has and has not been affiliated is extensive.

I turned our conversation to the cross burning. According to David, he didn't burn the cross to be malicious, but only to let people know that the Klan is still alive and well in the state of Maryland despite reports in the media that there is no Klan strength in this state.

David also insisted that he did not dislike Black people and that he had Black friends. He did, however, say that he did not believe in interracial marriage and miscegenation.

As I was about to leave, David and his father asked me if I had plans for the next morning, which would be Sunday. I replied that I did not. They then invited me to attend church services with them and the rest of their family that next morning.

At 10:00 on Sunday morning, accompanied by my secretary, Mary, we met at David's home. We attended their Baptist Church and enjoyed the service.

Following the service, Mrs. Black invited Mary and me to their home for dinner. We accepted. Apparently, Mr. and Mrs. Black invite many youngsters in the military whose homes are out of state to a nice home cooked meal every Sunday. That day, a young Black man, who apparently was good friends with David and his family, was there.

Mrs. Black is an absolutely wonderful cook and hostess. Mr. Black, David's father, is quite a good artist with a strong fascination and interest in Native American-Indians. He showed me some drawings he had done which were very impressive. Then David took me to his room. It was filled with books on the Civil War, race issues and the Klan. He showed me his robe and hood which he had gotten when he was in the military in North Carolina.

While David was in the service, he visited the continent of Africa. Very few, if any, Klansmen have been in Africa unless one considers the Klan counterpart in South Africa. In fact, I was discovering some common traits of the Klan members and one that surprised me was that hardly any Klansmen have visited places outside the United States and many have never gotten beyond the state in which they reside.

Mary and I left the Blacks' home, commenting to each other that everyone seemed genuine and that, while inconceivable, their hospitality didn't appear fabricated.

13

Marching with the KKK

Meeting with Klan members was teaching me a great deal about the personalities, economic status and home life of those in the organization which had caused so much fear and suffering for those of my race. In truth, some of my findings were similar to those written about by Morris Dees in a pamphlet put together by the Southern Poverty Law Center.

In it, Dees describes two men. One, Lloyd Letson is a Klan member; the other Bobby Person, is a Klan victim. Dees observes, "Except for color, Bobby Person and Lloyd Letson are little different. Both want better lives for their families. If they had been neighbors, they might have been friends."

It is a telling and insightful description.

Roger Kelly telephoned me that his group, the Invincible Empire, was going to march in my county the following month. "I wanted to let you know in case you want to come out and take some pictures." He said he would let me know the exact time and location when it was made known to him by the Montgomery County, Maryland authorities.

Daryl Davis

Normally, KKK groups like as much publicity as they can get. However, this time Roger notified the media at the last minute and they never came. I showed up at the starting point of the march with Mary and another lady, also named Mary, whom I was dating at the time, about a half hour before the Klan was due. We parked one car near the starting point and the other one at the ending point so we could ride back at the end of the march.

Not long afterward, two motorcycle officers showed up and parked about fifteen feet from me. Police cars began to pull in and park along the parade route. The Klan was to march on a path adjacent to the road. Joggers, bicyclists and passersby, noticing the commotion, began asking police officers what was going on. They replied, "Nothing is going on." One officer said something about a radar setup and when a civilian commented he didn't see any radar guns, but some video cameras, the cop shut up completely.

An undercover policewoman drove up in an unmarked car and spoke with the motorcycle police a few feet away from me. The two Marys were standing a few feet from me as well. I was nonchalantly standing by myself, although I guess to the police, there is nothing nonchalant about a Black man getting ready to be confronted by a group of Klansmen who were to show up at any moment. When it became apparent that I was not waiting for the light to change so I could cross the street, the lady officer walked over to me.

"Excuse me, are you waiting for something?"

"Yes, I am."

"What would that be?"

"The same thing you are waiting for."

"And what would that be?"

"Don't you know what you are waiting for?"

Frustrated with me, she went over to the Marys and asked them what they were waiting for. They told her they were waiting for the Klan march.

"How did you find out that the Klan was going to be here?" Both Marys raised their arms and pointed at me, so the police officer headed back.

"How did you hear about this?"

"They told me."

"Who are 'they?'"

"The same people who told you."

With a mystified look on her face, she asked, "Who are you?"

"My name is Daryl Davis. Who are you?"

Hearing my name, she smiled. "Oh, I recognize your name. You're the man who's studying the Klan. I'm Beth Taylor. Roger said some very nice things about you." Taylor walked over to her lieutenant, who was motioning his concern about me, to let him know that everything was okay.

I glanced at my watch. The marchers were twenty minutes overdue. The police were beginning to get fidgety. Moments later a large bus rode by. I recognized Roger behind the wheel and he waved at me in full view of the police. I returned the wave. One of the officers speculated with another officer as to whether or not the Klan would show. I informed him that the person who waved at me was the Imperial Wizard and that the marchers were in the van that just drove by. They looked at me as if to say, *You gotta be kidding. Why would they wave at you?*

Although Beth Taylor, the lady officer, did not recognize Roger as he drove by, she nodded her head to her partners to affirm that I was not joking. They began radioing the other police vehicles dotted along the route alerting them to get ready. Roger drove the three-mile route through the barren residential area to check it out and returned to where we were.

Roger parked the bus nearby. He and his Klan members got out and began to put on their robes and hoods. Others began pulling out placards with the State Office address for their Klan along with American and Confederate or Rebel flags.

Daryl Davis

People's faces had stunned looks as they came out of their townhouses and were confronted by this sight. Because the Klan was marching up a public path, they had to yield to the right-of-way to any pedestrians, bikes or joggers. Legally, I could have walked right alongside of them. I chose to walk in the median and take my pictures from there so as not to give the wrong impression to any passing motorists or Klan members.

Several bewildered joggers and bicyclists went by. Quite a few cars made U-turns to make sure that they were actually seeing what they thought they saw. I watched the reactions of the drivers. Many White motorists cursed at the Klan marchers or made obscene gestures. One of the cars, containing Whites, made a U-turn and shouted, "Why don't you get real jobs you fucking morons?" Only two Black motorists shouted their disgust. The other Blacks simply drove by and did nothing. There were two cars of White sympathizers who applauded the hooded marchers.

My secretary and I walked the entire three miles as did the Klan members. My date, Mary had to stop about halfway as the heat exhausted her. Shortly before the ending point, three residents who had apparently seen the marchers from their car, and had run inside their home to quickly create some anti-Klan signs, were standing in the median when the Klan marched by.

All of the bikers and joggers who passed alongside the Klan were White. I wondered what would happen if some Blacks happened along the path. I soon had my answer.

With about a half mile left, a Black man, his wife and small son, who obviously had not heard news of the event, were all out for a bike ride. They were on a path heading toward the marchers. Two police cars pulled ahead to where the cyclists were, got out of their cars and walked over to them. They remained with them until the Klan passed.

I turned to my secretary, Mary and said, "It was very ignorant on the part of the police to do that."

"It's the job of the police to protect the marchers."

150

"Why don't they walk over when Whites happen along the path. After all, it's mostly the White people passing by that are the most threatening. A Black man is not going to jeopardize the safety of his wife and small child by attacking a group of a dozen Klansmen."

"Perhaps," Mary suggested, "the cops went over there to protect the Blacks from the Klan."

Unable to conceal my anger, I blurted out, "It is not only impossible, but improbable that the Klan would attack the family in broad daylight and in full view of the police and other passersby without provocation. Certainly they had no reason to feel threatened."

I took a deep breath and went on. "It is called discrimination and harassment by the police."

We completed the walk in silence, picked up the other Mary on the way back and went home.

I had told Roger if he wanted to, he could drop by my house after the march since he was already in my county. A couple of hours later there was a knock on my door. It was Roger, his Grand Klaliff and another member. I invited them in, and we sat around discussing the afternoon's march.

Roger, asked me if I heard the guy yell out of the car window about getting a real job. I replied that I had, and Roger, laughing, asked me, "Do you think the guy was referring to you or to us." Then, commenting on the police coming over when the Black cyclists were on the path, Roger said he was disappointed that the officers had done that and saw absolutely no reason for it.

"Did you or any of your members feel threatened by the Black family?" I asked.

He replied, "There was no threat on either side. But the police, in doing what they did, could easily have created a situation."

"I could not agree more. If there wasn't a situation already, why create one?" I wondered what those same cops would think if they had seen these Klansmen at my house. I had a Black house guest upstairs and I wondered what he would have thought if he knew that the three men he heard laughing and joking downstairs were wearing robes and hoods only a couple of hours earlier.

The next morning, looking out the window, I saw two Montgomery County police cruisers across the street. The officers were observing my house. They obviously had trailed the Klan members here and probably wondered what on earth I could be doing. So they stayed all night in order to find out more.

14

The Dragon's Den

One day Roger called me and invited me to see the State Office Klavern located in the basement of his house. Roger's house sits on a large piece of property. The long gravel driveway leading to the house passes a full-size confederate flag on a tall flagpole situated in the center of his front lawn. At the end of the driveway is a chained up Doberman Pinscher. I got out of my car and couldn't help wondering, even though Roger and I were now friends, if the dog was trained to attack Black people. I walked over to the dog, and it eyed me up and down, but he did not even bark. So much for idle fears. Entering the Dragon's Den, I saw a poster with the words, "SAVE OUR LAND, JOIN THE KLAN."

The walls were adorned with various framed newspaper articles regarding rallies and marches in which Roger had participated. A large picture of Nathan Bedford Forrest, a picture of Ronald Reagan, various Klan plaques and Black stereotypical caricatures were grouped all over the room.

There were a number of chairs, arranged in rows facing a table in the front of the room, set up for meetings. On the table were a Bible and a gavel. On one side of the table was a cross about five-feet high with candles adorning the cross members. I assumed they were lit for certain Klan rituals signifying the flaming cross. On the other side of the table was a machine gun. Seeing it, I flinched and Roger, noticing my reaction, picked it up and put it away. He said, "It was not here to intimidate you, but for protection should anyone try to attack from the outside during the Klavern meeting." In the rear of the room was a porcelain Klansman figurine which, when plugged in, lights up. Elsewhere in the room was a display case containing Klan paraphernalia.

I knew, though it was not a place to induce comfort, that in revealing the Klavern for the first time, Roger was showing another sign of trust in me. About this, I felt good. He gave me a glass of ginger ale, and we sat down around the table, talking about everything from Ross Perot to interracial sex and to the taking of a human life.

We discussed Martin Luther King, Jr., Matthew Henson, the Black explorer who discovered the North Pole for Robert Perry, and Dr. Charles Drew, the Black doctor who had invented the process of blood typing and transfusion and whose invention has saved millions of lives all over the world. I was surprised to know that Roger knew nearly everyone I brought up.

I had thought we would talk for an hour or two. However, I got there shortly after ten in the morning and it was now almost seven in the evening when I got up to leave. I thanked Roger for inviting me. In truth, it was a most revealing visit, and I was grateful at having another layer of the secrets of the Klan peeled away before my eyes.

15

Reverse Discrimination at a Black Institution

Through our frequent interactions, our relationship grew to a point where Roger felt comfortable hanging out with me by himself. On one occasion, when Roger came alone, things took an interesting twist.

A friend had told me that the television show "IN FOCUS," which is broadcast by my alma mater Howard University in Washington, D.C., was looking for a studio audience. This particular episode was titled, "RACISM: WRONG OR WHITE." The panelists included the Reverend Jesse Jackson, D.C. Councilwoman Eleanor Holmes Norton and noted Black psychologist, Frances Cress Welsing, among others. All I had to do was call the station, put my name on a reservation list including the number of people in my party.

I called the station, reserved a seat in the audience for myself and some friends and acquired more information about the show. They were inviting any member of the public to attend free of charge to air their views on racism with the host, the panelists and the other audience members. I was also told that a Grand Dragon from a Klan faction would be phoning in during the show to air his views.

I thought of Roger and wondered if he would like to attend this program the following night. I phoned him and he said that he would, but would prefer to sit and listen to all the views rather than express his own. I told him that I would phone the station to see if I could add his name to my reservation list and then call him back.

I immediately phoned the producer to see if there would be any problem. She informed me that she knew who Roger Kelly was and that he was welcome to come but asked me to not have him come in his robe and hood. I assured her that he would not wear his regalia and was not coming to make a statement, but to merely be an observer in the audience. She reminded me to get there by 7:00 P.M. in order to secure our reservations. I called Roger back and told him to be at my house no later than 6:00 P.M., unarmed and sans sheet.

Roger showed up right on time the next day in a dark suit and tie. "Should I remove my Klan ring from my finger?" he asked.

I told him to leave it on since some people there would recognize him anyway. Upon our arrival, I saw the producer and introduced Roger Kelly. She shook our hands and thanked us for coming. A little while later, an associate producer led the audience to the studio. She insisted that Roger sit in a particular chair located in the front row closest to the host. Everyone else was permitted to sit wherever they chose. When we questioned why he had to sit there, she replied, "Because I said so." Minutes later, photographers and cameramen operating the studio video cameras began taking pictures of the Imperial Wizard.

I was sitting directly behind Roger. He leaned back and

asked me, very seriously, if I had set him up. I assured him that I had not, and if he wanted to trade seats with me, he was welcome to do so and anyone who objected would have to deal with me. I went and found the producer, reminded her that Mr. Kelly was not there to be the focus of the show. She assured me that I had no need to be concerned. I returned to my seat and told Roger if he was put on the spot, he did not have to respond unless he chose to do so.

Both the host and the producer gave the audience a pep talk while we waited for the show to begin. They insisted that anyone who had anything to contribute should speak up and "Let your feelings be known." The producer went so far to say, "There are all types of people here, some with opposing viewpoints. I encourage debate as long as it does not get out of hand. It makes for good television."

The audience was indeed made up of a good cross section of people: members of the NAACP, Anti-Defamation League, other Black, Jewish, Hispanic and minority organizations, the aforementioned panelists and interested people of different racial and ethnic backgrounds with no specific affiliations.

With two seconds to go before going on the air, the countdown was interrupted and three police officers came into the studio. One asked the associate producer a question. She pointed to Roger and the officer then came over and asked him to step outside. We both went out to the hallway with the officers. Another man, later identified as the assistant director, told me that I could go back in the studio to watch and participate in the program, but that the Klansman could not re-enter. When I asked why, I was told that he was not on the guest list. I asked the assistant director if he knew who Mr. Kelly was and he replied that he did. I asked him if he knew who I was, and he replied that he did not. I said, "Well, how the hell do you know that I am on the guest list?" and proceeded to correct the assistant director by letting him know that Mr. Kelly was indeed on the guest list. I informed him that Roger had signed it next to his name when we came in and the producer okayed my reservation for him the day before. The director said it was the station manager's order that Mr. Kelly be removed from the studio audience.

I asked to see the manager. He came out to the hallway. When I questioned him about this sudden move, he replied that Mr. Kelly was not on the guest list. I told him I had already heard that excuse, proved it wrong and demanded to know the real reason. He then told Mr. Kelly and me that he had it done it for security reasons. He felt he could not provide security for Mr. Kelly in the event something should happen. I assured him we did not come to make things happen.

The man replied, "I don't want him in there, and I have the final say."

I proceeded to question the manager on how he could provide security to Reverend Jesse Jackson, a former Presidential Candidate and a very high profile, controversial political figure who was going to be actively participating, and not provide the same to someone of less status who was not participating? "What happened to 'Equal protection under the law?' At no time did Mr. Kelly act in any adverse manner. He was very courteous and complied with all that was asked of him."

The manager retorted that if I wanted to return to the studio I had better do so then because he would not delay the airing of the live show any longer. He said he would permit Roger to sit in a room off to the side where Roger could watch the show on a monitor, but he would not permit Roger to return to the studio. "You go back in the studio," Roger insisted. "I'll be alright in the viewing room."

I refused. This was racism in the making by those who were supposed to be seeking solutions and ideas from the studio audience. The topic of racism is rarely discussed without it at least mentioning the Ku Klux Klan. They kicked one Klansman out, then talked about the Klan without allowing one of its leaders the opportunity to respond had he wished to do so.

Roger did not come to the show to recruit. He did not come to be converted. He simply came for the experience of learning firsthand what Blacks and other victims of discrimination feel. Well, the occasion sure as hell provided that feeling, although I did not think the teaching method was appropriate.

Roger Kelly came a long way, not so much in terms of the distance from his home near Thurmont, Maryland, to Howard University in Washington, D.C., but in terms of racial ideologies. For an Imperial Wizard of the Ku Klux Klan, by himself, to accompany a Black man to a predominantly Black environment shows a great deal of trust, willingness to learn and a desire to be exposed to the other side. Roger entered this anti-Klan environment with no one to protect him but me, a Black man. All Klan doctrines teach and preach that Blacks and Jews are threats. Many fears and problems existing between the races stem from the lack of exposure to each other. Mr. Kelly made quite a commendable, positive step forward, only to be pushed one hundred steps back. Instead of allowing him this experience and exposure, he became, at the hands of a Black man, the victim of the very thing Blacks have fought so hard in this country to abolish.

I am not advocating the views of Roger Kelly and his Klan. How could I, a Black man, do so? But can reverse discrimination be justified by assuming the posture, "Well the Klan has done it to us before, so now we are going to do it back to them?" That is one way to look at it, but that also can do more to polarize the races instead of allowing all races to be educated about one another's fears and concerns through communication.

Roger and I went to the viewing room to watch the fraudulent fiasco while two other people waiting outside entered the studio and sat in the seats that we were entitled to. The producer had prearranged to have Chester Doles, the Grand Klaliff of the

Daryl Davis

Invisible Empire Knights of the Ku Klux Klan, speak by telephone with the host during the airing of the show. This was Roger's old faction before he pulled away to form the Invincible Empire Knights of the Ku Klux Klan. For whatever reason, the producer had billed Chester Doles as the Grand Dragon. It was apparent that neither the host nor the Klaliff knew how to conduct this type of interaction.

Doles became very volatile and obscene, and the host disconnected his call in less than a minute. Of course, this achieved the host's intention and left the audience to believe that this Klan representative's attitude was reflective of all Klansmen and Klanswomen.

As I have alluded to before, Black people would become highly upset if the White media was to lump all groups that profess to promoting the advancement of the Black race, such as the NAACP, CORE, Black Panthers, SCLC, Black Muslims, etc., as one and the same. While some of their causes may be similar, no one group can represent the views of all the others, only themselves. Even then, there have been differences in opinions, policies, and practices within the same organization. Likewise, no one Klan faction can represent all the others. If this program was to be really instructive on the Klan movement and its leaders, it would be crucial for the host and audience to understand the contrast between two Klan leaders. It would have been a unique opportunity if Roger Kelly could have spoken up if questioned about what he thought of the other Klan leader's views and stated his own views, but he was denied his rights.

Having experienced discrimination enough times myself as a Black man, I could understand too well the hurt, confusion and frustration Roger was experiencing. I asked him if he wanted to leave. He said that it didn't matter to him, but he felt badly that this happened and blamed himself. I told him to be rest assured that he had every right to be there, and that I would fight this matter and bring it to the attention of the president of the University.

The entire event was badly handled. Had the general manager really been concerned about an attack on the studio from outside viewers because a Klansman was just down the street, there were measures he could have taken to prevent this. As I stressed before, Roger did not come to be an active participant or a television star. If the general manager, who had the authority to do so, had instructed the host not to question Mr. Kelly and instructed the cameramen not to concentrate their video cameras on him and had let him sit where he chose as did everyone else, the security problem that worried the manager would not have occurred. Instead, he and the producers insisted that Roger sit in one of the most obvious seats in the studio before removing him.

The next day, I phoned our local affiliate and told them about the incident. The news reporter thought it would make a great story, not only from the angle that a Klansman had been discriminated against, but from the angle that a Black man was willing to stand up for this Klansman. He was very excited that I had contacted him and no one else. He asked me if I could get Roger and me together for an interview. I got everything set up with Roger as the newsman requested. He called me back and said that he would have to postpone the interview because Presidential Candidate Bill Clinton was in town and all the cameramen were covering that. So, we rescheduled, only to be postponed again. This happened a couple of more times and finally the reporter told me that the news department was not going to do the interview because it was now yesterday's news.

Several months later, Carl, a friend of mine who works at the television station, showed up at one of my gigs and told me that the real reason the piece was never done was because the senior news editors decided that my standing up for a Klansman's rights would make the Klan look good. My friend did not agree with the decision makers, and felt that I should know what really happened. I only wished the public had; for how can we deal with racism effectively if we are not exposed to the truth?

After I spoke with Carl, I contacted the American Civil Liberties Union and asked them to get involved in this case of discrimination. They acted interested at first, and then afterward dragged their feet and declined to get involved, citing that they were too busy as the reason. Our system of equal protection and justice for all is, as we all know, flawed. Discrimination is the rule if you are a minority, either by virtue of race, ethnic origin, religion, physical handicap, sexual orientation, controversial affiliations or social views. Those who could be instrumental in changing the situation often manipulate it by: (1) dragging their feet; (2) creating bogus red tape; or (3) draining your pockets on legalities to the point where you are forced to give up the fight for the issue. While many traditionally blame Conservatives for the lack of change and progress, I have found that there are just as many Liberals who are guilty of the same thing. The only difference is that the conservative stance is well known, but often the Liberals do not put their money where their mouths are. It's an unhappy surprise. So much for slanted justice.

Interestingly enough, the ACLU did get involved with one Klan group, the Invisible Empire Group in Maryland. When Grand Dragon Kelly left this group, it's Imperial Wizard had to appoint a new Grand Dragon as a replacement. This new Grand Dragon was a "silent" Dragon in order to protect his identity from aliens—any non-Klan people. It was rumored that this anonymous Dragon was a well-respected professional, but I located him and found out that was really a myth. He allowed his Grand Klaliff, Chester Doles, to assume the role of Grand Dragon for most public events.

The Grand Klaliff, taking advantage of this opportunity, immediately began to create a name for himself by becoming loud and outspoken in the community and distributing flyers filled with hate literature. Upon checking into Doles' background, I found that he had served prison time and had been a cocaine addict. He was considered a "loose cannon" by the police.

Grand Klaliff Doles wanted to have a march in the town of Elkton, Maryland, on April 4th condoning the death of Martin Luther King, Jr. and celebrating his alleged assassin, James Earl Ray. Most Klans in one way or another celebrate April 4th, known as James Earl Ray Day, for the same reason. The town granted a parade permit to this Klan and then revoked it due to public pressure. The ACLU became involved in representing the Klan against city hall. The Klan and ACLU eventually won the suit and the city had to pay $61,000.

PART IV

STEREOTYPICAL KLUXERS AND OTHER RIGHT-WINGERS

16

Grand Klaliff
Chester Doles

I couldn't forget Grand Klaliff Chester Doles. From my research and other media reports, he was the stereotypical image of a Klansman, full of hatred and violence. I obtained his address and wrote to him requesting a meeting. I had begun to think of doing a book and told him so.

In the interim, I met with some other Klansmen and in the course of conversation, I mentioned that I was going to meet with the Grand Klaliff. I was advised to go armed, to take somebody and to inform someone of my whereabouts. In fact, to my surprise, one of the Klansmen volunteered to go with me as my protection. When I declined, he offered to lend me his nine-millimeter semi-automatic handgun. I declined that as well.

A couple of days later, Doles phoned me. "I have a lot to say."

He gave me his phone number, and we set a time and date to meet. He volunteered to come to my neck of the woods if it was more convenient for me. I told him I would come to his. He instructed me to drive to the city in which he lived, and upon exiting from the highway, to pull over and phone him with my location. He and his Grand Knighthawk would get me and lead me back to their home so we could talk. As with Roger Kelly, he did not ask and I made no mention of the color of my skin.

I was told that Chester did not like to see a Black man with a White woman and more than likely would explode if faced with this. Because something dangerous could happen, I decided not to take my secretary Mary with me this time. I did not want her to get hurt.

I had performed with my band the night before. After getting off the bandstand, packing up and making the three-hour drive home, I pulled into my driveway at six in the morning. Instead of trying to lie down and get two hours sleep, I nervously agonized about the upcoming meeting with Chester Doles scheduled for 10:00 that morning. The only protection I would travel with was my belief that God would watch over me. I took a shower and left my house at 8:00 A.M. in order to be at my appointment early.

About 9:45 A.M., I saw the exit for Doles' town and drove my car down the ramp. Seeing a shopping center, I pulled in. I got out of the car and walked into a drug store. It was early so, being friendly, I wasted some time making small talk with a cashier, who happened to be a young white woman. As I stood there talking, two white men entered and flashed me dirty looks. Suddenly, thoughts of Emmett Till ran through my mind.

Promptly at 10:00 A.M. I phoned the Grand Klaliff, told him where I was and what kind of car I was driving. The Grand Knighthawk got on the line. He said he knew the shopping center and instructed me to park my car in the center of the lot where there were no other cars. "We'll be there in fifteen minutes."

I did as I was told. To see better and be seen more clearly, I decided to get out of my Lincoln Town Car and sit on the hood of the car while I waited. As this was a rural shopping center, there was only one entrance.

Fifteen minutes later, two carloads of men drove in, one car behind the other. I had a strong suspicion that this was my Klan party. Any doubts that I may have had were erased when both cars began circling me at a distance. Some of the occupants of each vehicle, seeing me atop my vehicle, stared in disbelief while the others looked around to see if there were another Lincoln Town Car containing a White man that fit their assumed description.

Parking their cars about fifty-feet away, they sat inside them looking at me, still not sure whether I was the man behind the voice on the phone. I gave them an assuring wave. Seeing it, a big, burly biker-type got out of the first car. Even at that distance, I could see the Ku Klux Klan insignia on his tee shirt. He pulled a large buck knife from a sheath attached to his belt, opened it to a forty-five degree angle and hooked the blade through one of the belt loops on his blue jeans. Then he started to walk towards me.

I got off the hood and met him halfway. Introducing myself, I extended my hand. He shook it and said, "I'm the Grand Knighthawk."

Then he added, "Mr. Davis, we have a problem here."

I replied coolly, "What's that?"

He hesitated, then blurted out, "Well, you see, we didn't know that you were a non-Anglo-Saxon."

"Well, that's not a problem for me," I smiled. "I've been this way all my life and have gotten used to it."

His face flushed. "We have to be careful because we are being threatened by the Black Panthers, the NAACP and everyone else. We were going to take you back to a private residence to meet with the Grand Klaliff, but we can't do that now," replied the Knighthawk.

"I've driven two hours to get to this meeting."

While he went back to the car to consult with the Klaliff,

Daryl Davis

I thought to myself, *Does he not think that there are any Anglo-Saxons who would pose a threat to him if they knew where he lived?*

He returned to the car and said, "Follow me and we'll go to a park and you can meet the Grand Klaliff there."

I agreed, got in my car and pulled it behind his while the other car pulled behind mine. It was quite an entourage.

The irony of the situation in view of all I knew about the Klan's history of spiriting away Black men accosted me. Yet I did not want to turn back. I had come too far to yield to fear now. We reached our destination and slowly I got out of my car. The Grand Klaliff and Grand Knighthawk got out of theirs and walked over. As I shook hands with the Grand Klaliff, I noticed the words, "White Power" tattooed on the back of one hand and a swastika tattooed on the other. For a moment I involuntarily stiffened, but told myself to relax.

Doles immediately demanded to know why a Black man was interested in the Ku Klux Klan and who did I work for.

"I'm interested in the Klan because of their history of adverse interest in the Blacks, and I do not work for anyone but myself."

He said in total disbelief, "You said in your letter that you had met and talked with Roger Kelly and Tony LaRicci. They actually talked to you?"

I assured him they did and produced some pictures of me with Roger Kelly and Tony LaRicci which I had brought with me for credibility.

The Grand Klaliff stared incredulously at the pictures while repeating, "I don't believe this," and showed them to his Knighthawk. He then said, "Roger Kelly is a White Separatist. I am a White Supremacist. I could never pose for a picture with you. In fact, I am not sure I can even talk to you without Imperial authority."

"The photographs simply indicate that these particular

Klansmen did indeed meet with me, they don't mean that we've got some type of intimate relationship going on," I explained.

He told me to have a seat at the picnic table while he went and called the Imperial Wizard J.W. Farrands in North Carolina for permission for our talk.

The Knighthawk and I sat at the picnic table. I told him that I had been at the Howard University television station with Roger Kelly when the Grand Klaliff had called into the show.

The Knighthawk responded, "We were supposed to be on the show and had rented a limousine to make the two-hour drive to Washington, D.C., but were informed at the last minute by the producer that the plans had changed and it was going to be a phone-in instead." He expressed his discontent with the way it was handled by the producer.

Relaying Roger's and my experience to him, I concurred.

A short while later, the Grand Klaliff returned and told us that the Imperial Wizard was not in. Then he suggested that we head over to the house anyway and stop along the way to phone the Wizard again. Climbing into our cars, we did the convoy thing again. As we drove through the small, predominantly White town, many people recognized the Grand Klaliff and waved and offered friendly greetings. These people not only included common pedestrians, but policemen and firemen as well. I was disturbed, but impressed. We stopped at another phone. Doles hopped out and a few minutes later came over to my car, followed by his Knighthawk.

The Imperial Wizard had still not returned. Chester reconsidered his intent to meeting with me without Imperial authority and decided against it. He apologized for my having to drive so far for nothing and said that if the Wizard would approve it, he would be glad to come to me at a later date and save me the drive. "I'll call you as soon as I find out either way what the Imperial decision is."

We chatted a few more minutes, and I noticed a guitar

shaped belt buckle on the Knighthawk's belt; so I asked him if he played the instrument. He replied that he did and enjoyed playing Country and Southern Rock. I suggested that we get together and jam sometime.

Reaching out to my bag positioned on the seat beside me, I took out some of the Klan memorabilia I had collected. Seeing a "KKK MEMBER IN GOOD STANDING" medallion, Doles became upset.

"Where did you get that and how?" he demanded. "You should not have it, it is sacred to Klan members."

I explained I couldn't tell him who'd given it to me, "but you may be sure it was freely given. I didn't take it." He glowered at me.

I made the drive back to my neck of the woods and went over to a friend's house. About 11:30 that evening, I called my answering machine from my friend's house to retrieve any messages. The Knighthawk had telephoned, asking me to give him a call at his residence. He said he had some information for me. A couple of messages later, the Grand Klaliff's voice came on the machine identifying himself and saying he finally reached Imperial Wizard Farrands. He also said he had run my name through the KBI (Klan Bureau of Investigation). They would have nothing to do with me since I was talking to other Klan groups. They were the biggest and the true Klan, and if I wanted to meet them to know the truth about the Klan, I could contact them at that time. Then the Grand Klaliff added a message of his own in a steel cold voice, "As far as that medallion goes, I don't suggest you come back to Cecil County with it."

I phoned Doles and questioned him about the Wizard's denial of permission.

"I don't know any reason for the denial, but the Wizard has the final word," he said.

I told him as far as the medallion was concerned, it was given to me by a former Klansman. It was his choice to give it to me, and my choice to do whatever I wanted with it, not his.

"I phoned Roger Kelly," he said in a disgruntled voice, "and denounced him for posing in a picture with you."

I told him if he changed his mind, I still wanted to talk to him.

Afterward, I called Roger and asked him if the Grand Klaliff from his former organization had phoned him. Roger replied that the Grand Klaliff had cursed him out and called him a race traitor for associating with the enemy. The enemy being me or any Black person.

"I'm not concerned," Roger said, "about the barrage of obscenities, insults and threats."

Later that day, I called the Imperial Wizard, James Wentworth Farrands, at his home in North Carolina and asked him why he would not let his members meet with me. He said he wanted absolutely nothing to do with Black people. He did not want a Black person making money off of him or his people. I asked him if he would like to make a statement. He said he had none to make and that if I slandered him, he would come after me.

17

Music, Fireworks and the Klan

I was scheduled to perform at a seaside resort on July 4th. The town attracts an additional 100,000 or more people every Independence Day. As coincidence would have it, Chester Doles' Klan group was scheduled to have a recruitment drive that afternoon, two blocks away from the club in which I was performing that evening.

The city reluctantly granted the Klan faction a permit. They were to arrive at 3:00 in the afternoon, stand in a thirty-square foot area, pass out their literature and leave an hour later.

I walked over to the area around 1:00 P.M., figuring there would be some Klansmen there undercover, scouting the area beforehand. I was right. The Exalted Cyclops from Roger Kelly's group was there—not to participate but to observe the event. He recognized me. More Klansmen showed up undetected. They wore nothing identifying them as Klan. The Cyclops recognized three of them. The group to which they belonged was once headed by Roger Kelly. When Kelly split off and formed his own group, The Invincible Empire, some of the members went with him and others remained.

Daryl Davis

Since the men did not walk over to where we were standing, the Cyclops decided to walk over and speak with his friends from the rival faction. I asked him to find out whether they would meet with me. As he talked with them, they became more vocal and gestured towards me. I wondered what their reaction was regarding the Cyclops being with me. In a couple of minutes I found out when he came back and told me they had heard about me and did not want to meet me and derided him for associating with me.

"They asked me, 'Is Nigger Daryl your Knighthawk?'"

They also made some derogatory remarks about their former Grand Dragon, Roger Kelly.

"It seems they were told that Roger posed for a picture with you with your arms around each other's shoulders."

The Cyclops asked me if it was true about the picture of Roger and me.

I shook my head. "Come to my gig this evening, and I will show you the picture and let you determine if it's true."

Police in uniform and undercover began milling around the area. The Klan assembly point was strategically chosen. It was directly in front of a two-story observation booth. Behind the window, one could see video cameras trained on the area below. Also in the observation booth was the town mayor.

Two skinheads swaggered up. One was a heavyset guy wearing a tee shirt emblazoned with a large swastika across his chest and a Klan patch on his arm. The other, a tall thin man, was dressed in similar regalia. I went over to talk to them.

"How are you guys doing?"

"Fuck off!" the tall one replied.

"Are you all waiting on the Klan?"

"Yeah," the same man said with hatred in his voice.

The beefy guy thrust out in chest. "We don't want to talk to you, so get the fuck out of here!"

I stood my ground and met his angry glance. "I don't have to leave. In fact, I am staying right here whether you like it or not."

"Fuck you!"
"Fuck you, too!"

When the skinhead movement was first formed in England, it was not a racist movement. It was simply youth rebelling against the establishment, much like the hippies of yesteryear or the punks of more recent times. Even today, there are many skinheads who are not racist who retain the original ideology. Unfortunately, when most "establishment" people think of skinheads, they think of neo-Nazis and other racists. In fact, because of the bad rap non-racist skinheads have received, some of them have formed an organization called SHARP. The acronym stands for: Skin Heads Against Racial Prejudice.

Although many Klan groups and White Power Skins, as they are called, share many of each others' viewpoints, not all Klan groups welcome skinheads. Roger Kelly's group does not. Chester Doles' Klan group does.

Soon some pro-Klan bikers showed up. One of them kept flailing a large cloth Confederate Flag with the inscription, "The South Shall Rise Again." I overheard another one telling the news media, who had arrived, that they were there to protect the Klan from violence perpetrated by any anti-Klan people.

By now, tourists and passersby were beginning to stop and crowd around to see why all these police officers, bikers and skinheads were standing around glaring at each other. When told that the Klan was expected momentarily, their reactions ranged from, "I'm gonna stick around and see this!" to "Are you kidding, this is the Nineties. Are they still around?" to "I can't stand those people, I'm getting out of here."

The awaited moment arrived. In the distance, I could see a group of police officers marching toward the site. Directly behind them was another group of people, some with tall, white, pointed hoods. Some even had matching white masks covering their

177

faces. The thirty by thirty-foot pavilion was cleared of spectators except for police, reporters and me. A police officer walked up to me and said, "Get out of the pavilion."

"I know some of these Klansmen," I replied to his order.

He was not quite sure how to react to this statement. Just then the Grand Knighthawk, the Grand Klaliff and the Grand Dragon arrived. The Grand Klaliff said, "How are you doing Mr. Davis?" The police officer's eyes opened wide.

After the Klan members walked away, he asked me, "Just whose side are you on?"

Meeting his eyes I replied, "Our future's."

The Klan members began to distribute their literature, complete with applications to join, to the spectators who were within arms reach of the pavilion. Many of the papers were torn to pieces and thrown back at the Klan as confetti. There were jeers from the anti-Klan people in the crowd and cheers from Klan supporters. Every now and then I would catch the skinhead, whom the police did not permit to enter the pavilion, looking at me. He mouthed the words, "Fuck you," to me. I simply smiled.

I talked with the Knighthawk, who gave me some literature, the Dragon and the Klaliff. All were pleasant and cordial. The irony of it didn't escape me. The Grand Dragon, who was wearing a face mask, said he was sorry he could not meet with me due to Imperial orders, but wanted to know when I had talked to his predecessor, Roger Kelly. I told him, "frequently," and asked him if he was on good terms with Roger. He replied that he would like to think so.

When the gathering was over, the Klansmen and Klanswomen started walking with a police escort to the parking lot where their cars and pickup trucks were parked. I walked along with them.

A young male spectator had managed to elude the eyes of the police and passed through the escort accompanying the unknowing Klansmen back to their vehicles after their demonstration on the boardwalk. He crouched down behind one of the Klansmen's cars. When a Klansman got within reach, the spectator sprang up and snatched the hood from the head of the Klansman. Several police officers ran after the hoodsnatcher and apprehended him. While they were in the process of handcuffing him, a Klansman who had joined in the chase attempted to retrieve the hood which was now on the ground near the scene of the arrest. This Klansman was also immediately shoved to the ground, handcuffed and, in kind of a perverse equality or police overreaction, he too was arrested.

After the excitement had ended, I spoke to the Grand Knighthawk and invited him to come to the club where I was to perform that evening. He said, "I'd like to, but we have a crosslighting we have to attend in another town." It was one of those times that I acutely felt the incredibility of my position.

The Klansman from Roger Kelly's group, who had brought his girlfriend, and I went to ride on some of the carnival rides less than a block away. Later that evening, they both attended my performance and seemed to enjoy it. On one of my breaks between sets, I showed the Klansman the picture of his boss and me. It was obvious to him that neither one of us had an arm around the other. He realized that the rival Klan was spreading false propaganda in an effort to undermine the group to which he belonged.

When I returned home the following day, I called the Grand Knighthawk and asked him if he'd gotten a copy of the newspaper. He said he had not; so I told him I would send him an extra copy that I had. He said he was flattered that I had called, and I reminded him that I wanted to jam with him sometime. He said he was pretty busy but would try to arrange it. I hoped that was true. If so, I theorized my music might once again act as a bridge to communication. At least I hoped so.

The resentment of Doles' group toward their rival Klan

group continued. Roger Kelly began receiving insults through the mail from the Grand Klaliff's group, which he showed me. These letters called Roger a "Niger Lover." You would think that someone who uses the word, "Nigger" so much, would know how to spell it. The letters continually referred to the picture of Roger and me, calling him a traitor to the White race and encouraging his members to join the real Klan—their Klan, of course. Roger quipped in a candid moment, "While many Klan groups send out hate mail, I, a Klan Wizard, am now a recipient."

18

Trial of a Klansman

Several months after the incident on the Fourth of July, the arrested Klansman was to be tried. I made the three-hour drive to the resort town so I could observe the trial.

Getting there early, I spotted the Klansman who had been arrested and the Klansman whose hood had been snatched. I took a seat behind them in the courtroom. Tapping the defendant on the shoulder, I introduced myself to him. He shook my hand and told me he remembered having seen me that Fourth of July and that he was aware that I was gathering material about the Klan and might write a book. He then told me he had quit the Klan because it was not the Christian organization it had claimed to be. I had heard a rumor that the Grand Knighthawk had also resigned from the Klan and I inquired if that was true. He confirmed that it was and said the Grand Knighthawk's reason was the same as his.

I asked him, his girlfriend and the other Klansman if they would like to have lunch with me after the trial and we could talk in-depth.

The defendant replied, "I would like to, but you might want to go ahead and talk to me before the trial begins."

There seemed to be a prophetic ring to his words, as though he felt he might not be in a position to talk with me after the trial. Just as I was about to answer him, the judge made his entrance.

The case of the Klansman was the first to be called. He was charged with one count of assault on a police officer and one count of hindering an arrest. He pled not guilty to both charges.

A police officer took the stand first and testified that some of his fellow officers had pursued and apprehended the hood-snatcher. He was standing by watching his colleagues affect the arrest when this Klansman ran up and jumped on the back of the officer who was placing the handcuffs on the arrestee.

I could not believe what I was hearing, for this was not at all what I had seen. It didn't even make sense that this Klansman would jump on the back of a uniformed police officer who was arresting someone who had stolen Klan property.

About this time, Grand Klaliff Chester Doles entered the already packed courtroom. I had a little bit of space next to me and motioned to him to come and sit beside me so he would not have to stand. He gave a polite wave back and shook his head no. As I peered behind him, I could see a woman and another Klansman standing with him.

The Klansman whose hood had been ripped off now took the stand. The judge questioned him as to what had been taken. The Klansman replied that it was the headpiece worn with the traditional Klan robe. The judge feigned ignorance and asked if it was like a baseball cap or a hat or what. The Klansman said it was a hood to which the judge asked for a description and definition of a hood.

The Klansman replied, "Well, it's sort of like a dunce cap."

The spectators roared with laughter, and I turned and looked at Chester who was smiling, but was red with embarrassment.

The defendant then took the stand and denied that he had jumped on the back of the officer or had in any way hindered the arrest. A newspaper photographer who had no affiliation or affinity with the Klan had witnessed the incident and captured the entire sequence on his camera, proving that the Klansman was telling the truth. The judge refused to believe that the film captured everything and produced the criminal record of the Klansman, courtesy of the prosecuting attorney.

The judge held the first page in his hand and let the rest of the pages unfold like an accordion for emphasis. The record consisted of many burglaries, assaults, drugs and other criminal activity, much of it non-Klan related.

According to the testimony, this Klansman had come from a dysfunctional family and had spent eight of his twenty-four years on this earth in prison. Despite this plea, the judge found him guilty on both counts and sentenced him to two three-year sentences to be served concurrently. His freedom had been short-lived. He was taken into custody and escorted out of the courtroom by deputies from the sheriff's department. His girlfriend burst into tears, and Chester and his entourage stormed out.

Was this why the Klansman wanted to talk with me before the trial? Did he have an eerie, yet accurate premonition, or was he so used to going to prison, he thought that would be the result? Whichever, he had been right.

The whole trial seemed theatrical. The man who snatched the hood was not present. Most surprisingly, the best witness for the prosecution, the police officer whose back the Klansman allegedly pounced upon, was not present at the trial either, nor was any written affidavit on his behalf presented. It was obvious to me that while this Klansman did have an extensive criminal history, he was convicted and sentenced this time just on the basis of his being a member of the Klan. I could see no merit or reason for this. I thought perhaps the judge was trying to teach him a lesson by giving him a dose of the Klan's own medicine: guilty for being Black; guilty for being Jewish; guilty for associating with a Black, Jew or homosexual; guilty for being anything but a Klansman or Klanswoman.

Outside, Grand Klaliff Chester Doles was standing a few

feet away, besieged by the media who wanted his reaction on the verdict. Doles referred to the judge as a "race traitor," who had now brought the ire of the Klan upon his town. Doles vowed to return and to conduct regular marches and rallies there referring to it as "a new hot bed for Klan activity." He then said he had no more comments. I had walked over and stood right next to him. He turned to me and asked how I was doing and if I was still gathering research about the Klan. I replied that I was and he smiled for a moment and then turned serious.

"My group, as well as chapters from several other states, have pulled away from The Invisible Empire Knights of the Ku Klux Klan under the leadership of Imperial Wizard J.W. Farrands."

I knew Farrands was under investigation for Civil Rights violations and had been accused by his own members of misappropriating Klan dues and donations. Doles also told me that Farrands had given $20,000 they had worked so hard to raise to Tom Metzger of the White Aryan Resistance for his court battle with Morris Dees of Klanwatch instead of using it for his own court battle with Dees, as he had led his members to believe.

The Grand Klaliff went on to tell me that he had taken his group and formed a new organization called TKA, Territorial Klans of America, of which he was now the Imperial Wizard, adding that he would like to talk to me. He gave me his phone number again and I agreed to meet with him. We then walked over to a bar on the boardwalk.

On the way he kept telling me that this member was convicted only because he was a Klansman.

"You mean the same way Blacks are convicted because they are Black," I said quietly.

He nodded, "That's exactly right. That was the way it used to be."

"It still goes on today in many instances," I reminded him.

Before we parted, we made plans to meet the next day.

19

The Imperial Wizard

I set out the next afternoon for the two-hour drive to Elkton, Maryland, located about an hour north of Baltimore. A few miles before reaching the exit for Elkton on Interstate 95 North is the exit for the town of Havre de Grace, where the first Klan Church of Maryland was established in the 1920's under Maryland's first Grand Dragon, Frank Beall.

A few miles farther is the exit for the towns of Northeast and Rising Sun, Maryland. This was where Maryland's original Klan had been headquartered and where now, generations later, Klansmen are trying to reestablish their organization, much, I have heard, to the dismay of many local townspeople. However, Chester Doles would dispute this. He claims that these towns are very much Klan-oriented but prefer to keep low profiles.

I arrived at the designated tavern to meet Doles a few minutes early and walked in carrying my satchel. Everybody in the musty, artificially illuminated place stared at me. In that minute, I realized everybody was Klan. My heart began to race and beads of perspiration formed on my forehead.

Daryl Davis

I recognized many of the men and women from the Fourth of July boardwalk gathering. Those I did not recognize were easily identifiable as Klan by their tee shirts which read: "Knights of the Ku Klux Klan," "It's a White Thing, You Wouldn't Understand," "White Power" and "The South Shall Rise Again."

Almost immediately one of the Klansmen got off his barstool and said, "You must be here to see Chester," as if there was any doubt. I certainly wasn't there for my health.

I nodded affirmatively, and he led me to a back room where other Klansmen and Klanswomen were shooting pool. The room had that typical smoke and beer saturated smell that old bars and poolrooms get after years of drinking and games. He told me, "Chester will be here in a few minutes."

I took a seat next to a young woman, and she struck up a casual conversation with me. The bartender came in from the other room to politely ask if I wanted a drink. I declined.

A few minutes later, Chester Doles, the former Grand Klaliff and now Imperial Wizard, strode into the room dressed in his work clothes. Like many Klansmen, he held a blue-collar job. Chester was a road maintenance worker. He apologized for his appearance, explaining that he had just come from work and had not had time to go home and change.

As we shook hands, I noticed his right hand was bandaged and I inquired about it. He curtly replied, "I had a little incident."

I didn't pursue it. He then immediately addressed the dinner invitation I had extended to him the previous night on the phone.

"I appreciate the invitation, but out of no disrespect for you, I will have to decline." He explained that it was the policy of his Klan not to socialize in any form with Black people. A breach of this policy by any member was grounds for immediate banishment. His Imperial Klaliff, Wayne Brannon, the man who had led me to the back room, interjected that he had kicked a member out

186

just the other night for being too friendly with a Black man at another bar. Chester said that he wanted to meet with me, but he had to keep it on a "professional" level. I told him that I understood.

I began to ask him some questions about himself, keeping them rather informal. "How old are you?"

He answered in short, clipped replies. "Thirty-two."

"How did you first become interested in the Klan?"

"I'm a fifth-generation Klansman," he said proudly. "As far as I can remember, my father, my grandfather, my great-grandfather were taking me to Klan rallies and meetings, and it's always been a part of my life since I was a child."

Fifth-generation, I thought . . . *this guy has deep roots into the Klan.*

As we were carefully positioning and volleying the ball back and forth across an invisible net, I went on. "To which Klan organization did your parents and grandparents belong?"

"UKA, United Klans of America, under Robert Shelton. My grandfather and great-grandfather belonged to other Klans before the UKA. I don't really know the names. It may have been the National Knights under James Venable. I couldn't tell you for sure."

I wondered how I could get him to relax. "What is the main objective of TKA, the Territorial Klans of America, as opposed to the objective of the Invisible Empire of which you were formerly a member?"

He made a face. "Well, our goals are the same as the Invisible Empire, but we had a disagreement with J.W. Farrands. He hired an attorney to represent his case which he is involved with Morris "the Sleaze" Dees. He took $20,000 that we donated to him for his attorney, who we didn't know was Jewish, and we later found out that he gave it to Tom Metzger to help him with his court appeal of WAR, White Aryan Resistance. None of this was told to us, but we found out. That's just not the way things are done. You don't take Klan money and use it for another purpose and then turn around and ask for another $30,000. It's no use to try to stay on a ship that's sinking."

He was outwardly calm, but I could tell he was mildly agitated. His was the toughest veneer I had as yet tried to penetrate. He obviously kept his feelings under tight control.

"Are you more White Pride or White Supremacist?" I pursued, knowing this would give him an opportunity.

"Well, I have a lot of White pride. See this tattoo here?" He showed me the tattoo on his hand with the words, "White Power."

I said nothing but gave him a long look and nodded.

"I'm definitely a White Supremacist. I believe that the Anglo-Saxons are the sons of Abel and are the chosen race of God, and that the Anglo-Saxon is the true Israelite, not the Jew."

I wasn't going to let him get off on an anti-Semitic tirade, so I changed the topic. I asked, "Why are there so many different Klan groups? What causes them to splinter off like they do?" *Were they really as cohesive as they claimed to be?* I wondered.

"Well, I just told you why we did," he said in a booming voice. "It's not just the state of Maryland. Florida was the first state—Virginia, West Virginia, Georgia, Pennsylvania and any state that was in the Invisible Empire under Farrands that had any kind of leadership or membership. You're still Klan, but did not want to quit and wouldn't quit. So you had an excuse to get adopted by another Klan organization. Since we have such good leaders here in this state and the manpower, we can get the finances. We get it through membership funds and donations, and we have some big business people that even make anonymous donations. We have the power and the money where we can go on our own. I know how it works, and I know how to do it." He was obviously proud of his Klan group.

"How does your group differ from the others?" I asked, trying to draw him out.

"Like what others? Like Mr. Kelly's group?"

"He would be one, and say Tony LaRicci's old group or whomever."

"Our group differs from Kelly's because Kelly calls himself a Separatist. I definitely believe in separation of the races, racial separation. Not just for, say the White race, but also for the Black race, the Hispanic race, the Chinese, anything. You can break down each other's ethnic cultures and break down your heritage by mixing. So, definitely, we believe in separation. But, at the same time, Kelly's group is a Separatist group, and we are a White Supremacist group. We are a Christian group. We are not a militant group."

Now his voice took on a razor-sharp edge. I leaned forward to watch his body language closely.

"Now I believe a race war is inevitable." He sat up rigidly. "I know it's coming in this country. When it comes, we have a plan. We have a plan where to meet. It's not illegal, you know, to own a few weapons. We don't stress paramilitary training. We do have security guards that do get the security training and things. We stress Christianity, and we are even attempting to build a church. I've just leased sixty acres for a dollar a year, and I'm working on a ninety-nine year lease. We are going to build our own church and a Klavern Hall on this property here in Cecil County." His face glowed with pride. Looking off in the distance, he seemed transfixed.

I wanted to diffuse the moment. "That reminds me," I recalled, "the First Church of the Klan was around here in Havre de Grace."

He nodded, paused for a moment and then answered in a more conversational tone. "Yeah, that was back in 1926, but it burned down or something. I'm not exactly sure. Ours is going to be secured with guard dogs, and it's going to be called the Sons of Abel. We are going to have regular Sunday meetings. I mean church services, and then have our Klavern meetings in the building to the side. We won't hold our Klavern meetings in the church."

Daryl Davis

He was adamant in separating the church and Klavern functions, but I wondered why if his Klan was Christian.

"Did you know that the American Legion Building down the street was originally owned by the Klan?" I asked.

"No, I didn't know that. I'll be damned," he replied.

Was there some connection between the two organizations? I speculated. I put my thoughts aside and continued.

"Is there any camaraderie among the Maryland Klan groups?" I was more curious to know if the Klan groups had more in common than just Klan name.

"What do you mean by camaraderie?" He seemed genuinely puzzled.

"Do you all get along and hold joint activities or whatever?" I clarified.

"We should. We do practice unity. Like the march we had to take a stand against drugs. We had neo-Nazis, skinheads, members of the SS Action Group, members of the Posse Comitatus and members of the Christian Identity Group. I learned through the experience. And I was glad to have all their support, but at the same time, I told them we were going to stick to two chants: 'What do we want? White Power!' and 'Hey, hey, ho, ho, the drug dealers got to go!'

"I told them that's all I wanted chanted, but the Nazis and the skinheads started hollering, 'Kill the niggers, kill the Jews!' They will not march with us again!" he said forcefully, jabbing his right index finger in the air for emphasis. "If they want to hold their own march and chant things like that, fine. But, they will never march alongside the Ku Klux Klan if they are not going to follow orders. This was a Klan march. The Klan was in charge. If I was at one of their functions, I would have respected their orders. But, we do practice unity. I correspond with many different groups, especially the SS Action Group. Their National Director, Ted Dunn, is an excellent man."

"How about the Church of the Creator?" I cited another violent Right-Wing racist group.

"That's Ben Klassen's group out of North Carolina, but they have a chapter here."

"Now, when you had the rally on the Fourth of July, there were some members from Roger Kelly's group who were there, not participating but observing, and there seemed to be a lot of rivalry, back-biting and back-stabbing going on." I knew I was probably probing a sore spot.

"It's a shame, but that is the way it is. Kelly's way of doing things and ours are different. Mr. Kelly's letters, his literature, some of it's misworded, it's not neat. We should get along with any White Supremacist group by all means. His style of things is not up to our quota. He calls himself a Separatist because I think he's backing out. He wants to make it easier because when you call yourself a White Supremacist, you catch a lot more ridicule or whatever. That is what I am, and we say it everywhere we go. And we'll never stop saying it. We are a very good Christian group. We have a very good chaplain. He attends church twice a week with his wife, and he preaches for us. He has a real spiritual aspect of the organization."

A few weeks after this meeting, their chaplain was arrested and charged with committing a "peeping Tom act."

"Roger Kelly can come all the way down here to Belair. That's the nearest town he can come to. If I've done anything, I've helped Roger Kelly by making the Klan visible again. Roger Kelly seems like he's some kind of leader that sits around and waits for things to happen. I go out and make things happen if they're not happening," Dole frowned.

"I think this organization right here in Cecil County is one of the most active Ku Klux Klan organizations in the United States. We've now had nineteen recruitment drives in less than one year. We've probably had twenty crosslighting ceremonies. We've had marches, we've had rallies. Every time we get together for our monthly Klavern meeting, everybody's there. We don't just say, 'See you next month.' We got out and we hit the streets every month. We have picnics. We had a great picnic with a fifty-four-foot crosslighting. It was excellent!" he said excitedly.

"Why do some Klan groups allow skinheads to join, neo-Nazis, Catholics, American-Indians, like Virgil Griffin's group, and some don't allow these people to join?" I was puzzled by the apparent contradictions in what Doles had said to me a few minutes before.

"We allow Catholics, we welcome Native American-Indians, skinheads, if they cool their tempers and abide. They're welcome. If they want to keep up their more radical ways of hanging down in the malls and aggravating people, we're not going to tolerate that. If skinheads want to mature and act like a Klansman, fine. But if they don't . . . it's up to them.

"If you're an Anglo-Saxon and you want to join and you're Catholic, that's fine. The reason Catholics at one time were not allowed in the Klan started during immigration time when Catholics were coming over here from Rome, Italy, whatever. Yeah, Roman Catholics. They were putting the Pope in their country above the President of the United States, but yet they wanted to be American citizens. That's when the Klan took the stance against all immigrants and said that you had to be a true Anglo-Saxon." He wasn't indignant, but he clearly wanted to make the point about allegiance to America as a Klan principle.

"What you are saying is they were over here and had their allegiance over there?" I asked, clarifying.

"Right, and that's wrong. Today we have Catholics. That was their forefathers three generations ago."

"Tony LaRicci told me he was the first Grand Dragon of Italian and Catholic descent."

"He might have been." This appeared to be the first time he had heard this information. Chester's former Imperial Wizard,

J.W. Farrands, was the first Catholic Imperial Wizard and one of the few, if not the only, Northerner to assume national leadership.

"Do you know Bob White?"

"I know who he is, but I've never met him."

As we were talking, Wayne Brannon, the Grand Klaliff of the TKA, came over to the table to join us.

"Tell me, where do the American-Indians fit in? They're not Anglo-Saxon." I wanted to pursue the seeming contradiction of a pro-White Klan with members of non-White origins.

"But, they have to take a side. They are the Native Americans. We have people with Indian in them, part Indian. I don't think we have any full-blooded Indian members."

"Do you have Indian in you?"

"No," he shook his head. "Wayne has some Indian in him."

I turned to Wayne, who seemed to be caught somewhat off guard by this line of inquiry. "What do you have Wayne?"

"Cherokee," he shifted in his seat.

"I have Cherokee in me, too. So does that mean that somewhere along the line, you and I are related?" I have to admit I wanted to see him squirm a bit.

"No!" he almost shouted.

"Are you sure?" I teased.

"I'm positive."

"Well, we both have Cherokee in us," I noted.

"That's a big reservation, isn't it?" Doles interjected, clearly trying to "rescue" Wayne.

"Yeah, man."

"Well, somebody got around," I joked and then became more serious. "Tell me some more about this notion of a race war."

"I think before the year 2000, there will definitely be a race war. That's due to the government's politics of catering to minorities instead of the majority. I say equal rights for all and special privileges for none!"

Daryl Davis

"Does that 'all' include Blacks?" I prodded.

"That's all," he shot back. "Equal rights for all. But this catering to special programs and this crime by the NAACP and the Anti-Defamation League has gotten so far out of hand. Every time I pick up the papers, it's the crime, the poor Black youth. They blame the past, they blame society. Now you've got this reverse discrimination and that's the most racist thing that's ever come up. If a man comes up for a job and he's Black or whatever he is but he's qualified, give it to him. But don't give it to him just because the government says you have to have so many of this minority and so many of that minority. That is totally bullshit. The young White man is having a struggle for opportunity today in the career world because of that." My question had clearly touched a nerve.

"Sort of like hiring a Black woman to kill two birds with one stone?" I pursued.

"That's right. She's Black and a woman too."

"But, if she's qualified, then it's alright. Now, you said that you don't preach violence." I met his eyes, two flaming cauldrons. "Do you preach hate?"

His voice, however, was cold and steely. "We don't preach hate, and if anyone goes out nightriding, they're out of here. We don't have that in this organization."

"The Klan, from it's beginnings, has always been viewed as a violent and hateful organization. It hated Blacks, Jews, homosexuals, etc. Now in the Nineties, you say you are trying to work more politically . . ."

He interrupted. "You have to go with modern times. We are a pro-White, political action, Christian group."

"Since the name 'Ku Klux Klan' has such a negative image, why not change the name of your organization so you won't be associated with its past?" I suggested.

"Because I think it's one of the most patriotic organizations in the world, and I think that the Knights in the Klan are the ultimate American patriots. The violence and things that might have happened . . . " He paused, clearly seeking the best way to phrase what he wanted to say.

"Might?!" I asked incredulous.

"Okay, that *did* happen. The violence that *did* happen in the past. I think that the attitude of America at the time was different than it is today. You could do certain things then, and at the time, it was condoned. When the Klan was started, the Jews were the carpetbaggers that came down to the South and took all their money and took everything away from them. So why not hate them? Then you got the Blacks. They gave them the right to vote. For hundreds of years, the South had been fine. They came down on the Southerners because they were slave owners. Who do you think rounded up the slaves in Africa? It was the strongest tribe over in Africa that rounded up the weak tribe and herded them up to have them ready for the Jews that were bringing them over here to sell them." He was indignant, but calm.

"How do you feel about the Black and White soldiers who went to Vietnam or Iraq and had to defend each other on the front line against the enemy, only to come back here and be each other's enemy?"

"I don't really perceive it that way. I work with Blacks. Work's work. Being in the Army is a job. You got a job to do, you do it. Some of your Blacks are Black Power. They belong to Black organizations. They've got their Martin Luther King martyr. They've got the Malcolm X martyr. We've got David Duke and the Klan. We're just the other side of the coin. I work with Blacks all day long. I can carry on a conversation. I got no problem with it, but I'm not going to invite them home or go out drinking with them. Work's work."

"Outside of work, it's separation," Wayne interjected.

"I got a problem being in the military with them myself," Doles continued. "I am proud to be an Anglo-Saxon, and I'm going to do for the betterment of my race what I can. Just the same as a Black man would do to keep his blood as pure as possible. Why mix it? Our cultures are definitely different. Our music, our guidelines, the way we bring our children up are totally different. Not that it's wrong. You have your culture. Indians have their culture. Chinese and Mexicans have their culture and Anglo-Saxons have their culture. If you mix them together into one culture, you weaken both of us." Again he emphasized the issue of separateness and the need to avoid racial intermixing.

"If you were the leader of this country, what would you do to solve the racial problems?" I inquired.

"First, stop all immigration into the country and stop all aid to Israel. Take care of America first. Get rid of the job discrimination quota system. Definitely get rid of that right off the bat. Reform the welfare system. I read in the paper the other day that poor Whites make up one of the largest poor sections of the country today, and they are being ignored because of who they are.

"I think if I had the power to actually call the shots, I would make it so Indians have reservations. I would let them pick their states. Give them a place. Blacks can have Washington, D.C. They should all move there."

That would be a tidy, if somewhat congested solution, I thought.

"I don't think we ever should have done away with segregation as far as we should have had our White restaurants and you've got your Black restaurants. I mean they would both be the same. Like you would have one McDonald's on one side of the road, and we'd have another one on the other side of the road. But the Blacks wanted to come and eat with Whitey. They got their own restaurant, so why did they want to come and sit with us? Just because someone said they couldn't! I think it would be excellent to go back to segregation. Don't deny them anything. Don't take nothing from them. Have a White school, have a Black school, have a multiracial school, have a three-tier school system. Don't knock them out of anything, but have a choice where you want to send your kid. Have a choice for separation!" he argued.

"What about the homosexual issue?"

"It's ungodly. It's wrong! It's biblically wrong! Thank God for AIDS."

Shocked, I stared at him but held my tongue. Instead, I went on to ask, "Do you believe homosexuals are born that way, or do you believe they choose that lifestyle?"

"I'm not a psychologist or a doctor. I don't know. I just think that it's because someone is sick or diseased. I don't know."

"It's wrong!" Wayne proclaimed.

"It's just wrong." Chester echoed. "I don't know if it's a disease. I think you can quit being a queer."

"What if they can't quit, if they are born that way?" I asserted.

"Isolate them or put them in an institution like they used to do when they thought it was a disease," Chester responded without missing a beat.

"If you can't teach them the right way," Wayne announced, "they need to be institutionalized. It wouldn't be any different than a man who can't stop from committing crimes like sexual assault or burglary. If you can't teach them, put them in a place where they need to be." he sniffed.

Chester broke in, "It's morally wrong. It's supposed to be man, woman and kids. Some people can be rehabilitated. My God, I've got a prison record. I've got a criminal record." Chester had served time in prison for carrying a loaded handgun without a permit.

"I walk the straight and narrow now. I get up and go to work everyday. I've got six kids, and I love my kids. I'm in the PTA at their school. I go to all the parent-teacher conferences, and I go to open house meetings at the school. Me and my wife are separated and she doesn't participate in none of it. I do it all with my children," he said with obvious pride.

"What would you do if you found out that one of your kids was homosexual?"

"My God, forbid. I'd disown him!" he avowed.

His fervor, the fire in his eyes, took my breath away.

"What if they decided to mix with another race?"

Chester stiffened. "I don't see that happening with my children, with their upbringing. They are all in our Klan Youth Corps. My youngest ones are not old enough to comprehend yet. But, if they ever did that, I would disown them."

It was the defining moment. Everything he'd said previously crystallized for me. "You would disown them? A minute ago you were saying everybody should have the choice to choose Black, White or multiracial." We both tensed. I at the contradictions, he at my recognizing them.

There was a long pause. Then he said unapologetically, "Sure, but not my kids. I believe that my son will be a Klan leader of his generation in his time." A look of pride flushed his face.

"Absolutely!" Wayne concurred.

Doles went on. "He's done everything. He's been down to Stone Mountain, he's been everywhere." (Stone Mountain, Georgia, has hosted Klan conventions, or Klonvocations as they are called, every year. Klans from all over the country get together there to practice Klanishness or Klankraft. It is one of the few times rival factions share a rally. It is hosted by Imperial Wizard James Venable of the National Knights who lives on Stone Mountain.)

I thought it best, in view of Doles' emotional reaction to even the idea that his children could discard the Klan's views, to change to a more dispassionate topic. "Of all the Klan leaders of the past and recent times, who do you think has the best and most effective objectives?" I asked.

"I respect Thom Robb the Imperial Wizard of the National

Albert Pike statue in Judicial Square, Washington, D.C.

A protest sign in front of the Pike statue.

A right wing protest
of the Holocaust
Museum in
Washington, D.C.

Daryl meeting with Black Separatist Dr. Robert Brock and
New York Grand Dragon for the Invisible Empire Knights
of the KKK, Bill Hoff.

Daryl talking to right wing attorney, Kirk Lyons, at the Holocaust Museum protest.

Daryl pictured with the head of the Right Wing Liberty Lobby, John Nugent.

Daryl Davis pauses from conversation with Dr. Edward Fields, founder of the National States Rights Party.

National Knights of the KKK Imperial Wizard, Thom Robb, talks with Daryl Davis.

Daryl visiting the incarcerated Imperial Wizard, Chester Doles.

Thomas Tarrants and Daryl Davis relax in Tarrants' home.

Roy Frankhouser, Daryl Davis and Mark Thomas behind the scenes of the cable access Klan show.

Daryl appearing with Roy Frankhouser on Frankhouser's Klan TV show.

One of the Klan robes Daryl was given by a member who has quit.

Jammin' with the Prez: Judy Collins, Bill Clinton, Dionne Warwick, Daryl Davis and Chuck Berry.

Daryl Davis in tux with Linda Evans.

Ray Charles and Daryl Davis.

Daryl Davis at the piano.

Daryl Davis and his friend Jerry Lee Lewis.

Actor Bruce Willis with Daryl Davis.

Daryl Davis joins Liberace laugh.

A young Daryl Davis with Willie Nelson.

Jammin' with the King: Daryl Davis on stage with Chuck Berry.

Daryl Davis and Dolly Par

Knights out of Harrison, Arkansas, a lot. Do you mean White Supremacist or Klan leader?" he asked, seeking clarification.

"Either or both," I shrugged.

"Well, let's see. I used to respect J.W., but I think he forgot where he came from and handled things wrong. I lost respect for him." He became somewhat pensive as he spoke.

"I've heard a lot of complaints about J.W. misusing Klan funds and other things," I suggested, opening another line of inquiry.

"I was very loyal to him for a couple of years. I always will be. But when somebody slaps you in the face, you'd be a fool to hang on," he snapped.

"I remember your loyalty, and I respected your wanting to get his permission before you talked to me," I said.

Once again that look of pride appeared. "Yeah. After this thing happened, I decided I would talk to you. Bill Wilkinson did a lot. David Duke did more than we could do in just a few years because of his political standing. I have an article that was put in the paper here that says David Duke and Chester Doles should team together and form the Republican Klan party. I'm running for County Commissioner here in Cecil County. I am going to run for the Cecil County Republican Commissioner of the Second District. Whether I win or not, I think they are going to be very surprised at the number of votes that comes in here in Cecil County. I had a march through Elkton recently."

"Were you there?" Wayne asked, turning to me.

I shook my head, "No. Roger Kelly had a rally in a public park on the same day down my way also. I was going to try to make both yours and his, but I had to play a wedding that day and couldn't make either one."

"There were at least two thousand people at this march. I didn't know what to expect when I came up around the street. People were applauding and cheering. There were maybe a dozen poor people, anti-Klan people who had some signs there. Every time they tried to say something, the crowd just over-cheered them and clapped and drowned them out.

"There were some Blacks that chased us around shaking their dicks at us and pulling down their pants. The cops didn't do anything. They harassed us the whole parade route. These were the local drug dealers. I've been down there many times checking it out. They stand out there with their hand in their pocket full of cocaine bottles. They're the ones who got right up there in front of the cops' eyes, and the cops didn't do one thing to them. Then the NAACP says we're picking on the poor Black youth over here. Give them a reason to get one of us, they ain't gonna hesitate to nail my ass."

"Do you think that there are any White drug dealers around?" I asked, looking at him intently.

His candor surprised me. "Oh, absolutely. Sure there are, definitely. But, I don't know any that stand out there in front of a bar and stand out there for ten years every night of the week."

"Or write prices on the street curb," Wayne added. I noticed how at every turn he backed up what Doles said.

"Yeah, they had prices written on the telephone pole and on the curb. You pull up and you looked at the prices and stuff right there," Chester remarked.

"They got it marked down, what a gram sells for," Wayne chimed in.

"Do you know J.B. Stoner?" I inquired.

"Yeah, J.B. Stoner and I have sat down and talked before."

"How about Bobby Shelton?"

"I got lucky. I met Robert Shelton," Wayne declared.

Doles shrugged. "I don't know nothing about Shelton's doings. If you want to know which Klan leader I most admire in all of history, it would be Sam Bowers." (Sam Bowers was the Imperial Wizard of the White Knights of Mississippi. His Klan, along with Shelton's, were considered the most violent Klans since the Fifties. It was his group that was thought to be behind the murders of three Civil Rights workers: James Chaney, Andrew Goodman, and Michael Schwerner. His Klan was responsible for more than three hundred bombings, burnings, beatings and murders during the Sixties.)

"Have you ever met Bowers?" I asked.

"No, but I would *love* to talk to that man. Sam Bowers took control and said, 'We don't care about the rest of America, we care about Mississippi.'

"The things he did or might have done were radical. They sound so radical and violent now, but you have to put yourself back in that era of the Sixties when they were going about their business and everything was fine. Then all of a sudden, you got these Jews and Blacks coming down from Chicago and other cities saying, 'We want to go to your college.' Why? Cause it's all White. They came down looking for trouble and they found it." His eyes flashed with anger as he spoke.

"I don't know any Whites that ever went up to Harlem and wanted to go to the University of New York City or something. They don't want to go to it. Just because they were all White down there in Mississippi, they went all the way down there in the heart of Mississippi. People had their own culture, their own way of life for years and years, and they come down and stir it up," he said excitedly.

"Look at all the shit that's happened in the country since Civil Rights. Blacks and quota laws and the doing away with segregation. That's the way I look at it. They say the reason Sam Bowers doesn't start the organization up again is because they might find some more skeletons." He laughed. "No disrespect to you, but you asked me, and I'm telling you. When the United States Constitution was originally written, Blacks weren't citizens. At that time, they were property. So how could they fall under the Constitution. It wasn't written for them. It was written by the White man of the White man."

"But as you said earlier, we've got to move with modern

times. Blacks are citizens now, and we can vote," I reminded him.

"Right." He nodded. His face momentarily sagged with the thought and then it brightened. "So we've got to get a man in office who is going to look out for us. Not condemn minorities, but be fair and go by the Constitution as it was originally written and intended. Like the Fourteenth Amendment is an illegal amendment. It was supposed to be ratified by the majority of the states, but it was only ratified by twelve states in the Union. At the time, there was only twenty-six states. Rhode Island was in the Union, but didn't sign it, and the Southern states didn't even have a vote in it. You can go out there, stand out there and shout, 'Black Power, I'm Black and I'm proud,' and people like you, they want to recognize you. They'll put you in the paper and call you Citizen of the Month. But, if I go stand out there with my Ku Klux Klan hat on that says, 'White Power,' people will call me a racist, bigot bastard. That's crazy bullshit.

"I'm proud and I'm teaching my children to be proud of where they come from. I went to my kid's eighth grade social studies class during parent-teacher school night. She was going down the list of what they were going to talk about this semester and she said they were going to discuss Native Americans, African-Americans, the Civil War and all this. Then she asked if anyone had any questions. I asked her if she was going to talk about the European-American. Now she's a Black teacher and was caught off guard. I told her the majority of this country, let alone this county, was White. Didn't she think she should teach them about European-Americans? She said that came under 'Traditional.' I told her that I didn't know she thought of us as traditional. I want to push for a White History Month. She's Black and going to teach European history in school."

"How do you feel about Black History Month?" I asked, sensing his discomfort with the notion.

"I don't like it," he said unapologetically. "I'm going to take my kids out of school because they talk about Martin Luther

King, and they patronize him and talk about him like he's an almighty god. Maybe he was real good to the Blacks in their movement, but there are FBI documents where he was a White whoremonger and had White prostitutes. He was supposed to spread the work of peace, but everywhere he went, violence and race riots broke out in every town. There are even FBI documents, and I've seen 'em one time where his doctor's papers had been forged. There are proven facts that he was supported by communists and communist organizations. I don't know the names off hand, but they backed him." Reverend King was clearly a subject about which he held vehement opinions.

"You mentioned the FBI. Do you remember Gary Thomas Rowe?"

"No," he said, appearing to search his memory.

"Do you remember Viola Liuzzo?"

"The Black lady that sat in front of the bus?" Chester speculated.

"No, no. That was Rosa Parks. Viola Liuzzo was a White lady who was on her way through Alabama and . . ."

"She got shot," he suddenly blurted out. "She had the Black guy in the car. That's right. And the FBI had a guy in there (Gary Thomas Rowe), and then they turned around and convicted him for firing the shots."

"The FBI did a lot of illegal things against the Klan," I observed dryly.

"Oh, definitely. They were out trying to date our women and calling our bosses at work."

Here again were the blinders I'd seen in other Klan members. "So knowing this, why do you give credibility to the FBI when they are knocking Martin Luther King, but discredit them when they are knocking the Klan? Why are the records on King and Kennedy sealed until sometime after the year 2000?"

"I'll note that the country's a mess. The country is a real mess . . . " Chester reflected.

"Yeah," Wayne cut in. "We're all here to stay, but . . . "
Wayne trailed off.

"Maybe it shouldn't be you against me, but us against them . . . " I suggested.

"I agree with that, but the reason we have racial problems and those kind of things is because the government allows the minorities so much. The government has established a quota system and special programs. You have the Negro College Fund. Why don't we have a White College Fund? You don't think the poor White people need it? You have a Miss Black America Pageant. If they had a Miss White America Pageant, they'd scream racism."

"There was a time when the Miss America Pageant did not allow Blacks to compete," I reminded him.

"They have made a couple Miss Americas out of Blacks," he retorted.

"*Now* they have," I replied quietly, but could not keep the edge of sarcasm from my voice.

Doles didn't catch it. "I will tell you honestly," he said, caught up in expressing his own opinion, "it was only because they were Black. Because there were some women in there, my God, blondes and blue eyes that were tearing ass all over these people. I said no way they could win, but they catered to them because they were Black."

"Didn't you think Vanessa Williams was pretty?" I asked.

"No."

"No," Wayne echoed.

"She straightened her hair and stuff like that, you know?" Chester remarked.

"May I say one thing?" Wayne asked somewhat mischievously.

"Sure," I responded curiously.

"I heard an old Klansman say one time, 'I've seen some good looking Black ladies, but I think my dog's good looking.' I think some horses are good looking, but there are none I'd like to go to bed with."

"It's just like human nature, cats don't chase dogs, pigs don't chase cows," Chester added to emphasize the point.

"You got it," Wayne chimed in.

"You stick with your own," Chester affirmed.

At this point, we were joined by a woman who I had been chatting with while waiting for Chester to arrive. Although Chester and Wayne glanced at her, no one addressed her. "What are your views on women?" I asked, taking advantage of the moment.

"Women are the future of America. White womanhood is very, very important. If we have a lady who comes into our organization, who is very talented as Kimberly Brannon here is, I have no objections. They can have full say in meetings. I ain't going to say no names, but I ain't going to listen to all women. If they are talented and show me that they have skills and the know-how and intelligence to carry themselves and are well-behaved, intelligent women, I have no problem with that. We swear women in left and right. We got seventeen new members this past weekend and five of them were women and about a half dozen children."

"How about women who take on jobs that were traditionally held by a man, like police officers, firemen and so forth?"

"I work in the county roads department, and I have a woman that's out there with me digging ditches and stuff. The only thing I reject or object to about a woman doing is holding any kind of a minister's position because the Bible states in First Corinthians . . . "

I pulled out my Bible and handed it to him. The Klan has always used the Scriptures as the guideline for their beliefs—although they interpret the meanings to their liking. As he scanned over the First Corinthians he continued to express his opinions on woman and their duties.

"They should not be ministers. They let lesbians teach

205

Daryl Davis

Sunday school, my God! I don't know how any kind of congregation could ever have gay leaders. Here we go, I found it. 'Let your women keep silence in the churches: for it is not permitted unto them to speak; but they are commanded to be under obedience, as also saith the law. And if they will learn anything, let them ask their husbands at home: for it is a shame for women to speak in the church.' That's right here, First Corinthians, Chapter 14, verses 34 and 35 in the Bible. Now, if it's a shame for a woman to speak in the church, how can she be a reverend?

"As far as homosexual women and homosexual men teaching any kind of religion in the church, I don't care what religion it is, it's totally ungodly! What kind of moral respect is that if you've got a queer Sunday school teacher teaching your kids? My God!" Chester said with a flash of emotion.

"By the way, Daryl," said Wayne, "this is Kimberly Brannon, my wife." Wayne turned to the woman who'd been standing silently next to us. "She's the Grand Secretary." ("Grand Kligrapp" in Klan terminology.)

"Hi, Kim. Pleased to meet you." I stood and shook hands with her.

"Hi, you too," she responded cheerfully.

"Well, Chester, that's it for me," I said, ready to bring our conversation to a close.

He wasn't ready to end our talk. "The Territorial Klans of America under the leaders we have here in the Realm of Maryland are strong. The Grand Dragon is a good, excellent, prominent, wealthy man from Delaware who'll help make the TKA group the largest Ku Klux Klan organization in America. We are going on a campaign tour with what has worked. We have several hundred members here in this county alone. I say we are going to be the largest, most respected organization in the United States as a Christian Ku Klux Klan organization. But, if we're pushed, we'll push back," Chester declared.

Chester, his diatribe over, became more friendly and his

mood more easy. "I can't let you buy me dinner, but you can buy me a beer if you like."

I laughed and bought a round of beers for Chester and the Klan members who were present. He promised to mail me some pictures of himself. I started the long drive home, my head swimming with thoughts of all we had discussed and the mercurial man I had begun to know, if not understand.

20

Let's Try It Again
(The Klansman's
Appeal)

A couple of months after the trial of the Klansman who pursued the stolen hood, I returned once again to the Eastern Shore—this time for the trial of the hoodsnatcher.

I left my home at five in the morning, figuring that I would get there by eight, run into Chester Doles and some of his constituents and have time to chat with them before the trial. I had phoned Doles at his home the night before to see if he was going, but got no answer at his home. I arrived in plenty of time before the trial, but saw no sign of Doles or any Klanspeople in the lobby outside of the courtroom. I also saw no sign of the young fellow who snatched the hood.

Entering the courtroom, I took a seat in the front row. The prosecutor was talking about the case of the hoodsnatcher with another attorney and they both were laughing. I overheard the prosecutor say that he would call that case first and get it out of the way. Still no sign of the Klan or the defendant who was charged with "Misdemeanor Theft."

The judge entered, we all rose, sat back down and came to order. The prosecutor immediately addressed the case of the hoodsnatching and told the judge that the state wished to nolle prosequi (unwilling to prosecute) that case. His Honor granted it and the next case was called. Just like that. The charges were dropped, the case was not tried, the defendant was not guilty and he wasn't even there.

Shelly Bowman, a detective that I know, came into the courtroom a couple of minutes later to see the trial. When I told her what had taken place, her mouth fell open. Once again, the whole thing seemed preorchestrated for the benefit of legal formalities or observers in the courtroom.

A few months after I met with Chester Doles, the date for the Circuit Court appeal of the Klansman who was arrested and found guilty arrived. Fortunately for me, I happened to be performing nearby that evening.

I got to the courthouse about twenty minutes early and was told by a reporter friend of mine, Tony Wilbert from the *News Journal*, that he had heard that the charges against the Klansman were going to be dropped. He said that because they did not prosecute the hoodsnatcher, they felt that they couldn't very well prosecute someone trying to retrieve the property.

I walked through the metal detector, into the courtroom and took a seat on the very front row, as had become my custom. As it neared nine o'clock, spectators began streaming in. I overheard one young woman seated in back of me tell the person next to her, "The Klan's here. There's a bunch of them walking down the street towards the courthouse."

Leaning over, I asked her how she knew it was the Klan? She replied, "They're wearing their stuff."

Thinking she meant they were enrobed and that this would be a spectacle to see, I got up and walked out to the hall to find a window. Just as I turned the corner, I was met head on by Chester and seven members of his entourage. They were not wearing robes and hoods. All but one were wearing Klan tee shirts and blood drop emblems. The odd man was dressed in a suit and tie.

"There he is. How're you doing?" Chester asked amiably.

"I'm doing fine, Chester," I replied in kind as we shook hands. We all walked toward the courtroom together. I went inside and reclaimed my seat on the front bench while Chester and the other Klansmen stopped so they could all get through the checkpoint. It seemed to take forever for these Klansmen to get through the metal detector.

The first one, who happened to be the man in the suit, took a seat on my bench a few feet from me. I noticed his tie was embroidered with the letters, "KKK." I said, "How are you?"

With a distant, but piercing look in his eyes, he replied, "Fine."

The rest of the men began filing in and Chester motioned for all of them to sit a couple of rows behind me. My bench neighbor stood up and quickly relocated to the rear bench. I couldn't help thinking about Rosa Parks and the segregated bus seating arrangement, which had not so long before existed in the South. It was now reversed, with a Black man in the front and the Ku Klux Klan in the back. I laughed to myself, perfectly content. Chester called out my name and struck up a long distance conversation with me. People in the courtroom who didn't know that we knew each other watched, their faces reflecting total shock and surprise.

A moment later the bailiff announced the judge's entrance. We all stood up and then sat down again as the clerk started calling the cases. Most of the cases on the docket were for people who had been charged with "Driving While Intoxicated" or "Driving Under the Influence." When the Klansman's case was called, the prosecutor, with a slight scowl, informed His Honor that the state wished to drop the charges.

"We've located the police officer on whose back the Klansman had allegedly jumped. He is now residing in Pennsylvania. He has told us that he remembered the arrest, but could not recall anyone jumping on his back."

The prosecutor told the judge that without any witnesses, they would be unable to proceed against the defendant. The judge granted the dismissal much to the shouted glee of the Klansmen and much to the dismay of one policewoman who had attended to observe.

The people who had looked shocked and surprised to see a Klansman and me conversing in a non-hostile manner were equally, if not more surprised, to see me walk out of the court-room with them when the case they had come to see was dismissed.

Outside the courthouse, Chester, surrounded by the media, held a short interview. He stated that he was glad that the judge had done the right thing and how it was proven that the cop who testified in the first trial had lied.

Chester told the news media that he was prepared to announce a date for another Klan function nearby had the judge not dismissed the case and stated that a Klavern had been formed in that town as a result of the arrest. He then announced its post office box number, and encouraged all White people to join. He passed out his new card proclaiming him to be the Imperial Wizard of the Knights of the Territorial Klans of America. I asked him to give me one, which he did. They went off to a bar to celebrate, and I went back to where I was staying before my gig. And what of the Klansman who had been exonerated? He didn't make it to his trial. He was in the Cecil County jail on other charges.

As a Black man, I found it very informative to see the

array of events surrounding this incident unfold. For once, this was a situation involving the Klan which was not racially motivated and all the parties—the Klan, the hoodsnatcher, the police and the judge—were White. My feelings on the whole matter were something of a dichotomy of both amusement and sadness. On the one hand, it was bitterly amusing to see White people convict another White man who had committed no crime, for no other reason than the fact that he belonged to the Klan, while exonerating another White man who, in front of numerous people including police officers, had indeed committed a crime. On the other hand, it was sad to see that if someone belongs to a minority group or holds beliefs that are not in alignment with the general sentiment of the majority, they will not find justice; at the same time those who uphold the sentiment of the majority can count on the support of the legal system to allow them to commit "permissible" unlawful acts.

I went to my car and headed towards home. For the next three hours, I thought about how this particular Klan was in the same position in the judicial system as Black people have too often found themselves: unfairly accused. It is often said, "What goes around, comes around," not to say that what came or comes is justified. Also, I wondered what the outcomes of both court cases would have been had the hoodsnatcher been Black.

That evening, I phoned Imperial Wizard Chester Doles and asked him why he had not been present at the court. He said that he had to work that day and that it had slipped his mind. He asked me what the outcome was and I told him.

"I'm disappointed, but not surprised," he said. Chester thanked me for letting him know, and I suggested that we set up a day and time to meet. He mentioned a place and told me it was the only one among the ten area taverns from which he had not been barred. I told him not to eat and I would buy us dinner while we talked. This time, he didn't refuse.

21

Albert Pike, Hugo Black and Robert Byrd

One Friday, I headed for Washington, D.C. to see the followers of Left-Winger Lyndon LaRouche protesting the statue of Albert Pike in Judicial Square.

Albert Pike was an ex-Confederate General. He was also the editor of the *Memphis Appeal* during the Reconstruction. Various sources identify Pike as a Klansman who drafted their original KKK prescript and served as the Chief Judicial officer for the Klan.

The statue is surrounded by various courthouses including the Supreme Court. A number of various groups continually hold protests near the statue, calling for its removal and claiming that it represents Klan justice instead of equal justice. On a recent night some demonstrators had dressed the statue in a white sheet and hood.

I have always viewed Lyndon LaRouche as somewhat of a racist. It seemed odd to me that his group would be calling for the removal of the Pike statue. I asked some of the pro-LaRouche people to explain this, commenting, "that his teaming up with a Black to run for office seemed a tactic to acquire publicity and votes. A similar tactic," I went on, "was used by David Duke when he posed for a picture with James Meredith, the first Black admitted to the University of Mississippi."

The ones with whom I spoke were friendly, but appeared to me to be brainwashed; they had the same monotone answers to my questions as many of the Klansmen with whom I had spoken.

This is certainly not the only instance of a Klansman being in the judicial system. Many Southern judges of years past were also Klansmen. This was not limited to rural towns. Supreme Court Justice Hugo Black had been a Klansman in Alabama in the 1920's. Senator Robert Byrd from West Virginia, who is still a Senator today, had been a Klansman in the 1940's. To my knowledge, no attempt has been made to remove Justice Black's picture from the Hall of Justice. That cannot be said for Senator Byrd.

While in Washington, D.C. in the 1980's to check out a Klan rally in Lafayette Park in front of the White House, I had met a young woman who belonged to the John Brown Anti-Klan Committee. She was handing out "Death to the Klan" literature. Subsequently, I would see her from time to time at Klan and Nazi gatherings, and we always spoke cordially to one another. The next and last time I heard her name was when she was arrested along with some others in the bombing of Senator Byrd's office in the United States Capitol Building. The Senator was not in his office at the time.

22

Roy Frankhouser

Roy Frankhouser has been in various Klan groups since the Fifties. Over the years, I have become well acquainted with his name. He has been arrested close to one hundred times for various charges. Frankhouser was never one to leave unchallenged a law he felt to be unconstitutional.

Many of the demonstrations he led as Grand Dragon of Pennsylvania resulted in violent disturbances of the public peace. He quickly acquired the nickname "Riot Roy." During a barroom brawl, Roy lost one of his eyes. He now has a glass eye in its place, which once during a conversation with me, he popped out and set on the table. One of his glass eye replacements had been auctioned off at a Klan rally, and I happen to know the Klansman who now has it in his possession.

In addition to the charges of "Inciting to Riot" and "Disturbing the Peace," he has been arrested for possession of explosives. Although never convicted, Roy has been a suspect in bombings and murders.

As a young man searching for a sense of belonging, Frankhouser became friends with George Lincoln Rockwell and joined his American Nazi Party. Wanting to be a part of organizations with similar philosophies, he also joined the National

States Rights Party, the Minutemen, the National Renaissance Party and the United Klans of America, among others. Being a liaison between various Right-Wing extremists, Roy developed exceptional organizational skills in putting together joint functions involving various groups.

Roy then became a personal bodyguard and chief of security to Left-Winger Lyndon LaRouche. Roy was also arrested for trying to "fix" a grand jury investigation of the credit card fraud scheme that raised more than $1,000,000 for LaRouche. Frankhouser also cooperated with Black community activists in an effort to reduce crime and unemployment. All this time Roy Frankhouser was a known Klansman and never renounced his membership.

Although many Klans still respect and cooperate with Roy, many other Klans now consider him to be an informant after it was found out that he had at one time cooperated with the government on certain matters.

However, during the 1966 House Un-American Activities Committee Interrogations, Roy refused to disclose any information. At another point in time, Roy was also questioned about the Martin Luther King, Jr., assassination and supposed assassin James Earl Ray. Roy had been in contact with Ray. James Earl's brother, Jerry Ray, had served as a bodyguard to well known racist J.B. Stoner, who headed the National States Rights Party.

Dan Burros was one of the United States Army National Guard soldiers assigned to help integrate Central High School in Little Rock, Arkansas amidst violent racial protest. He said he quit the Army because he objected to "protecting niggers."

It was determined that he was unfit for service after he attempted suicide and left a note signed "Heil Hitler." Somehow, which was not uncommon in that period, Dan Burros received an honorable discharge.

Upon his release, he promptly joined the American Nazi Party and, like Roy Frankhouser, joined many of the other

Right-Wing organizations. One of Dan's favorite pastimes was fighting with Blacks and Jews and defacing Jewish establishments with swastikas. Roy recruited Burros into the Klan. He was eventually made a King Kleagle, or recruiter, and a Grand Dragon in New York. In October of 1965, the *New York Times* discovered a startling fact—unbeknownst to the Nazis or the Klan, the anti-Semitic, anti-Black Dan Burros was half-Jewish!

Knowing that this revelation of his secret would cost him most of the friends he had made and, being of very low self-esteem, on Halloween 1965, Dan Burros blew his brains out in front of Roy Frankhouser at Roy's Pennsylvania home. Although it was ruled a suicide and many confirm that they were good friends, there are those who believe that Frankhouser took the life of Dan Burros.

Now Roy Frankhouser was about to be released from jail. He had been serving time for stabbing another Klansman in a dispute. A Klansman who is a close friend of Frankhouser's told me that Roy would not have a problem talking with me and volunteered to give him my phone number. I told him to go ahead.

Shortly after his release, Frankhouser phoned me. We must have talked for an hour. He was a very well-spoken, highly intelligent man which fascinated me a great deal because of his history. He said he wanted very much to talk with me and invited me to his home. After setting the date he gave me directions, commenting I couldn't miss the place.

As I drove that night, I was surprised to see the address Roy had given me was leading me into the heart of an integrated neighborhood made up of Blacks, Whites, Hispanics and Asians. I thought for a moment that I had not followed the directions properly or he'd given me the wrong ones. Then I remembered him telling me that I could not miss his place. So I drove on until I reached the address. And he was right! I couldn't miss it. Right there on the front wall of his row house was a Klansman on horseback with a flaming cross.

Daryl Davis

I had arrived a few minutes early, but I went ahead and knocked on the door anyway. No one answered. A little Hispanic boy who appeared to live next door, said from his front porch stoop, "Mr. Frankhouser over there," while pointing at a laundromat. "He said he'll be right back."

A moment later the boy pointed across the street, looked at me and smiled. I looked and saw a man in his fifties wearing headphones with a Walkman type apparatus in one hand and some laundry in the other, walking in my direction. He waved and I returned the gesture.

"You must be Mr. Davis," he said. As my odyssey had become better known, so had the fact that I was Black, so he was not surprised.

"I'm sorry I was not here to greet you. Have you been waiting long?"

I assured him that I had just gotten there and no apology was necessary and to please call me by my first name.

As he led me inside I was once again in a Klan den. It reminded me of Roger Kelly's meeting room complete with rows of chairs, an altar, a five-foot cross and all the other essentials.

"Do your neighbors know who you are?" I asked.

He assured me they did. "We all have a mutual liking and respect for one another and look out for each other which is why I sometimes leave my door unlocked," Roy said with a slight smile.

I looked around. The walls were decorated with all types of certificates indicating his membership in the organizations and different ranks in the organizations. He led me upstairs through his bedroom to his sitting room. Swastikas and other SS Nazi memorabilia as well as a wide assortment of Klan paraphernalia were part of the decor.

Roy also had quite a collection of books and little figurine soldiers from different wars. He offered me a seat and a cold drink, both of which I accepted. Although I must admit it felt eerie, Roy Frankhouser was a most hospitable and gracious host. However, he didn't make me anymore comfortable when I asked him about the Dan Burros incident.

"Burros shot himself in the very spot you're sitting in." He then told me that one of the Nazi flags on the wall was covering some of the bloodstains that remained there as a result of Burros blowing his brains out.

"Would you like to see them?" he asked.

"No, I don't think so." I said firmly. Crazy, adventurous, bold, and brave are some of the adjectives people have used to describe me—macabre is not.

Roy hosts his own local public access television show promoting various Right-Wing groups and White Supremacists and Separatists. He invited me to be a guest on his Klan show. He says that ex-Klansman and current White Aryan Resistance (WAR) leader Tom Metzger got the idea for his similar show, "Race and Reason," through Roy.

Tom Metzger, by the way, denies that Roy founded the show. Tom told me that he created the show in 1984 and since that time other Right-Wingers have followed in his footsteps in the public access and cable television markets.

Not long after we'd met, I appeared on Roy's show along with Right-Wing Pastor Mark Thomas. The three of us had a very lively discussion concerning racial issues. Whether agreeing or disagreeing, everyone was very cordial and respectful of one another.

At one point, after Roy had introduced me on air as a musician researching the Klan, I spotted a piano. I asked Roy if I might play it for his viewers, and he agreed. I performed "Fur Elise" by Beethoven and Pinetop's "Boogie Woogie" by Black Boogie Woogie pianists Pinetop Smith and Pinetop Perkins.

Daryl Davis

The spirit of the rollicking piano reminded Roy of Jerry Lee Lewis, and he rose from his chair and began dancing. It was quite a sight to see. Only moments before, a very serious discussion on race had been going on between a Black man and two Klansmen. Moments later, one of the Klansman was dancing to the music being played on the piano by the Black man. I thought for sure that this unplanned, spontaneous happening would be edited out of the broadcast. It was not.

23

The Holocaust Museum

The long awaited Holocaust Museum was to be dedicated on April 22, 1993, in Washington, D.C. This was to be a private ceremony by invitation only to survivors of the Holocaust and other dignitaries. President Clinton and the president of Israel were on the invitation list.

I had been told by a Klansman from New York, with whom I communicate quite frequently, that there was going to be a protest across the street from the museum during its dedication. He told me that representatives of different Right-Wing groups would be there to participate in the demonstration. He named a few of the people he knew would definitely attend. I decided to meet them in order to learn their views.

Information on the upcoming dedication and opening filled the media, but no mention was made of any protest. The day came and I drove to downtown D.C. I had to park my car several blocks away and walk because the streets near the museum had been sealed off for the President and other dignitaries.

Tourists crowded the area, as well as people who did not have invitation tickets, but just wanted to stand, listen and watch the dedication on the big screen provided for just that purpose. The event was to be held outside. The rooftops in the area were lined with federal agent sharpshooters with binoculars.

As I got within a block of the museum, I asked a burly, red-faced policeman where the protesters were. He replied that there were three different groups, named them and told me their locations. One group contained the Nazis, Klan and similar types. This was the largest group of protesters. Another group consisted of Black Nationalists led by Dr. Roger Brock, a Black Separatist who believes in the repatriation of Blacks to Africa. He and different Klans have met several times on a friendly basis because of their common beliefs. The other group was comprised of young Jewish people who were protesting the presence of the other groups.

Approaching the first group, the first person I saw was Thom Robb, Imperial Wizard of the National Knights of the Ku Klux Klan based in Harrison, Arkansas. He was standing within a fenced off area with about seventy-five other Right-Wingers. He was holding a placard denouncing Jews.

I walked up to him, told him I was gathering information about the Klan and other racist groups, reached across the fence and shook his hand, much to the astonishment of the police and surrounding passersby. At his invitation, I walked around to the opening in the fence and entered the protesters' arena.

People on the inside and outside seemed to be having a field day taking pictures and videotapes of me. From their point of view, my presence must have looked rather odd. One protester even offered me a sign to hold. I politely declined. Several protesters came over to me and said they were happy to meet me. They thought I was a Black Nationalist from Dr. Robert Brock's group on the next block. I let them know that I was not from Dr. Brock's group.

Looking around, I thought the fenced-in area, which was about 1,250 square feet, resembled a Who's Who Right-Wing convention. Some of the groups represented were the Aryan Nations, Posse Comitatus, Church of the Creator, Invisible Empire Knights of the Ku Klux Klan, National Knights of the Ku Klux Klan, some neo-Nazis, White Power Skinheads and various other Right-Wing groups. All these protesters were brought together and organized by a group called the Liberty Lobby.

Among the people I saw were: Thom Robb (Imperial Wizard, National Knights of the KKK), Bill Hoff (Grand Dragon of New York, Invisible Empire), John Nugent (Head of the Liberty Lobby), Kirk Lyons (Right-Wing attorney), Willis Carto (Founder of the Liberty Lobby), Dr. Edward Fields (New Order Knights of the KKK and National States Rights Party co-founder), Mark Thomas (Posse Comitatus, ex-Invisible Empire KKK, Christian Identity minister) and various other unidentified Right-Wingers.

I chatted with Thom Robb for a few minutes, and we exchanged phone numbers. Then I approached Dr. Fields. I was not quite sure how he would react to me. In the 1950's and throughout the 60's, Edward Fields was one of the most outspoken racists to walk the face of this Earth. He and J. B. Stoner, an equally vehement racist, formed the National States Rights Party.

Many ex-Right-Wingers allege that Fields had information about various bombings and that he, J.B. Stoner and Klansman Robert Chambliss made the bomb which killed four young Black girls at the Sixteenth Street Baptist Church in Birmingham, Alabama on September 15, 1963.

Fields created an anti-Jewish week and was also arrested for violent interference with school desegregation. After the 1979 shoot-out in Greensboro, North Carolina between Virgil Griffin's Christian Knights of the KKK and the Communist Workers' Party, which left five CWP members dead, Fields held a banquet honoring the Klansmen and neo-Nazis who had participated in the murders.

Despite the difficulty, I tried once again to put my own

feelings and prejudices aside in order to understand his views more fully. I walked over to him and introduced myself. He was very pleasant and receptive, even after I told him I was not a Black Separatist. After talking with Dr. Fields, I spotted Bill Hoff and moved towards him.

William Hoff first joined the Klan in the Sixties under Robert Shelton's UKA. In 1965, he became the King Kleagle for the state of New York. During the race riots which followed the assassination of Dr. Martin Luther King, Jr., Hoff threw a grenade into a Black bar, wounding two people. He was arrested in 1968 for giving dynamite to an undercover officer to blow up certain homes. Hoff was charged with conspiring to murder 158 leftists and civil rights activists. In addition to being involved with the Klan and the National Rights Party, Hoff was linked with the Minutemen and the American Nazi Party.

Most recently, Hoff had been seen on many television talk shows. Not long before, he had been working for a Black-owned company and had a Black boss. He was fired when the boss found out his employee was a Klansman. According to the boss, Mr. Hoff was an excellent worker and pleasant person who presented no problems, but the fact that he was a Klansman did not sit too well.

I introduced myself to Hoff, and he acted genuinely pleased to meet me.

"I've heard about you through various Klan channels," he said. We talked for quite a while. I asked him about his violent background. He did not dispute it, as do many Klansmen who have been charged or convicted of violent hate crimes. He said that his stay in the federal guest house was the best thing that ever happened to him. He now denounced violence.

A short time later, the group of young Jewish protesters was leaving and walked near the Right-Wing arena. Immediately almost everyone in the fenced-in area rushed in that direction and began shouting slurs and giving the "Sieg Heil" or "Heil Hitler" salute. Just as quickly, the police on horseback came between the two groups. Bill Hoff refused to participate in this interaction and stood next to me telling me that this was not the proper way to achieve anything.

Hoff said he still holds the same Klan ideology, but now believes that there are better, more peaceful ways of achieving his goals. One of the ways he hopes to do this is by working with Black Nationalists and Black Separatists. He expressed a great interest in meeting Dr. Brock and asked me if I knew him. I replied that I did not, but that I believed Brock would talk to me since my information-gathering about racism was becoming well known.

I walked over to Brock's designated protest area. Catching sight of him, I introduced myself and we chatted for a few moments. "There is a Klansman who wants very much to meet you." I said.

"I'll be here for a few more minutes before I have to leave," Brock replied.

I went back to the Right-Wing arena, found Bill Hoff and told him, "Dr. Brock's agreed to meet you. Please come with me." We walked there together as I mused that had to be an odd sight for anyone who observed us and recognized Bill Hoff as the Grand Dragon of a Klan group.

And so my odyssey produced another first for me. I introduced a Black man and a White Separatist. They shook hands, exchanged phone numbers with a promise to keep in touch and arranged for some future discussions. We posed for some pictures, then I walked Hoff back to the rest of his Klan members. He thanked me, and asked that I keep in touch with him.

By this time things were winding down and everyone was leaving. Thinking over the strange events and experiences I had since starting my quest, I walked back to my car, got in and headed home. As I drove, I flipped on the radio and tuned in the news. Suddenly an announcement blared: "A warrant has been issued for the arrest of Maryland's Grand Dragon of the Ku Klux Klan. He is wanted on charges of 'Assault with Intent to Murder.'"

PART V

SELF-DESTRUCTION
OF A KLAN

24

Assault with Intent to Murder?

Although the radio broadcast identified him as a Grand Dragon, I realized even before his name was spoken that the man they were seeking was actually the Imperial Wizard, Chester Doles. Stopping at the next turn-off, I got a newspaper. Headlines reported the case. The article went on that on Monday afternoon, Chester and his Exalted Cyclops (head of local Klavern), Raymond Pierson were riding around in their cars. At an intersection, they spotted a vehicle containing two Black men and a White woman. The Klansmen got out of their pickup truck, pulled one of the Black men, whose name was Peters, out of his vehicle. Doles punched and kicked the man while Pierson hit the man on the head with a bat. The Klansmen fled the scene leaving the Black man for dead in the street. Fortunately, the man did not die. The pickup truck that was used by the Klansmen in the incident was later found by the police burned out.

When the Imperial Wizard found out he was being sought by the police for a simple assault, he phoned his attorney and stated over the phone that he had been fishing with some of his

Daryl Davis

White Supremacist friends in Delaware and knew nothing about the incident. However, Doles was told that he had been positively identified by at least six witnesses. He said he would turn himself in to clear his name.

Doles then found out that the charge was really "Assault with Intent to Murder" and changed his mind about turning himself in. He fled the state, but was picked up on a traffic violation in Delaware four days later. Raymond Pierson also fled, but turned himself in a week later.

A couple of days after the arrest of Chester Doles, I made up my mind to go to the jail and talk with him. I didn't know whether or not Doles would see me, but I decided to take the chance.

At the jail, the first person I saw was the girlfriend of the Klansman who had been involved in the Fourth of July hood-snatching incident. She recognized me, told me her name was Tina and said "I'm waiting to see my boyfriend." I told the guard who it was I wanted to see, and Chester was notified that I was there. He agreed to see me.

Doles was being held in maximum security. The entire visiting area had to be cleared of people before he could be brought to the visiting booths. Since there were quite a few other visitors there, I had to wait a while before seeing him. I took a seat next to the Klansman's girlfriend, who informed me while she waited for her boyfriend to be brought from his cell, "He's now an ex-Klansman." We continued to chat.

"He's due to get out in a few weeks" she said, "and he won't be rejoining the Klan. You know Chester has never even come by to visit him at the jail."

"That kind of disproves the theory of Klan brotherhood," I said softly. She did not reply.

When her name was called, Tina waved and went in to see her boyfriend. After her time was up, she came out and said goodbye to me. "All the best," I said. "I hope you and your boyfriend do well after his release."

Shortly after Tina left, Chester's mother, pregnant girlfriend and one of his daughters arrived. I didn't comment on their strange cooperative effort to see Chester. Instead, I introduced myself to his mother.

A thirty-minute time limit is imposed upon the visits and if there is more than one visitor for an inmate, the time is split among the visitors at their discretion as long as the visit is completed in the thirty-minute allotment.

Mrs. Doles went in first, followed by Chester's girlfriend. When she came out, I went in. Chester and I were separated by a metal divider in which there was a small glass window so that we could see each other but not touch. There was a phone on both sides of the divider through which we communicated.

The Imperial Wizard seemed happy to see me and wanted to know if there was anything I could do to get him out of jail. His bail was set at $750,000. His nineteen-year-old girlfriend was going to give birth in about a month and a half. "I wanted to see my child being born," he said. This would make his seventh; he has six children by his ex-wife.

Chester then pointed to a slight cut about two-inches long just under his chin. "A Black Muslim in the holding area of the Delaware jail tried to kill me by attempting to cut my throat with a razor hidden in the bristles of a toothbrush."

I did not want to take anymore time away from his family, so I told him that I would come back again, probably the following week.

"I'll request," he said, "you be given press status and be allowed access to me with no divider and allowed more than thirty minutes." He asked me to phone the administration office to see that it was approved. I told him I would.

On my way out, I stopped to talk with his girlfriend for a

moment. "I had to move out of Chester's home after the burglary in which mostly Klan paraphernalia and documents were taken. Chester said he knew who had done it because I was receiving death threats from certain Klansmen," she confided, "and I feared for my life."

25

Déjà Vu

This time I was slated to be with the prisoner face-to-face rather than talking by telephone while separated by a glass partition. As I was led through the automatic sliding steel doors of the jail, my mind spun backwards to my own arrest. A guard brought me to a secured area and left me alone saying he would return with Chester Doles.

As I heard the steel bars and doors clanging shut, I just hoped the guard would return, period! I couldn't help remembering the jarring images of being held in a similar jail and the guard who had told me that he would lose my papers for three days so I wouldn't get out. This time there was no need for my anxiety. The guard returned momentarily with Chester and Director Clewer. We were led into the chapel where we could sit and talk.

Director Clewer was going to leave a guard in the room with us, but I assured him that it would not be necessary. "I'd appreciate being alone with Chester since there might be some things of a confidential nature discussed."

Clewer complied with my wish and said, "I'll post the guard outside the door." He showed me a button on the wall to press. "In the event you need the guard to let you out before the two hours have expired."

I thanked him, and the door to the chapel closed and locked. Chester, the man I'd once labeled stereotypical of the worst element of the Klan, who'd once antagonistically met with me as he'd put it on a "professional" basis," and I were alone in a prison where he was incarcerated. He had nothing to lose.

Chester reiterated that he did not provoke the encounter with the Black man and had no idea that Raymond Pierson would hit the man with a bat. He claimed that his first knowledge of Pierson's past was when he read it in the paper a few days prior to my visit. He stated that Pierson, as long as he had known him, was always very polite, respectful and kind to children. He did remark, however, "Pierson is the type who would not fight you if a conflict arose. He would instead try to kill you."

Doles insisted, "I had never seen this guy Peters before in my life. They are actually trying to say that this was racially motivated. I didn't even know there was a White girl in the truck with the two Black guys until I read it in the paper the next day. I heard screaming, but I didn't know who was in their truck. It was around 3:30 in the afternoon and Raymond and I were on our way that day to the courthouse on some other business. I was trying to get some permits for a rally ground. I was in a three-piece suit and tie."

He paused, as if to make sure I was listening. I leaned forward to indicate I was and he went on.

"Anyhow, we were stopped at an intersection. Peters must have recognized me as a Klansman." *Something that is not hard to do,* I thought, *because Doles' picture is in the local paper every other day it seems, in conjunction with something he has done or is doing.*

"He was looking at me and flipped me the bird and was saying, 'Fuck you, I'm not scared of you.' I looked at Raymond like, 'What the hell is with this guy?' I cracked my door and Peters cracked his door. We climbed out and met. He got a couple of shots to my head, and I knocked his glasses off of him and that was it. I threw maybe two punches."

He took a deep breath and fidgeted a little. "Raymond came flying out of nowhere. I didn't see him coming. Raymond just bashed him. Raymond just snapped. I was in total shock. That was against everything I've been preaching for the past five years. We are trying to stay away from violence because the Klan has such a violent background. When Raymond hit Peters in the head with the bat, he fell to the ground and didn't move. Raymond said, 'Let's get out of here!' I was still in shock, but since I was riding with Raymond, I got back in the truck and left. I called some of the bros (fellow Knights or Klansmen) and they met us over in Delaware. They said that the cops were looking for me for simple assault. They told me to tell the police I was fishing with them over in Delaware at the time of the incident and they would support my alibi."

Doles was a lot of things, some of them pretty awful, but he wasn't a fool. I wondered if he was telling me this story purely for public relations or because he believed it.

"I was going to turn myself in to clear my name, but, when I called my lawyer, he told me that witnesses had positively identified me and gotten our tag number and that I was being charged with 'Assault with Intent to Murder.'

"I took off and went down near Rehoboth, Delaware, and was staying with this girl at her place back in the woods. I could have stayed there for a year before the cops ever found me."

I nodded and motioned to him to go on.

"Raymond and the other guys went to burn the truck to destroy any evidence. I don't know where Raymond went after that. How I got nailed was on a traffic violation.

"About ninety-eight percent of your hate crimes is Blacks against Whites—your muggings, robberies, rapes, burglaries and carjackings. Why aren't the Blacks charged with a hate crime? This hate crime law was only made up for the Blacks to go

Daryl Davis

against the Whites. Eighty-five percent of people in jail are Blacks. The people they committed the crimes against are Whites, or they are in there for dealing drugs. Why isn't this hate crime law put against them? Because the politicians are so pro-Black because of the pressure put on them by the NAACP and the Anti-Defamation League that they are fucking scared to stand up for their own kind. That's what makes me sick."

He looked at me curiously but remained silent.

"This isn't right. I get into a little scuffle and the authorities want to throw this Civil Rights violation and hate crimes law on me. Why didn't they look into what was going on with that White girl? Here she is with these two Black guys and she's only seventeen-years-old. She's a minor. These guys could get nailed for statutory rape or contributing to the delinquency of a minor.

"I just thought that this thing with Peters would be a little scuffle, the light would turn green and Peters would get back in his truck, and I would get back in Raymond's truck and we'd go on about our business. Raymond changed the whole tune of that and now he's changed the whole course of my life over this stupid thing." Color suffused his face and his eyes narrowed.

At the last trial I attended for the appeal of the Klansman, I had sat for a few minutes near one member of Chester's entourage who had dressed more neatly than the others. This older man wore a gray suit and white tie embroidered with the letters KKK in red. He had remained very quiet and even when we spoke, had a somewhat disturbing look in his eyes.

I had phoned Chester at home that evening and asked him who this mysterious man was. Chester would only say that he was formerly with UKA and was a very, very serious individual and apologized for not being able to say anymore than that. Chester now confirmed that the man I had asked about a month earlier was indeed Raymond Pierson.

Our time was up. The guard came in to take Chester back to his cell and escort me out. I told Chester that I would set up another appointment with him within a week or two and that I would like him to let me take some pictures of him. He agreed and even said he would pose for one with me. Previously, he had been adamantly opposed to posing with me in any way, shape or form. He said, "I'll talk with my old lady," as he referred to his girlfriend, "and have her get my extra Imperial Wizard robe and hood like the one that was stolen from me to wear for the picture." I was to call her and let her know when I was going to return to the jail to see him.

As Chester and I shook hands, the guard walked up and said, "Deputy Ordway would like to see you for a moment if you have the time."

I stopped by the Deputy's office, sat down and talked with him for a while. He knew that I was a musician and he was a big music fan. I had performed with some of his favorite entertainers, so I shared some remembrances about them with him. He was also fascinated with my odyssey among the Klan. He, in turn, had some dealings with the Klan a while back. Now he shared his remembrances with me of how he helped in the arrest of Bob White.

On my drive home, I thought about Chester's version of what happened. In my eyes, it was false. I highly doubted a Black man would get out of his vehicle by himself and initiate an attack on two men in another vehicle he happened to recognize as Klansmen, especially when his back-up—the seventeen-year-old White girl and the other Black man—remained in the truck. Yet by allowing Doles to express his version of the truth, I had learned a great deal about a man whose ideas and beliefs had a major impact on a segment of the Klan. I would have to see later whether our meeting advanced my cause.

26

More Conversations
in Jail

Again I was led through the clanking steel doors and down corridors filled with video monitors, this time to the chapel. Another guard brought Chester to me. Chester told me that his own officers, including Wayne Brannon—now promoted to Grand Dragon—had put a hit out on him and had been conspiring with the other Klan officers for some time to overthrow him and take over the organization. Chester said that when Brannon and the other officers, including his Imperial Klaliff Bob Tweed, found out about his arrest, "They broke into my home and stole all of my Klan paraphernalia." This included robes, Klorans (Klan handbooks) and various other things he had collected over the years. His girlfriend was not home when the burglary occurred.

"Perhaps," I suggested, "they wanted to get the records and anything that could link them with the Klan out of your home before the police got to it." Chester informed me that he had taken precautions for that already. He had phoned his girlfriend from the jail and told her to give all the records, membership lists and other such documents to the Imperial Klaliff (second in command on the national level as opposed to the Grand Klaliff who is second in command on the state level), which she had done.

I asked him to tell me more about this accusation of infamy within his organization. Anger showed in his eyes.

"They accused me of misappropriating Klan money and womanizing. They would see me with two or three girls at a time. I don't think it's any of their business. I like women, cold beer and cigars. I am going crazy for a cigar right now. If I have another week of solitary confinement, I'll go crazy.

"When I got into this trouble, I asked them to rally to my support. Instead, they ransacked my home and stole $50,000 worth of stuff. They stole my United Klans of America collection which belonged to my grandfather, my Invisible Empire collection, Klan paraphernalia from all over the country, about twenty robes, Klan Youth Corps certificates, my Klan sword and my Imperial Wizard's robe. They took advantage of the opportunity and went wild. They should have rallied to my support. They should have had tee shirts made up saying, 'Free the Wizard.' They should have been putting money in my account and taking care of my old lady. They should have been having public protests."

He flashed a look of disgust. "They are doing everything wrong. They want a Ku Klux Klan Motorcycle Club. Out of about 350 members, they will probably wind up with 75. They are destroying the Klan and they don't even see it. That's what they are doing by making splinter groups. They forgot where they came from. I made each and every one of these men. I swore them in and dubbed them with the sword under the fiery cross. I am the one that made them Knights and gave them their officer positions. As Imperial Wizard, I have now officially disbanded the Territorial Klans of America forever, never to rise again in the United States of America." His voice quivered emotionally.

"Bob Tweed, the Imperial Klaliff, is telling the press that

they are not accepting that. I don't know how he made it through the Marine Corps. He has no respect for the chain of command. I'm not a follower, I'm a leader."

His words hung in the air for several moments. Then he said, "I spent $7,000 or $8,000 out of my own pocket building this organization from two people to well over 300. My reward was seeing it grow. I saw six Klaverns spring out of this. I took maybe $20 out of the Klan fund for my kids to have milk and bread. Ten dollars of it went for gas so I could go to work. I always put that money back when I cashed in my paycheck. That's where they come off with 'misappropriating' Klan funds. They forgot about the thousands of dollars I spent out of my own pocket and didn't ask for it back. They didn't even have a tribunal for me. They even banished my old lady. She spent countless hours helping out the Klan. She kept the records straight and helped me write letters. I knew what I wanted to say, but I would get migraine headaches trying to word it just right because I can't spell. My old lady would go over it and correct it for me.

"They will see how hard it is to try and run it by themselves. They have no clue how to run an organization. You can't run it like a motorcycle gang. I know that some of these people are involved in selling drugs and fighting in bars. I've screamed and yelled a thousand times that they are giving us a bad image. I don't want to pick up the paper and see where one of my men has been busted for selling drugs. I've told them if they want to fight, then go down on Bou Street in the Black section of town and get their hands full instead of beating up on White people. We are getting a bad reputation."

I wondered if he understood the irony of his words and realized, of course, he didn't.

"They are going down a road of self-destruction. I am not saying that because I am mad at them. I am saying that from an intellectual standpoint because I've been there. I know what I'm talking about. My track record speaks for itself. I did things that

243

became historical events like the first march in Elkton and the first march through North Delaware.

"We were pulling in 200 people at a Klavern meeting. A Klavern is only supposed to be a dozen members. We were holding our meetings at the Cecil County Community Center. I had arranged to hold meetings there one Sunday a month for the rest of the year. During the summer, we held meetings in the park at the pavilion. (The same park pavilion I was led to, no doubt during our first encounter). I was making a legend out of myself."

When Chester mentioned some of his members being involved in drugs, I asked him about his own previous involvement with cocaine.

"That was a youthful error. I had my bouts with it. I look back and can't believe I ever let myself get like that. It almost killed me a few times. I did it every way you could, but I will never touch it again."

Chester Doles was facing a possible forty-five year sentence. I asked him about his plans for the future, whether he stayed in prison or got out.

"I really want to get out of here and take care of my old lady and my family. I want to be there in a month and a half when my seventh child is due. I helped deliver four of them.

"I am planning to run for County Commissioner on the Republican ticket even if I am still in here or any other prison. If Lyndon LaRouche, who is in federal prison, can get on the ballot for President, I can certainly run for County Commissioner in jail. There are a lot of people around here in the First District that would cast their votes for Chester Doles. I also have a lot of silent support. I envision one day starting a third political party called the White Unity Party.

"If I could get out of here, I could have a Klan group put

together in twenty-four hours. I still have some very loyal followers, and I owe it to them to keep it going. I may run an underground Klan and be its silent Wizard and advisor. If this doesn't happen, I would encourage my members who want to continue on with the Klan, rather than go with Wayne and Bob's renegade group, to join Virgil Griffin's Christian Knights of the Ku Klux Klan out of North Carolina. I've always had a lot of respect for Virgil Griffin.

"When I get out of here, what I really want to do is form a chapter of the NAAWP (National Association for the Advancement of White People) like David Duke did and go more the political route. I will also go to a Fellowship Baptist Church. I think it's time I get into a more settled, acceptable, recognized organization as David Duke did. He ain't done bad in his life."

I looked at him soberly, listening to this line and noted that as he spoke, his voice gathered more momentum, changing his remarks about getting out in the future from the vacillating "if" to the dictatorial "when" as if just voicing them to me made the questionable attainable. It was an interesting metamorphosis.

"There's a lot of money to be made in racial politics for profit. I will follow in the steps of David Duke. I've always been in correspondence with Duke and his organization."

Then his voice reached full power. "I will never denounce the Klan. I think the Klan was really a stepping stone for me to reach my full potential. You can only do so much and get so much attention lighting crosses in corn fields...not that I don't love a good crosslighting. My heart used to just flutter when I heard them singing Amazing Grace and the cross would glow up through the night, lighting the true way through the darkness, to Christ. I used to love it. I think I had to go through that to get the experience I got. I am going to get my hair cut and start wearing a shirt and tie."

I told Chester that I had heard from reliable sources that

David Duke is an atheist, which is completely contrary to the Christian belief the Klan claims it stands for.

"David Duke—money and power is his god."

"Remember," I said quietly, "our first talk before you were incarcerated, our discussion that the name, 'Ku Klux Klan' has a bad connotation and deservedly so. I am not trying to encourage your pursuit of racial politics, but trying to understand why you think you can achieve your goals with such a violent, hateful name. That is why Duke maintained his beliefs, but changed the name of his organization to the NAAWP even though it still shared the same post office box as the KKKK (Knights of the Ku Klux Klan)."

"You could not have told me that five years ago. I lived and breathed the Klan hard. I've been raised Klan all my life. I have shook the Eastern seaboard with White Power. I've given it hell. We've had thirty-nine crosslightings in two months. That's more than most Klans have in their entire existence. The three nights before this incident, we had a crosslighting each night. We were out Kluxing one hundred percent. I kept preaching that we got to do it all legal and non-violent.

"Now, I'm not turning the other cheek. If push comes to shove, I'm gonna push back. But, I'm a hard-head. I had to learn it and experience it for myself. I organized this whole organization.

"We didn't have enough investigators to check out people's backgrounds. This person would say, 'This is a friend of mine,' so we'd let him in. The next thing you know, we had 350 people. I couldn't babysit all of them. A bunch of them would go and get in trouble. I wish I had just kept it to twenty people. I could have got a lot more done. But, you know, you need the numbers and the power for the marches."

I had heard that Chester had to be rushed to the hospital a few days before our meeting. He had suffered a mild heart attack brought on by stress and anxiety. I asked him about it.

"I was so stressed out by all of this, I started getting chest pains and fell on the floor. The nurse here at jail is a big Black woman. I kept passing out. She had this oxygen mask that she was about to put on me. She said, 'Now, look what you've done to yourself. If you die, the last thing you're going to see is a big Black woman!' She had me laughing."

The moment of levity relaxed us; we both laughed. Then I asked him about J.W. Farrands, the Imperial Wizard of the Invisible Empire Knights of the Ku Klux Klan. He had just lost a civil court case which had now put him out of business. Both Roger Kelly and Chester Doles had been Grand Dragons under Farrands.

Farrands did not want his Maryland group associating with other White Power Organizations, which contributed to the reasons Chester had left the Invisible Empire KKKK and formed the TKA. Farrands did, however, recruit neo-Nazis and White Power Skinheads and allowed other chapters to hold joint functions with such groups.

"Farrands let the Grand Dragon of Florida, John Baumgardner and his Klan members march side by side with a Black Nationalist group in full African attire. They marched together against ZOG (Zionist Occupied Government). It was all over the Invisible Empire's newspaper, *The Klansman*. But he wouldn't let me march with other White Power groups. My members would never understand that, marching with a Black organization, but not a White one. It goes against the Bible. It says it right in Leviticus 19:19 and Genesis 9:27."

I am a deacon in my church and feel as familiar with scripture as he appeared to be. I wanted to find out where he thought scripture dictated such racist messages. I pulled my Bible out of my bag and handed it to him.

He turned to Leviticus 19:19 and read: "Ye shall keep my statutes. Thou shalt not let thy cattle gender with a diverse kind: thou shalt not sow thy field with mingled seed: neither shall a garment mingled of linen and woolen come upon thee."

Daryl Davis

Then he moved to Genesis: "God shall enlarge Japheth, and he shall dwell in the tents of Shem; and Canaan shall be his servant."

He paused and said, "We don't allow anyone but Klan to come to our Klan Klavern meetings, but we welcome neo-Nazis, Aryan Nations and any other White Power groups at our rallies. We are for just about anybody who is against ZOG. We shake hands with them and practice White Unity because we believe that in the next upcoming battle, (the Race War) your skin color will be your uniform."

His piercing eyes met mine as his voice took on a razor edge.

"This country is run by the Jews and ZOG. I don't really have anything good to say about Saddam Hussein, but every time he sent one of them Scuds over to Israel, I was cheering him on. I'm not saying that a race war is really going to happen, but if you look at the way this country is going, it's a good possibility. I thought the Los Angeles riots were the start of the Race War, especially if it spread across the country like the fags have from California.

"We had a rally in front of Delegate Ethel Murray's house last month. She's the Black NAACP woman who introduced some kind of anti-mask law. Stupid ZOG bitch."

He was becoming more agitated; I decided to change the subject for the time being. "What's your opinion of the beating of Black motorist Rodney King by four Los Angeles police officers?"

"Maybe Rodney King could have been subdued quicker, handcuffed and thrown in the car. But it seems like people are putting a limit on the cop's use of force. From what I hear, this Rodney King was a pimp and a drug dealer. Still, I don't think that gives them the right to beat the hell out of him that bad. But it still sends a message and cops are scared about what force they can use. It's got cops afraid to enforce stuff. Now, we do need to keep them in check because some of them do go overboard."

248

"Do you think the four White Los Angeles police officers went overboard?" I said, feeling my lips tighten.

"I don't know if they went all that overboard. Well, maybe a little, to some extent. But, I didn't want to see them found guilty. I was disappointed in the guilty verdict. I know that a couple of them had to be found guilty in order to pacify people. They didn't want their city burned down again."

Our conversation turned back to the incident that led to my coming to see him in jail in the first place and whether or not he knew Peters' side of the story. Peters has refused to make any public comments.

"Peters sent word to me that he wished the incident had never happened. He said that he does not want to testify, but he will be subpoenaed to testify. He's talking about not even being around when the court case comes up. Rumors are he is a major crack cocaine dealer.

"I know the apartments where he lives. There are mostly Whites living there. I know the exact apartment he lives in. His wife is pregnant and furious because he had a White girl in the truck with him. A White nurse who took care of me in the hospital lives right over the top of him. She says he's got people coming in and out of there at all hours. The word around the apartment is 'The Ku Klux Klan got a hold of his ass.'"

I questioned Chester about his Inner Circle and nightriding. There had been a series of incidents in which local Black taverns were shot up in drive-by shootings, Black people allegedly selling drugs on Bou Street were grabbed by White occupants of a car and dragged then let go into the street at forty miles per hour. The front of a synagogue in Pennsylvania was bombed and a sign was left with the message, "Gas a Jew for Jesus," and about a dozen crosses were burned on the lawns of Black families or Black-owned businesses. I also asked him about his arms stockpile in which I understood he had access to grenades, automatic weapons and the plastic explosive known as C4.

Chester did not deny that there might be members of his Klan who participated in these night missions and had access to these weapons and explosives in preparation for the Race War. He described, in an emotional voice, how an eight-foot cross could be made with a hinge so it could be folded and put in a car trunk. It would also have a railroad tie affixed to it. That way the cross-burner could quickly hop out of the car, unfold the cross, pound the railroad tie into the ground, set it on fire and leave the scene.

He casually mentioned that one of his favorite activities was going out in a field and shooting guns at life-sized, stand up cardboard displays of the Black men featured in the movie, "Boyz in the Hood."

I stared at him for a long moment. Perhaps it was a stroke of luck or the same Divine intervention which I believe had occurred so many years ago when a ten-year-old child had called me a Nigger, but at that moment, the steel doors clanged, signaling that my time was up; the guards were there to escort Chester back to solitary confinement and me to the outside. As I was about to leave, Chester called to me.

"The first day we met, you had us worried as shit! We were not expecting you to be Black. We Klansmen looked at each other like, 'What's going on?' Man, that was a trip! You've always been straight with me, so I've got to be honest with you. You have shown me that you are more of a friend when I'm in a jam than half the Klan. It's a shame, but it's true."

A part of what Chester was referring to, with respect to my support, was an incident that occurred a few weeks before this meeting. I had called his girlfriend and asked her to meet me. I didn't tell her why. When she showed up, I gave her some money. Chester obviously could not bring home his weekly paycheck from work while he was incarcerated. I knew that it was rough on her, at age nineteen, helping to care for his other children and about to bear another herself in a few weeks.

Whether or not Chester Doles ever changes his feelings towards members of another religion or race, one thing is for sure; he is a Klansman who will never forget and can never deny that a Black man helped keep food on his children's table. Another thing that's for sure: he will definitely have some time to think about it.

PART VI

KLAN-DESTINE RELATIONSHIPS

27

My Friend Tom Tarrants

When Thomas Tarrants is spoken of or written about, his name is usually preceded by the words, "former Klansman" or "ex-Klansman." People, in most cases, are given titles preceding their names because they have earned them through something they have done, be it positive or notorious. I, however, believe Tom has earned the omission of the title, Klansman.

Thomas Albert Tarrants III is a native of Mobile, Alabama. In the early Sixties as a youth, prior to becoming the person who authorities referred to at the time as, "the most dangerous man in Mississippi," Tom was a scofflaw always in trouble with the local police. Often when he was pulled over while driving and arrested by the police, a sawed-off shotgun or a submachine gun was found in his possession.

As a youngster, Tom was exposed to the Right-Wing initially through the John Birch Society. Soon he was aligning himself with Dr. Edward Fields and the National States Right Party.

A few years later, just before the end of that decade, Tom moved to Mississippi and joined the White Knights of

Daryl Davis

Mississippi, under Imperial Wizard Sam Bowers. This organization was known to be one of the most feared and violent Ku Klux Klan groups ever known.

Among the many murders believed to be committed by the White Knights, some of the most infamous are: the 1966 murder of Vernon Dahmer, a Black Civil Rights activist; the murder of three Civil Rights workers, James Chaney, Michael Schwerner and Andrew Goodman in 1964; and the 1963 murder of Medgar Evers. It is thought that these murders were authorized by Sam Bowers and committed by his Klansmen which allegedly included Mississippi law officers.

Tom Tarrants' specialty was bombs. Between 1967 and 1968 in Mississippi, numerous Black and Jewish homes, churches, synagogues and businesses were bombed or torched. The man chiefly responsible for most of these atrocities was Tom Tarrants, by then a staunch, anti-Black, anti-Semitic, White Supremacist terrorist.

Eventually, Tarrants was caught and imprisoned. Assisting in his capture by the FBI and the Meridian, Mississippi police were Alton Wayne Roberts and Raymond Roberts, two Klansmen brothers. Alton Wayne Roberts was a triggerman in the murder of the three Civil Rights workers.

The FBI paid the Roberts brothers over $30,000, largely collected by the Jewish community to "set up" Tom Tarrants and his partner in crime, another violent extremist by the name of Joe Daniel Hawkins, often referred to as Danny Joe Hawkins. The Roberts brothers, although they still held their racist beliefs, succumbed to the temptation of the money offer and set up their fellow Klansmen to be ambushed.

At the time, Tarrants needed little encouragement and was ready to bomb the home of a Jewish businessman. After the date had been stipulated, the Roberts brothers informed the FBI and collected their money. When the appointed date and time arrived, the FBI and police hidden away, waited for the mad bomber.

Tarrants and his bombing partner arrived as scheduled. He

drove up and down the street in front of the targeted home to check out the area. Just prior to his arrival, the authorities had been informed that Tarrants had a woman in the car and not Danny Joe Hawkins as expected. But the authorities determined it was too late to abort their mission.

Satisfied that he could plant the bomb and make his get-away, Tarrants parked the car and got out, carrying the bomb which consisted of twenty-nine sticks of dynamite and a timing device. As he walked up the driveway, a hail of bullets struck him. He dropped the bomb, dashed back to the car and started the engine.

A high speed chase ensued with the pursuing police hanging out the window of their police car, firing into the vehicle and striking the female occupant.

They shot out the tires in Tarrants' car, forcing him to stop. Exiting the car armed with a submachine gun, Tarrants returned the fire, shooting one officer critically in the chest.

Ironically, as Tarrants tried to escape on foot, he ran into an electric fence, put there to keep Blacks off the White owner's property. The electrical shock knocked Tarrants' already bullet-riddled body to the ground.

As he lay there, four police officers approached, firing their revolvers. Though gravely wounded, Tarrants survived, as did the officer he shot. Such was not the case for the female accompanying Tom. She died in the car during the chase. Later she was identified as Kathy Ainsworth.

Kathy Ainsworth was somewhat of a mystery. She led a double life. Young, very attractive, pleasant and very well-liked, she taught school by day and was a Klan terrorist by night. She was considered to be the most violent and dangerous Klanswoman in the history of the KKK. Her bombings and other acts of extreme violence were not known to authorities or her husband, but only to the top leadership and Inner Circle of the White Knights of the Ku Klux Klan of Mississippi.

Thomas Albert Tarrants III, entered Parchman Farm Prison

in December of 1968 to begin his thirty-year sentence for the attempted bombing of the Jewish businessman's home.

Tarrants immediately began planning his escape. Within six months he was ready. With the inside help of some of his fellow inmates and the outside help of some of his fellow White Knights, Tom successfully executed his escape plan. His success, however, was short-lived. Two days later, he was captured by the FBI and one of his escapee companions was shot and killed when he engaged in a shootout with the agents.

Back at Parchman Farm, while not planning another escape and not reading racist literature, Tom began reading the Bible and asking God for guidance to be shown the truth. Not long afterwards, he underwent a miraculous transformation. His hatred for Blacks and Jews vanished and he began, for the first time, to feel remorseful about the things he had done. He decided that God must have spared him for a purpose and that purpose was to help others and to spread the word of God.

Since many prisoners go through religious transformations, prison authorities are often suspect of the prisoner's motives as to whether or not the transformation is genuine. However, so convincing was Tom Tarrants in explaining his conversion that he was released from the penitentiary in December of 1976.

When I heard about him, I knew I wanted to meet him. Obtaining his phone number, I called him. "Would you consider giving me some of your insights into the Klan?" Tom was reluctant and politely declined, stating that he wished to put that part of his life behind him and did not keep up with current Klan activities.

I phoned Tom again and asked him if he had any speaking engagements coming up. He informed me that he would be preaching at a church on a particular Sunday and invited me to attend the service.

On the Sunday Tom invited me, I arrived early at the

church. Looking around the large congregation, I saw a wide mixture of people with different ethnic and racial backgrounds, including interracial couples. I couldn't help wondering if the congregation knew the background of the man who was going to preach that day.

As my eyes scanned the front pews, I spotted Thomas Tarrants III. He looked like the old pictures I had seen in the newspapers, only a little grayer and more mature. I studied him as he greeted people around him. Then I walked up to him and introduced myself. He took my hand warmly in his as we shook hands. I could tell that he was genuinely happy to meet me. I couldn't stay long enough to hear him speak, as I had to leave for an out-of-town gig. I phoned Tom the next day and asked when he would be returning to that particular church to speak. He gave me another date, and I made sure that my secretary kept that day free of any bookings.

I attended the church service again. Tom was indeed a very impressive and sincere speaker. At the end of the service, Tom shook my hand, placed his other hand on my shoulder and told me that he was very busy doing community work, but he would try to accommodate me as soon as he could find some free time. I was very happy to know that he believed in what I was doing, as I believed in what he was doing. We kept in contact by calling each other and finally were able to find a day that was suitable to both of us.

I traveled to the city where Tom indicated he would be. We met at the address he had given me and took a walk to a nearby restaurant where we had lunch. Tom was very generous with his time and knowledge and was eager to know more about me. He asked if the Klansmen I had already met with had been cooperative.

Though, as he'd told me earlier, Tom does not keep up with any Klan affairs, past or present, he remains concerned about possible retaliation from the Klan. There are two major reasons that his is a realistic fear. First, Tom denounced the beliefs and activities of his former colleagues. Second, and even more importantly, they would retaliate because he no longer believed in exterminating Blacks and Jews and instead believed in working for the benefit and the unity of all races.

I asked Tom if he had tried to share his new found philosophy and changed attitudes about the races with some of his former Klan friends. He told me that he had written to Sam Bowers, but he did not think the former Imperial Wizard would ever change. He explained to me how the Klan takes verses from the Bible out of context and distorts them to their own ideology. I had already seen this in meeting with Chester Doles. This twisted interpretation is repeated so many times to the members that they become brainwashed.

Tom said an example is the Klan's belief that the curse of the Biblical character Ham was that he was Black and all Blacks are his descendants. Therefore, all Blacks bear his curse.

My talks with Tom added a new dimension to my odyssey. For the Southern Klan group of which he had been a catalyst was reputed to be the most violent and murderous one of all. Studying and listening to him, it was hard to believe he was once called, "the most dangerous man in Mississippi," who some years ago would have as soon killed me as to look at me. The change in Tom Tarrants is perhaps the best argument that with God's help, all is possible.

Like Tom, I believe the healing power of God is so great, a person, organization or even a nation can be reborn.

28

The Silent Klanslady

All Klan factions have what are known as silent members and some of these are women. Shortly before Christmas, I told a Grand Dragon that I really wanted to speak to a Klanslady. A couple of weeks later he phoned me and told me the best spoken of all the women in his group, and a silent member, had agreed to meet with me if I would protect her identity. "She's expecting your call," he said. He also told me that she would agree to meet with me under the condition that I come to her house and we talked there because she did not want to be seen out in public with a Black man. He then said something I will never forget, "Daryl, don't be offended, but she hates Blacks more than I do."

I phoned Karen right around Christmas to wish her a Merry one and a Happy New Year, but also to let her know that I would be happy to wait for the holidays to pass before we met. She said that would be fine with her, to call her and let her know when. I gave her my phone number in case she needed to reach me for any reason.

No sooner had I hung up the phone with Karen, she called me right back. She asked me if the Grand Dragon had told me that she did astrological charts. I told her that he had not. She then told me that she would like to do my chart. I agreed and furnished the information she requested (my full name, birthdate, time of birth, etc.).

Daryl Davis

I phoned Karen just after the holidays in mid-January. She gave me directions to her house. I arrived at our scheduled time of 7:00 P.M. It was twilight. Her home, a rustic cabin set deep in the woods was bathed in a blue-orange glow. Karen, a petite blond, was at the door. She welcomed me inside and offered me a drink. I followed her from the living room to the kitchen where she poured me a soft drink, and herself a cup of coffee. The kitchen was small but tasteful, the fruit and vegetable wallpaper slightly faded from sunlight. The smell of brewing coffee filled the room, making it seem even more cozy. We sat across from each other at the pine table and after a few minutes of chit-chat, I got right to the point. "What was it that got you interested in the Ku Klux Klan?" I asked her.

She paused for a moment, her delicate features pensive and then answered, "I have always been interested. I was never able to join before because of being married to a man in certain positions. It would have been bad if his wife was a member. Now that I am free to do as I want, so I joined."

"How old are you?" I asked, hoping she wouldn't be taken back by my direct questions.

"Forty," she said without hesitating.

"How long have you been in the Klan?" I leaned forward in my seat, resting my elbows on the table.

She thought for a moment and responded, "About two years."

I looked straight into her eyes and asked, "What was the main reason you decided to join the KKK?" She returned my stare and unblinking, gave me her reasons.

"I don't like the way the world situation is going. I'm very patriotic. I feel that it is not so much the Black and White issue, it's what is good for the country. Your chart shows that you are a good person and that you are looking for fairness. But, I have found that most Blacks are only interested in what is good for them. They only vote for the person who can do the most for them. They don't vote for the person who does the best job for what they are hired for." She took a deep breath and continued to explain her position. It was almost a recitation. "I feel that more people have to stand up no matter what color and get this nation back on track. I don't believe in the violence, I just believe in what is best for the country. I don't really believe in all equal rights for women. I feel that if men can do that particular job better, then they should be the ones doing it. I just want the best for the nation."

Karen's comments on equal rights for women aroused my curiosity. "Different Klansmen I have spoken with appear to be male chauvinists, in that they don't believe a woman should be a police officer or a firefighter or run a bulldozer. Do you go along with that?"

She quickly responded, "No, I feel that if a woman qualifies, then, yes, she should get that job. If she doesn't qualify, then she shouldn't. Sometimes women are more emotional and if there is no room for emotions in that job, then they should not get it. They should leave that to a man who is more logical."

Although I wasn't totally satisfied with her answer, I didn't want to get too far off track, so I let that topic go for now and got back into racism and the Klan. "Do you believe in White Pride or White Supremacy?" I asked.

Her response was immediate and passionate, "White Pride."

I sipped my soda and then said, "Some Klans often talk about a race war. Do you think that will happen?"

"It wouldn't surprise me," she sighed. I felt like we were beginning to get somewhere now.

"Do you believe the Klan preaches hate?"

"Some members do and some don't. It's individual." she said matter-of-factly.

"Are you referring to members of the same organizations or members of different Klan factions?" I hedged.

Daryl Davis

Karen took a sip of her coffee before answering and setting the cup down with a clank. "Well, sometimes I see some members of our organization doing that and our leader tries to weed them out because we want law-abiding people, not 'Hey, I want attention' type people," she explained.

I shifted a little in my seat, realizing how hard it was before going on. "Is this the only Klan group in which you have belonged?"

"Yes," she replied.

I really wanted to understand the dynamics of her feelings about Blacks, so I asked, "How do you feel about Black and White United States soldiers fighting together in say, Vietnam or Iraq, having to be responsible for each other's safety, only to come home and be each other's enemy?"

She had her eyes fastened intently on my face. I wondered what she was thinking. Then she said, "Okay. I feel that Blacks and Whites can work together as long as they work equal. I'm not finding that. To me, you do not look like a typical Black, only because I did your chart. But from what I see, most Black people are violent and it's 'Give me, give me,' without working for it and 'I will be loud and I will get my way. I will get a house by destroying it first rather than building it with my own two hands,' like I did with this house. I built this house with my own two hands," she said, raising her hand up as if she was displaying her house on a game show. She was obviously proud of her work and her efforts to make it what it is today, and I could not blame her for that.

"It's beautiful," I told her.

She nodded and went on, "As far as working together, I see nothing wrong with that. I worked at a large company at one time. There was one Black girl. I was the supervisor. I knew what the paychecks were. That one Black girl who had one year of college got a higher paycheck than the girls who had three and four years of college," she said, hinting of something more.

I leaned forward and asked, "Are you saying that this was because she was Black and would have made a big stink?"

She seemed relieved to unburden herself of this troublesome knowledge. "Yes. I guess it's okay to tell you, it was the phone company. I had six years of service there. In this particular company, and I have heard it from other companies as well. If they want to fire a Black person, they have to come up with about three or four good reasons and they don't have to do that to fire a White person," she said angrily.

"Is this so that the company won't face a discrimination suit?" I asked.

"Yeah, and White people don't have an organization that backs them up like the Black people do. We are almost on our own. This is where I feel like the Klan is all we've got going," she said, coming full circle with her explanation of why she joined the Klan. However, her next statements revealed her problems with the Klan itself.

"It's not exactly the way I would like it to be. I would like to see it . . . well it is a legal organization, but I would like to see it upgraded to where we can protect the White people like the Black people are."

I couldn't let her forget the way Blacks were treated in the past, so I said, "Would you say that twenty or thirty years ago it was the Blacks who were getting treated the way you say the Whites are today? That unqualified Whites were getting the good jobs because they were White, and Blacks did not get those jobs because they were Black?" I paused then added with a mocking smile, "The only jobs the Blacks could get, say in the phone company for example, might have been cleaning the bathrooms."

"Well, actually, she had a better position than that," Karen said referring to the Black woman she supervised at the phone company. "As for how long ago Blacks were treated unfairly," Karen said, "I'd have to say farther back than twenty years.

Daryl Davis

Twenty years doesn't seem too far for me, possibly thirty-five years."

She paused, looked at me and then continued explaining her position. "I feel that in trying to right what was done in the past, we have brought the quality of this country down. We now have Black people who are hired because they are Black, who do not qualify for the job. We have Black people who are pushed through school with better grades than they deserve. The standards have been lowered for the Black people. I really don't think that I would want a lower graded Black person being my doctor because I feel that he would not be as good a doctor. With jobs that matter, that would worry me. That's detrimental to the United States," she said resolutely. She seemed sincere in her concern.

"So what do you think can be done to correct this problem as you perceive it?" I asked.

She had obviously already given a lot of thought to what needed to be done and quickly responded, "I'd say, make all applications exactly even. If the Black person is getting the grades to go on to the next grade in school, they have to accept it. I feel that when Black people get loud, let them get loud, don't give in. You know, the loud people are the one's who get their way no matter what race. I feel we have to stop doing that. It's the same with the White people who are loud, they get their way," she added disgusted. "I just read in today's paper that President Clinton hired a lesbian almost simply for the fact that she was a lesbian. He said that he was going to hire a minority, so he hired a minority, and I can't tell you how many better qualified people were turned away. That to me is racist," she said, displeasure written all over her face. She sipped her coffee and there was a moment of silence.

Then I asked, "Would you be opposed to integrated schools if you thought that the Black people going to the White schools were willing to meet all the qualifications and standards of education that the White students have to meet?"

"No," she replied. She got up to pour herself some more coffee.

"How about interracial dating?" I asked.

"No, I do not approve," her voice rose. Even with her back to me, pouring coffee, I could tell the depth of her feelings.

"Why?" I asked, wanting to understand her position on the subject. She turned back from the coffee maker and sat back down at the table before answering. Her words showed more introspection than most Klan members to whom I'd talked.

"That I would have to say is because of the way I was raised. I was raised prejudiced. My feeling about being prejudiced now, well the dating thing has stayed with me, but I have gone from the emotional end to the logical end," she paused and looked at me apologetically. "I don't include you in this and I know there are a lot like you, I'm sure. I find that most Black people are of lower intelligence and I feel that most Japanese people are of higher intelligence. I look up to them. I don't know about Russians or others. I see what people have done with their life. I look at the African nations who are mostly Black people and they don't have nice homes. They are in a nation where they do not have any White influence and they don't have the intelligence to do it on their own," she said with disdain. She gazed out the window into the night and looked thoughtful before going on. "I look at the Japanese and they have exceeded us in many ways. I look at areas where you have predominantly one race or another as to how I am prejudiced for or against depending on what they have done for themselves. I am also part Native American-Indian," she added in a way that sounded to me like she wanted to prove something.

I had been hoping to find common ground which would better establish our relationship on a less strained basis. *Momentous issues*, I thought, *can hinge upon the smallest quirk of fate.* "I am, too. I have Cherokee in me," I smiled.

She looked a little surprised, then smiled back. "I am

Iroquois," she said. "The Indians would not have progressed quite as far as the White man because they weren't quite as overbearing. White men are obnoxious and very strong-willed. I think with the White man, when their blood mixes in with any of the races, it brings out in them to go forward and learn and continually progress."

Considering her comments on other races, I was curious about her feelings on Native Americans. "How do you feel about the Native American-Indians?"

"I wish the White men weren't here because there was nothing wrong with the way the Indians lived," she said passionately. I couldn't let her get away with what seemed like an obvious contradiction to me.

"Well, there seems to be a contradiction in what you are saying. Many Indians lived in these tepees and mud and straw huts much like the way many Africans lived in their countries, and both races lived off the land by hunting and growing crops. Remember, it was the Indians who taught the first White settlers how to live off the land and rotate crops. Then, when the Whites no longer needed the Indians, they tried to kill them off. The ones who survived were put on reservations." I wondered how she would respond.

She quickly retorted, "The Indians did not abuse the land and have more children than they should have. I don't feel for the people in Somalia at all," she shook her head angrily. "I feel that if they were in that situation, then they should not have gotten pregnant. I don't feel sorry for any of the poor people who are poor and they have child after child. I come from a very poor family, and I'm the only child," she said, defending her statements.

"I am an only child too," I told her quietly.

"Oh, yeah?" She was still angry. "I only have one child. We have four generations of one child each. I feel that people should not continually reproduce, especially when there is no need for these children. They are of no use to anyone. I don't believe in continually having all these children. I don't believe in killing them off because they're no good, but I feel that they should not have gotten pregnant to begin with." Karen calmed down and spoke in a softer voice. "I just believe in whatever is best for the nation. I believe in going forward, and I feel that we are spending so much time and money on trying to right a wrong that was done a long time ago and making everybody happy. There are still so many things that have to be done and that's holding us back. There's space to explore, there are computers to better and there are just so many things to do yet and we are just wasting our time with each other," she lamented, her eyes were partially closed.

I sighed heavily, "A lot of Klanspeople and other Right-Wing types believe that Blacks should go back to Africa and Jews back to Israel and other minorities back to wherever they came from so that this country would be an all-White nation." My own strong feelings colored the force of my remarks.

"Some of these Whites think that this country should be divided up and that Blacks should be given certain states, Whites get certain states and so on. I think even if that could be achieved, the Whites would turn on their own eventually. The blondes with the blue eyes would probably discriminate against the redheads with freckles even though one group is no more White than the other. Anyway, this removal of minorities or total separation or segregation is not going to happen. So, what is your advice on how we all can get along because you are not leaving and neither am I?" I asked, my words almost running together, I was talking so fast.

She looked at me thoughtfully for a moment before answering with carefully chosen words. "My advice would be to forget about the skin color and hire only one who is qualified and not who is loud. Do not hire them because they are Black. I feel that if you take that completely away that will keep a lot of the

Black people from getting the jobs that they have now. They will have to work harder because I don't think they are really trying."

Although I thought I knew her answer already, I asked, "Do you think that they are using their color as an excuse to get ahead?"

Karen shook her head vehemently. "Yes, yes. Right now, we are in a world where minority rules. I don't know what happened to the majority rules but that seems to have gone out the window. It's unfortunate because it was the majority that used to rule who made this nation. This nation is going to slide right into the sea if we don't do something." Her voice had a bitter quality.

I continued, "The majority that used to rule were also the ones who made the mistakes by discriminating in the first place against the Blacks or against the women or whomever. I think Blacks have made some progress and women have made some progress, but in some instances Blacks and women are in the same boat in that they are discriminated against by the same people, the White males who make and enforce the laws in this country." I hoped my mention of women would encourage Karen to get back to that topic.

"I like it better that way," she told me.

"You do?" I asked, surprised.

"Yeah. I feel that too many women are overstepping their bounds. Again, I think that they are abusing the fact that they are women. I know that Clinton hired people because they are women. He said so."

Karen was obviously no women's libber. I wanted to find out more about her views on women's roles and men's roles.

"Now, when you go out on a date, do you like for the guy to open the door for you and bring you flowers and that sort of thing, very traditional?" I questioned.

Not surprisingly, Karen responded, "Yes. However, I do know what kind of strong-willed person I am and if I feel that he is not as good a person as I am, then I don't act the demure woman," she said, smiling conspiratorially.

"You just take charge," I said, laughing.

"Yeah, although I don't want that," her smile faded.

"Did you say you have a daughter?" I asked, serious again.

She leaned back in her chair and replied, "Yes."

"What would you do if you were to find out that your daughter was a lesbian?"

She leaned forward in her chair and thought for a long time. "Whew! I probably would not associate with her as much as I do," she finally said.

"Would you disown her?"

Karen had picked up her coffee cup, but she put it down without taking a sip. "No, she is still my daughter," she answered firmly.

I continued this line of questioning. "Would you try to change her?" I asked.

She shook her head, "No, you wouldn't be able to do that. But I would not welcome her lover into my home. My daughter could visit me on her own."

"What about if you found out she was dating a Black man?"

"Same thing," Karen answered resolutely.

I got back on the subject of homosexuality. "Do you believe that homosexuals can be born that way?"

Karen nodded over her coffee cup. "Yes and I think it should be kept hidden. It shows when they have homosexual tendencies. What they do about it is up to them. They can ignore it and just continue to live a straight life, or they can just follow their desire," she said, adding "And, I think if they follow their desire, they ought to do it in the closet."

I was a little surprised by her answer and let her know why. "Most Klanspeople I have talked with do not believe that people can be born homosexual. They think that it is some illness or something that has caused these people to flip."

"That's because I do astrology. Whenever Venus and Mars are conjunct when they're born, there is a potential of them becoming a homosexual. Even if they don't ever, it runs through their minds," she explained.

With all this talk of astrology, I wondered what religion she was.

"What is your religion?" I ventured.

"Methodist," she said, looking at the kitchen clock.

Thinking she didn't seem very interested in talk of religion and wanting to wrap things up, I stood up to get ready to leave. But Karen offered me another drink and seemed to want to talk more, so I sat down again and said, "What you think the future of the Klan is and what do you hope to get out of it?"

She thought for a moment and seeming as if she still needed to explain herself to me she said, "I like being part of what I would consider the new Klan. The Klan is not what I thought it would be. I was as surprised as you were. I joined because I am free to, now. There is no one holding me back. When I got in it, I was pleased that my Grand Dragon is who he is, and the rules that we are expected to follow pleased me. I am proud to join, but I don't tell everybody because some people are prejudiced against the Klan, especially my job. I need my job to keep my house. I certainly don't want to lose it. I work with a newspaper. I feel it is wrong that the newspaper ignores a lot of things. I have probably never seen as many news stories incorrectly printed as I have since I have been a Klan member. I feel that has to be taken care of. I think whether they like it or not, the truth has to be printed. I feel that the papers have gotten away from that." She had been looking out the window, but now she looked right at me and went on, "I would like to see everybody qualify for what they do. I am against Black people until I know that they qualify for my friendship. Guilty until proven innocent. The other way around."

"Do you have any Black friends at all?" I asked cautiously.

"I really don't see anyone anymore, but when I worked in the office, yeah," she responded.

After all the statements she made, I didn't know whether to be surprised or not. "They had proven their friendship?" I wanted to know.

"Yeah, they weren't the wild type. They earned my respect. My daughter was friends with a colored guy who got killed about six months ago," she said quietly. "He worked at a publishing house," she added.

"Books?" I asked.

"Yeah. He was killed in an accident. His two nephews who were in the car with him were killed also. It was headlined in the paper everyday because this man was so well-liked. My daughter cried and went to the grave, and she put flowers on the altar in memory of him. She explained to me why she did this and what kind of person he was, so I have no anger at her for this. I feel she had a reason. She told me that whenever she was feeling down in the dumps, he would always have something nice to say to her." She nodded a little to show she did not disapprove of her daughter's actions.

I wondered what her daughter was like? If she had Klan ideas implanted in her psyche or if she had moved beyond that.

Karen went on, "It was almost like he was a shoulder for her to cry on when she was having problems with her boyfriend or something," referring again to the Black man who had been killed. "I see nothing wrong with that," she said defensively.

I could see it was a subject she did not want me to explore further and I switched gears, wanting to know if her feelings and beliefs were the same for Black and Whites.

"Now, what about White people?"

"Same thing," she quickly replied.

273

Daryl Davis

I wanted to be sure we were on the same wavelength. "Do they also have to qualify and earn your respect?"

"Right. I admire intelligence and I admire a worker. I admire somebody who's not going to be sitting on the front porch that's falling down. This is because I, myself, come from a very poor family. I was the only one in school with mayonnaise sandwiches because I had nothing to put on them. I had an outhouse until I was fourteen. My mother worked in a factory, and before she retired, she became the secretary to the vice president of that large company. I haven't done bad, and I got all of this, not by being loud and saying, 'Gimme, gimme.' I don't take help from people. I did it all myself," she said, proudly adding, "My parents couldn't even help me, and I never expected them to. I feel like, 'Hey, I've come from the same side of the tracks that these people are still sitting on and I did it.' Because of that, I have no sympathy," she pounded her fists on the table for emphasis. She seemed like she had more to say so I waited for her to continue.

"I used to live in the Bahamas. I was married at the time and we had our baby down there. I was told not to have the baby down there, but to have it at home in the United States. But I wanted to be with my husband with our first child. The problem was because of the racism in the Bahamas. In the hospital, I was tortured. So much so that I had to have operations when I came home to the United States, and I could never have any more children," she said angrily.

Clutching her coffee cup, she went on. "A few years ago, I was biking on the Baltimore Beltway on a motorcycle and a Black man in a truck stuck his head out and spit on me. I had a full-face helmet, but it did get all over my neck. Now those are two things that have happened to me. Of course, the childbirth thing was the worst. I have never, ever done anything physical to any Black person nor have I ever wanted to, but I have been the recipient of racial problems," she confided, her voice filled with displeasure for memories she could not change.

I tried to reason with her, "The butcher in the hospital and the guy that spit on you should not be indicative of the entire race though. A similar thing happened to my mother. My mother was given an unnecessary hysterectomy back in the Fifties in Chicago. That's why I am an only child. There was a scandal in which a lot of White doctors were routinely performing hysterectomies on Black women whether they needed them or not as a form of Black population control. I think you can find wrongdoers in every race," I concluded, hopefully making my point clear.

Karen nodded her head sympathetically.

"Yeah. About six years ago I started going steady with a Cuban man who still lives about a couple of miles from here. He told me about how when he came to this country, the Klan came to the camp he was staying at and just shot everybody. He happened to be asleep in his bunk, so of course, he didn't get shot."

"Was this around here?" I asked, shocked by the shooting and that Karen would date a non-White.

She seemed not to notice my surprise and responded, "No, it was Arkansas or Kansas. He wasn't really sure what the state was. In checking into it, I found that apparently the reason was because of the Cubans who were coming into Florida. Fidel Castro had released all the prisoners and the bad guys. They came into Florida and just created havoc. When the second batch came in, the law couldn't do a whole lot, so the Klan stepped in. This is probably why the Klan has stepped in a lot of cases and took the law into their own hands," she explained.

I looked at her intently, wondering if she really believed her rationalization. Her eyes met mine. Her coffee cup was empty again, but this time she did not fill it. I leaned back, waiting for the rest of her explanation.

"Times are more strict now. I prefer it this way anyhow. I prefer law-abiding citizens. I don't think it's fair that the Klan has to obey the law and Black people in California don't," she said, referring to the riots which followed the criminal court acquittal of the four White police officers in the beating of Black motorist Rodney King.

She went on, cold and deliberate now. "I am talking about the ones who burned down their homes and things like that. I don't think they should be given anything. If anything else, I think they should be made to work with their own hands to rebuild their own houses."

"How do you feel about that first trial?" I asked, expecting some interesting insights.

"I didn't see it. I don't watch television," she shrugged.

A little disappointed but not daunted, I asked, "You heard about it, right?"

"Yeah," she said, without elaborating more.

I continued probing. "Did you see the videotape of the beating?"

Karen got up and carried her cup to the sink. She turned back around and answered, "No, I didn't. My first husband was a policeman. Although we were married a short time, he came home with a lot of tales, which only added to my feelings. They had their hands tied. As soon as they would get in a policeman who wanted to do his job and wanted law and order and say, 'Hey, you obey the law,' they hollered police brutality if he even touched them. The next thing you know, this policeman who was doing his job more than the other police, was out of a job," she said as she returned to her seat, her face flushed with anger.

There was an uneasy silence.

I glanced through the kitchen doorway towards the living room and suddenly noticed a small, portable keyboard. I asked her if she played. She told me she'd sung and recorded some Country and Western music years before. She said that nowadays she fooled around with the keyboard a little bit, but she preferred her piano. I did not see the piano and couldn't recall seeing it earlier, but I told her I would play it for her if she would sing. She hesitated a moment, then led me to the piano. It was located in her bedroom. When she saw me looking around, she laughed a little nervously.

I immediately took a seat at the piano and asked her what she wanted to sing. She replied, "I don't guess you know any Country."

I asked her to name some songs. To her surprise, every song she named, I knew and played for her. I let her know that I had played Country music for a number of years. I accompanied her on "Walking After Midnight" and "Crazy," both made popular by Patsy Cline and "You Win Again" and "Your Cheating Heart," both made popular by Hank Williams. She apologized for her singing, saying she had not sung in a long time, but she sounded great to me. During that time at the piano, we were not a Black man and a White woman divided by our skin colors. We were just musicians, having a good time. But, although her feelings of dislike for Blacks had momentarily evaporated, I knew that no matter how friendly she was or how hospitable, those feelings were deeply entrenched and alive. Nevertheless, it was a beginning.

29

The Exalted Cyclops

Raymond Pierson, the forty-four-year-old Klansman who had hit Peters with the bat, was also charged with "Assault with Intent to Murder." He was an Exalted Cyclops in Chester Doles' Territorial Klans of America. The state is divided into Klaverns. The Exalted Cyclops heads a local district or Klavern.

Pierson, who bears a strong resemblance to James Earl Ray, has a long history of Klan membership. He was formerly a member of the United Klans of America led by Bobby Shelton, and has a long history of violence, including murder, assault and battery and threatening people with guns. He has beaten most of these charges by pleading guilty by reason of insanity. He was diagnosed as paranoid schizophrenic with delusions of persecution. For the murder he committed by beating a man to death with a blunt object and dumping the man's body behind a high school, Pierson spent twenty-one months in a mental hospital.

After doctors determined he had made an excellent recovery and was no longer a threat, he was released. Not long after that, he was in trouble again for beating one person and threatening to kill another.

Raymond Pierson was now incarcerated at an undisclosed

location. I was able to track him down and a few weeks after his arrest, I drove out to the facility where he was being held.

A couple of minutes after I entered the lobby of the jail and told the guard who I was there to see, two women entered and announced that they were there to see Raymond Pierson. The guard told them that I was also there to see him. They both reeled back and became ugly and rude. Then they demanded to know who I was and what I wanted with him. When I asked them what it was to them, they informed me that they were his sister and his wife.

Because of their ill-mannered ways of addressing me, I refused to answer their questions. They told me that Raymond would not see me and told the guard not to permit me to go to the visitor's booth.

As a matter of procedure, the guard went to let the Klansman know the names of his visitors. When the guard returned, he told me that Pierson would not see me. The two women laughed and proceeded to go to the visiting booths with "I told you so" looks on their faces.

Several months later, my secretary Mary and I attended a court hearing in Maryland. The attorneys for Chester Doles and Raymond Pierson were attempting to persuade the judge to suppress the hate crime element in the charges against their clients. Both men were led into the courtroom in handcuffs and leg chains. Chester and I spoke briefly before the hearing began. Raymond just looked at me, but did not speak, nor did I make any attempt to speak to him.

Some members of Chester's family were present and were polite to me. Raymond's wife and his two sisters were also present. Their faces registered disgust upon seeing me.

At the end of the hearing, after the judge struck down the motion to suppress the hate crime charge, one of Raymond's sister walked by me and called out "Nigger!" Raymond's other sister then began calling Mary a "Nigger lover."

Mary and I walked outside to wait for the elevator. The two women saw us, changed their minds about riding the elevator and took the stairs.

30

Attacked

The Territorial Klans of America had become adversely divided with some members remaining loyal to the Imperial Wizard Chester Doles and others deciding to go with Chester's Imperial Klaliff Bob Tweed, who was now proclaiming that he was the Imperial Wizard and Doles was banished.

Then, another division occurred. In order to get a reduced sentence, Chester agreed to a plea bargain in which he would testify against his Exalted Cyclops, Raymond Pierson. As a result of this pending testimony, the prosecutor would not seek the maximum penalty against Chester.

When this revelation hit the news, many Territorial Knights from both sides of the now divided TKA turned against Chester. It is forbidden by Klan oath to reveal the secrets and deeds of a fellow Klansman. Personally, I did not think that this event was very secret, considering the fact that it occurred at a busy intersection in the middle of the day with many witnesses. Nonetheless, Chester was now labeled a ratfink and a stool pigeon. He and his girlfriend, who had just had his baby, began receiving death threats from his former KKK allies.

It turned out that Pierson, who was going to plead, "Not guilty," ended up pleading "Guilty." Therefore, Chester did not have to testify against his former friend. However, the damage was already done in the minds of those who condemned Chester for even considering testifying against a fellow Knight.

On the day of his sentencing, Chester's grandfather, an old UKA member, grandmother, girlfriend, ten-year-old daughter and some of his loyal Klanmembers came to the courthouse for moral support. Chester was sentenced to seven years to begin immediately. There were hugs, kisses and tears. Afterward, Chester was then led out of the courtroom in handcuffs and leg shackles. He shuffled over to me in the hallway, shook my hand, thanked me for coming and hoped that I would write about how he had been given a bad deal by the system.

Outside the courthouse, Chester's family and Klanmembers gathered together to watch Chester leave in the prisoner transport van. As the van began to pull off, several of the Klanmembers gave the White Power salute to Chester. His ten-year-old daughter had started crying as she stood there and watched them take her daddy away. I walked into the middle of the gathering and hugged her. Then I hugged Chester's girlfriend, who was also sobbing. His grandmother turned to me and hugged me. His grandfather extended his hand and said, "I won't hug you, but I would like to shake your hand." I obliged and also shook the hands of the other Klanmembers who were now finished saluting.

A few weeks later, the day of Raymond Pierson's sentencing arrived and once again, I attended. This time I brought Bob White with me because he had expressed interest in watching the proceeding as it was not so long ago that he also was sentenced for "Assault with Intent to Murder."

We arrived at the courthouse early and the doors to the courtroom were locked. Some law officers were setting up to search people coming into the room. We stepped outside to wait so Bob could smoke a cigarette. Also outside, were TKA Imperial Wizard Bob Tweed and Larry Sines, the Grand Kludd (Chaplain).

Tweed and Sines are brothers-in-law and are usually seen together. We spoke very briefly. Their conversation with me was geared mostly toward the idea that America is a White man's country and how I should know that their former leader Chester Doles was a race traitor.

They did not speak to Bob White appearing not to recognize him, although they knew very well by reputation who he was, as did any Klanmember in the Middle Atlantic States.

As the time approached for us to go back in the building, Bob Tweed said, "I know you are trying to get KKK information, but the family is under a lot of pressure right now. I would appreciate it if you would not ask them any questions."

I told him I would oblige his request, as I did not think they would speak with me anyway. He was well aware of the previous run-in I had with the family when I tried to visit Raymond at the jail.

We all entered the courtroom and took our seats. Pierson's attorney vigorously argued with the state's attorney and the judge to not impose a stiff sentence on his client. Despite this, Raymond Pierson was sentenced to fifteen years in prison.

When the sentencing was over, the Pierson family and other Klanmembers gathered in the hallway to answer questions posed by reporters. I stood away from the gathering, but not out of earshot and heard a good deal of loud, derogatory remarks about the judge. Once the konklave (Klan gathering) had moved down the hall, I chatted with Steve Chzarnowski, a reporter friend of mine who covers the Klan for the *News Journal.*

Bob White and I headed downstairs to leave. We walked down the hall towards the back door leading to the parking lot where my car was parked. Standing in front of the double glass doors were Bob Tweed, Larry Sines, Ray Pierson's two sisters and his wife.

Rather than try to walk through the middle, I chose to walk around them in order to exit the doors. As I passed behind one of

Daryl Davis

Pierson's sisters, she kicked me on my shin. She then attempted to kick me again, but I blocked her leg with the palm of my hand as her foot came up off the ground.

"This is not necessary," I said, and continued walking.

She shouted, "You're nothing but a fucking Nigger!"

Her younger sister yelled, "He looks more like a coon or an ape to me!"

At this point my temper flared. I stared at the younger sister and said, "And what do you look like?"

Bob Tweed said, "Hey, watch your mouth," to me and almost simultaneously, Larry Sines came at me with one hand outstretched to grab me and the other cocked back in a fist to strike me. I immediately prepared to deflect any blows and to be able to execute a quick attack on my assailant. Hearing the commotion, sheriff's deputies and police came running and Larry Sines was restrained from reaching me.

Upon seeing the police, the younger sister grabbed her face and began feigning a cry while saying, "He slapped me! That Nigger slapped me!"

The law officers asked each party to separate themselves to opposite sides of the hallway. Everyone did as told, and then we all were questioned as to what had happened. Naturally, the stories didn't match.

I asked one law officer to send Larry to where I was so that I could talk with him. Reluctantly, the officer complied. When Larry appeared I asked him why he had launched an attack on me. He told me that it was his duty as a Klansman to protect White womanhood and that I had violated this Klan doctrine by slapping a White woman.

"You know damn well I didn't slap anybody!" I protested.

In the meantime, Bob White, who had witnessed the whole thing, walked over to Bob Tweed to talk to him in an effort to diffuse the volatile situation. As Bob White approached Bob Tweed, the two sisters began calling him "Nigger lover." At this point,

286

Bob White turned to them and announced in a booming voice, "I am the Grand Giant!" The two women visibly trembled but said nothing.

At that moment I asked Tweed if we could confer. "Look Bob," I explained to him, "You know what I'm all about. This isn't necessary."

He said that he would talk with everyone involved and that if I would not press charges against them, they probably would not press charges against me. But I was far too offended to accept this appeasement.

"If the other side does not admit to starting the fracas and retract the statement about me slapping Pierson's sister, I'm going to press charges," I said in a flash of anger.

The two sisters weren't about to back down. Part of their feelings stemmed, I believe, from vindication for the stiff sentence imposed on their brother less than ten minutes prior to this incident and the rest from the fact that they could not accept a Black person being right and a White person being wrong, no matter what the circumstances.

The first I could understand but the latter I could not accept. I pressed charges against the older sister for "Assault and Battery" and against Larry for "Assault." More than thirty days after the alleged attack, the younger of the two sisters filed charges against me for trying to slap her in the face.

Bob White volunteered to come to court and testify as a witness on my behalf. It was an interesting idea—one Klansman testifying against another Klansman and Klanswomen on behalf of a Black man. I accepted his offer.

31

My Day in Court

On March 11, 1994, the case was tried before the Honorable Judge Harry Goodrick in the District Court of Maryland. I arrived with Bob White as my witness. Another Klansman, who shall remain unnamed, from another Klan group met me there; he had come for my protection. There was a strong rumor that Klanmembers loyal to Bob Tweed and Raymond Pierson had put out a hit on me.

Our konklave was indeed a strange sight to anyone who knew what was going on. One Klansman testifying on behalf of a Black man against other Klanmembers and another Klansman acting as bodyguard for the same Black man in the event some Klansmen might try to attack me again. My witness and my protector were from different Klan groups, as were my attackers. All together there were Klanmembers from three different Klan groups present. There was also another Klansman present who was there to face a charge of driving on a suspended license.

Larry Sines arrived at the courthouse just before Pierson's sisters. I nodded to him and he said hello to me. The two sisters soon arrived. Our case was called and the trial began. Noticeably absent were Bob Tweed and Ray's wife.

Daryl Davis

The judge read the elder of the two sisters the charges against her and informed her of the maximum incarceration time and monetary fine if she was found guilty. She pleaded not guilty to the charge of "Assault and Battery." I was called to the stand and was questioned by the state's attorney and the defendant's lawyer. The entire time I was on the stand, my opponent attempted to stare me down, but to no avail.

Bob White took the stand and testified to what he had seen. When the defendant took the stand, she denied kicking me. Her younger sister backed her up when it was her turn. They both denied having seen me before this incident and said that they did not know me from Adam. They claimed that I demanded to question them about their brother following his sentencing and when they declined to be questioned by me, I made obscene racial remarks to them.

His Honor asked the younger sister what I had said, and she replied that the language was too filthy for her to repeat. His Honor told her he would have to know what was said if I was to be accused of making racial and obscene remarks. She relented and said that I had called her and her sister, "fucking whores and White trash."

At the conclusion of the trial, His Honor found the defendant guilty as charged and asked me what I wanted to see done. I told His Honor that I was not injured by her kicks and I did not want her to be incarcerated or fined, but that I would be perfectly satisfied if he were to issue her a verbal reprimand.

His Honor kindly gave Pierson's sister probation before judgement, meaning she was let off the hook as long as she did not get into trouble during her probationary period. Stating that she was not guilty, she refused the probation! His Honor then fined her a total of $200.00. She claimed she would appeal her conviction.

I thanked the judge and left the courtroom satisfied that I

had made my point. I also won another case that day. The prose-cutor informed me that they would not try the case of the State of Maryland vs. Daryl Davis. This was the charge that the younger sister had filed against me, claiming I had slapped her. Larry Sines was never called upon to testify and later apologized. I dropped my case against him.

On the way back to Bob White's house, he told me that he was going to sign up to take some courses in order to do lapidary work. I felt I knew him well enough to mention the thought that went through my mind. I said, "What's the matter? You can't get away from the routine of chopping rocks? Nevertheless, I guess it's better to be chopping rocks on the outside of the joint than on the inside."

We both laughed.

32

My First Rally

Traditionally, Blacks are not permitted entrance to Klan rallies unless they are held on public property. There have been many instances when even then, Blacks were denied entrance.

However, Roger Kelly and I had grown much closer, and I knew he had one coming up at a public park near my home. This rally was not publicized in the media, but through the handing out of flyers and literature to White motorists and passersby at various street intersections. This is what is referred to as a "Klan roadblock." Roger gave me the date, time and location of the rally and told me the intersection where an hour long roadblock preceding it would be held.

That morning, my secretary Mary and her daughter Margaret accompanied me to the site. Several police cars and officers milled about in a nearby bank parking lot. We pulled our car into the lot and parked a few yards away from the police. They stiffened, but said nothing. While we were standing around waiting for the Klan to show up, a motorist drove by yelling, "Klan-Man," out the window of his vehicle. I assumed it was in reference to a recent newspaper article and picture of Roger and me. I was silent.

Daryl Davis

Shortly thereafter, a pickup truck and car slowed down. The truck driver tooted the horn and waved at me. I returned the wave, recognizing them as Klanmembers. Apparently, so did the police who stopped what they were doing and, as a unit, moved closer to observe. The Klan group pulled their vehicle over on the shoulder of the road catty-cornered to the bank lot.

I watched as the men got out and began donning their robes and hoods. Some wore masks as well. They split up, walked over to four corners of the intersection and stood there to hand out rally flyers. I walked over to some of them, talked for a few minutes and took some pictures before heading to the rally site.

Mary, Margaret and I drove to the park to get an early view as to what goes on before a Klan rally. At the entrance, we were stopped by a gray-haired police officer.

"Good afternoon, sir," he greeted me. "Are you all here to go camping?" he inquired.

"No, I'm here to go to the Ku Klux Klan rally," I answered.

Looking bewildered, he blurted out, "Only the camping side of the park is open and it will be another half hour before people are permitted to enter the rally side of the park."

When he asked how I knew about the rally, and I responded that the Klan had told me about the rally, he became even more bewildered.

The three of us returned to the park exactly a half hour later. The same gray-haired officer shook his head and handed me a parking permit, which read, "KKK RALLY TODAY," instructing me to place it in my windshield. He claimed it was a parking permit, but I suspected it was also used to identify the bearer's car so that another officer could run the license tag number for identification.

Apparently, the police officer at the entrance had radioed

the police in the parking lot. As we pulled in, police, firemen and paramedics scurried to get a look at me.

Mary and Margaret, with me trailing a few steps behind, proceeded towards the small amphitheater where the rally was to be held. A police officer with a camera had to step aside to let Mary and Margaret through. He then stood directly in front of me and took my picture before I could pass.

We were the first arrivals and sat down front row center, about twelve-feet from the podium at which some Klanmembers would be speaking. Shortly after the appointed time, the Klan arrived and marched single file to the rally area. Imperial Wizard Roger Kelly took a seat to my far right. The other Klanmembers sat to my far left. Music began blaring from the stage. I listened as songs were sung about "Niggers." I even heard the song "Ship Those Niggers North," the same one that had been played especially for me by the deejay at the racetrack when I had gone to see Jerry Lee Lewis' concert. Today, people in the amphitheater watched for my reaction when seeing that I was the only Black present. I simply patted my foot to the music and then looked back at them, noting their reactions.

The rally began. Various Klanmembers came to the lectern on the amphitheater stage and delivered speeches ranging from the history of the Klan to its virtues and why every White Christian American should join to the problems our great nation has acquired because of Black people.

At one point, during a Klansman's history speech, which he had obviously copied from a reference book, he referred to the second Klan leader in history, William Simmons as "William Simon." I looked over at Roger who was looking at me to see if I caught the blunder. I smiled and he shook his head as if to say, *Oh, well, you can't win them all.* I looked at the other Klan members and realized that none of them had registered any reaction to the mispronunciation of their historical leader's name.

The last speaker was Roger Kelly, who delivered the most

charismatic speech of the day. Though I could not agree with most of the things Roger Kelly said, I was very impressed with his take-charge command of the audience. His dramatic delivery reminded me of a Black Baptist preacher in the pulpit. However, Roger's message differed greatly from what I was used to hearing in church. This was a sermon preaching separation of the races instead of racial unity.

At one point in his speech, Roger shocked the hell out of me by pointing at me and introducing me as a friend of his who is Black. He then asked his members to give me a round of applause. I about fainted when all of his robed Klansmen stood up and applauded me. I turned around and looked at the contingency of police who were just as stunned as I was. Nevertheless, I stood up and took a bow.

When the rally ended, I walked over, mingled with the Klanmembers and posed for some pictures with some of them. As I left, I nodded and waved to a police officer who was also leaving. He ignored me and continued on his way.

As I continued walking, I recognized a red-haired police officer among the various others in attendance. This particular officer often stopped in a club in which I performed on a weekly basis. Though I'd never spoken with him, the regularity with which he came in made me think this may have been part of his regular patrol beat.

The Tuesday following the rally, I went to my weekly gig at the club. The club manager, who happens to be White, came over and asked if he might ask me a personal question. I obliged him.

"Daryl, I've known you for three years and you don't have to answer this if you don't want to. I heard you were a member of the Klan. Is that true?"

My eyes met his, "You've got to be joking," I said, taken aback. "Who told you that?"

He informed me that the red-haired police officer who regularly comes in the club told him. Nodding, I told the club manager about the rally and said that the officer was probably just kidding him to get a rise out of him and that there were no Black members in the KKK. He assured me that this officer was serious. I was determined that I would set this officer straight when he came in that evening.

Wouldn't you know it? He didn't come in that evening. However, as I was driving home, I saw him driving on a street near the club. I pulled behind his car and flashed my lights. He pulled over and I got out of my car and approached him. I questioned him about what he had said and he nervously denied saying it.

"I would appreciate you not saying anything that would lead to the spreading of false rumors," I said and walked away.

I didn't know it, but my presence at the rally left a lasting impression on more than the red-haired police officer. The following Christmas, I was invited to the home of a gorgeous model friend of mine named Sharon Branthover. She kissed me at the door and led me by the hand into the living room to meet her parents. Her father immediately said, "I've seen you before."

Thinking he had seen me perform somewhere or on television, as is usually the case, I asked, "Where did you see me play?"

He shook his head, "I've never seen you play. I saw you at the Klan rally. You are the first Black man I have ever seen get a standing ovation at a Klan rally. I'm Craig Branthover, Montgomery County Police," he said as he reached out to shake my hand. "I was there to monitor the rally."

As I clasped his hand in return, I realized he too looked familiar, but for another reason. Major Craig Branthover is the first White Montgomery County, Maryland police officer to ever receive the NAACP Man of the Year Award.

33

"Akin"

If a Klansman is unsure whether or not a certain person is a Klansman, he may attempt to find out by use of the code word, "AYAK," an acronym for "Are You A Klansman?" For instance, he may say to someone, "Do you know Mr. Ayak?" If the individual questioned is in fact a Klansman, he might respond with something, like, "Yes, I know Mr. Ayak, and I also know Mr. Akia," a countercode acronym for "A Klansman I Am."

Because the individual about whom I am now writing has asked me not to identify him for fear of repercussions, I have obliged his wishes. I shall refer to him as "AKIN"—my own acronym for, "A Klansman I'm Not."

I had seen Akin around at various places where the Klan appeared. Sometimes he was wearing his Klan regalia and other times he was not. We rarely had conversations and when we had spoken, it was generally just an exchange of pleasantries. Akin had been in the Klan for several years and was currently a Klan officer. He had been, at various times, an Exalted Cyclops, Grand Kludd, Kleagle and Great Titan.

One day I encountered him while he was tending to his own affairs in the same building.

Daryl Davis

"Hey, Mr. Davis, how are you doing?" he asked.

"Just fine," I replied. "How are you?"

"I heard you had some trouble recently," he said in reference to the incident at the courthouse in which I was attacked. He was not present, but apparently word travels quickly along the Klan grapevine. There is even, what can be referred to as an inter-Klan grapevine, in which news of what one Klan is doing somehow becomes known to rival Klans.

"I think that's a real shame, what happened to you," Akin continued. "I know they lied about you slapping the woman and I know that Pierson's sister did kick you and Larry Sines came after you for no reason. I know you don't agree with everything the Klan stands for, but I've never seen you get violent with any of us. I am tired of the lying and the hate. I am a Christian. I am thinking about dropping out."

I told him that I wanted to discuss this a little further with him and if he was not pressed for time, we could finish the business we had originally come to do and meet up in the lobby of the building afterwards. He agreed and we headed in different directions.

We rendezvoused in the lobby as planned. It turned out that a friend of Akin's had given him a ride into town and dropped him off. I offered him a ride home, which he accepted.

While in my car, he continued telling me that he was serious about quitting. He said that he knew there were some very good people who were Klanmembers, but every Klan has their bad apples. He reconfirmed that he was sorry to hear what had happened to me.

Akin had heard of a couple of favors I had done for some Klanmembers and was very taken by my gestures of goodwill. This, along with some other things, had led to his decision to give up the Knighthood.

We arrived at his apartment and he invited me in. Logic

warned me that this could be a setup since this was not on my agenda, and while there are some Klanmembers I can associate with, there are many that would probably attempt to do me in if given the opportunity. I guess my hesitancy was similar to that of the Klanmembers I met during my odyssey when they came to the surprise revelation that I am Black. Akin's intentions, however, seemed sincere and my instincts told me to accept his invitation.

We went into his house and were greeted by his wife. I took a seat and was offered a cup of coffee. Akin then asked me to follow him. I walked cautiously behind him as he led me to his bedroom. Once inside, he opened his closet and removed his Klan robe and hood and handed them to me.

"I'm getting rid of it. You can have it if you want it. Maybe you can take some pictures of it for your book."

I was absolutely shocked as I came to realize that he was indeed serious about leaving the KKK. I thanked him for the robe and hood.

He then pulled open all his drawers and removed all of his Klan tee shirts, certificate of membership, cards, jewelry and other Klan items, including newspaper articles with his picture in full Klan attire, and put all of this in a plastic trash bag and gave it to me.

Before leaving Akin and his wife, he told me that he would let the others in the particular Klan group to which he belonged, know that he was retiring. He would not let them know he gave me his Klan regalia and paraphernalia.

For his sake, I agreed not to reveal the source of my acquisitions. He asked me if it would be okay for him to keep in touch with me. I told him to please do.

34

Death and Life
in the Klan

As time passed and I continued my journey to get to the heart of racism, it brought high and low points. Some Klanmembers I have met remained devout racists and have threatened, kicked and spit on me. Others, like Akin, have left the Klan and made me gifts of their hoods, robes and other memorabilia. I do not think my vision has been clouded by a desire to see people as better than they really are. Racism is perpetuated when people have little personal experience with those they fear or hate. I only hope my relationships with Klanmembers can act as an antidote. You can't force anybody to change, but you cannot disavow a friendship when you see it in the making.

One day, I was away from home and phoned in to get my messages from the answering machine, as I always do. Roger Kelly had left a strange message. He said that he had something important to tell me, but would prefer not to leave it on the machine. I wondered what was wrong. I called him immediately, but he wasn't in; so I left a message saying what time I would be returning home.

Finally we connected and Roger relayed sad news. His

Grand Knighthawk, Dan "Shakey" Wantz had apparently committed suicide the previous night. This was the young man who frequently accompanied Roger and had escorted him the first time we met.

"He shot himself with his 9-millimeter semi-automatic. No one knows why," Roger said brokenly. "I wanted you to know of Shakey's death since you knew him and he liked you so much."

I expressed my sincere sympathy and asked Roger if there was anything I could do.

"Nothing that I can think of," he said sadly.

"Do you think it would be appropriate if I attended the funeral?" I asked.

Roger responded that he would really like to have me there and felt sure that Shakey would have wanted that. However, he felt that Shakey's parents would not understand, and it might be better not to get them any more unnerved than they already were. I certainly empathized with their shock and grief and would respect their wishes.

Then, with deep sincerity, Roger added something that touched me deeply. "If I should die before you Daryl, I would like you to be at my funeral and I'll put that in my will."

It was a measure of how far our relationship had come.

Later, Roger took another unprecedented step documenting our closeness. This time it was a life-affirming move which, I hope and believe, heralds a future in which "They shall beat their swords into plow shares. . . neither shall they learn war anymore." When I first met this Imperial Wizard of the Ku Klux Klan, he had become single after a difficult divorce. At times, when we'd get together, he'd tell me about the women he was dating. None seemed serious until he brought a particularly lovely young woman along on one of our outings. Her giving nature and obvious deep feelings for Roger impressed me a great deal. He later asked me what I thought of her. I told him, "This one you should marry." Fears of having another bad marriage stalled him for awhile, but finally he did.

Two months ago Roger and his new wife had a baby girl and named her Megan. Yesterday, I became Megan Kelly's godfather.

Afterword

Before I began my journey, I realized in seeking out the driving forces behind the racism found in members of the Ku Klux Klan, I would hear a lot of things that would bother and sometimes anger me. However, I decided to meet those who held views opposed to my own and get their side of the story. I did at times, after obtaining their confidence and allowing them to freely express their views, venture my opinions. Some Klanspeople I met were persuaded by my opinions and others were not. Nevertheless, I believe the best way to reach the hearts and minds of those who oppose you is to allow them to be themselves.

One of the questions I'm frequently asked is: "Did you ever get scared being around Klanmembers by yourself?"

My answer is that I have always felt in my heart that I was doing a good thing for the good of all people and God. The God they worship is the same God I worship. I had faith that God would watch over me.

Some who, like me, believe in tolerance between people

still say, "I hate the Klan! Don't you hate them? How can you stand being around those people?"

I reply that hate is a powerful word. Coincidentally, people who hate the Klan are doing exactly what they are accusing the Klan of doing—hating.

I remained honest with each and every Klanmember I met, and, most importantly, I remained honest with myself. I did not pretend to be anything other than what I am, and though I allowed each Klanmember to know where I stood, I never forced my beliefs upon anyone. Over a period of time, this, I believe, became the basis for their trust and respect for me.

Though the idea of being friends with a person whose belief system you despise sounds like an impossibility, I believe I have demonstrated that it is indeed, very possible for two diametrically opposed human beings to learn and accept enough about each other to co-exist without strife. And while I was learning about the Klan and its members, I was also passively teaching them without forcing myself or my beliefs and they responded in kind.

We are all human beings, though we may have some physical, cultural, sexual and religious differences. Often these differences seem monumental to those of us who are only accustomed to being around our own kind. We are ignorant in understanding these differences. Therefore, we are ignorant in understanding that these differences are only superficial. Though we are influenced by our backgrounds and our environments, as human beings we are fundamentally the same. I am not trying to downplay the Klan's atrocities, past or present; however, after more than 130 years of violence and hatred, I felt it was time we get to know one another on a social basis and not under the cover of darkness.

It is fear that is instilled in us through ignorance that often breeds hate. Hatred, if not kept in check, will sometimes escalate to destruction. We want to do away with the things we don't like, especially if they are things we fear. It comes down to getting rid of the source of our fear before it gets rid of us.

Putting aside fear and learning to present myself in a non-threatening manner allowed me access to some of the innermost workings of the Klan organizations and the minds of their members. Of course, this did not happen overnight, but over time, doors that had been locked to all Blacks and closed to many Whites, were opened. I have learned throughout my unique odyssey to discover the roots of racism, that any non-violent form of communication is a mutual, positive way to exchange information even if there is disagreement. Moreover, it is a beginning.

Each party has now found common ground on which to agree. It becomes obvious that all people want many of the same things; child protection, safety and awareness in the community and school system, etc. When opposing forces see that these goals can be achieved without short-changing themselves or the other party, fear begins to subside. The discussion can then turn to, "What can **WE** do to achieve these goals? Things are accomplished more quickly if **WE** work together." Once this point is reached, and each party becomes involved with the other for a common cause, respect, trust and friendship may ensue and former bottlenecks are often shattered or are at least unblocked.

Sometimes my approach raised eyebrows. Some people who don't know me very well angrily questioned my endeavors, criticized my methods and suggested that I was selling out.

However, I have Klan robes, given to me voluntarily, hanging in my closet. Klanmembers have invited me to their homes for dinner. And some members have quit the Klan as a result of getting to know and respect me and my non-racist beliefs. Time and exposure is a great healer—perhaps the only healer for irrational fear and hatred. Laws can be made to take people out of the Klan, but laws cannot be made to take the Klan mentality out of people. The best way we can learn to respect each other is to know each other.

Daryl Davis

There are people who feel that racism and those who propagate it should be ignored. They think that giving such beliefs any type of attention will only promote them. I believe some things can be ignored and will eventually go away, like the teaser or bully we have all encountered in grade school. However, I do not feel that racists fit into that category. Racism is similar to cancer; unless treated, it will spread and eventually consume the whole body. If the afflicted body procreates after being attacked with such a deadly malady, whether it be cancer or racism, there is a good chance that any offspring will be exposed to it as well. And the terrible process will begin all over again in a new generation.

Racism and prejudice, however overt or subtle, are rampant in our world today. They are most common in those with poor self-esteem. Until people feel positively about themselves, they will look for someone else to step on in order to negatively gain what they cannot positively achieve.

Based on my research and association with members of the Ku Klux Klan, personal feelings, experiences and the teachings of some representative men such as Martin Luther King, Jr., Harvard Law professor Randall Kennedy and others in which I deeply believe, I have become more introspective and have composed a code by which I live my life.

One important part of my code is to try to cut down on the polarization and isolation of races by focusing on how I identify myself. You will notice I have not, in this book, used today's politically correct term, "African-American." I have chosen to call myself and others of my race, "Black."

First and foremost, I consider myself an American. If further description is warranted, then I am a Black-American. Over the years, there have been many acceptable terms: Negro, Colored, Black, Afro-American, People of Color and so on. As far as being politically correct, I don't think we will see the NAACP—the National Association for the Advancement of

310

Colored People—changing its name to the NAAAAP—the National Association for the Advancement of African-American People. I do not find the terms "Negro," "Colored" or "Black" to be offensive. In fact, I prefer them to be used in descriptions of me or in my descriptions of other members of my race if race must be distinguished or is being discussed. To me, an African-American is a person who, in a matter of speaking, recently emigrated from Africa to the United States. My ancestors, like the ancestors of most Blacks in this country, got off a boat many centuries ago, thus making the nationality of their descendants just plain American and their race Black. I feel the same way about White Americans who have been here for generations and see no reason to call them Euro-Americans.

Though at times, since my journey into the heart of the Ku Klux Klan the charge has been hurled against me, let me emphatically make the statement that I am in no way ashamed of my African heritage. Unlike most Black Americans, I lived in Africa for ten years and am very glad to have descended from such a great continent and magnificent people. However, I long for the day we can all just call ourselves "Americans" without any racial, ethnic or origin prefix. This declassification will surely cut down the feelings of isolation we all are currently experiencing in our society. This is not to say that we, whatever our heritage, need to forget where we came from. We should learn about individual backgrounds and acknowledge them by sharing our histories with others, both in and out of our individual races so that everyone may learn and not let his or her heritage be forgotten. In this country, with the exception of the first Americans, the Native American-Indians, we are all composites. America cannot be defined as consisting of any one type of people. It is comprised of people whose history reaches to every corner of this planet. That is America's real strength if only all citizens could recognize it.

I believe one must strive to make the world a better place

by accomplishing those things that will benefit our future rather than trying to reactivate the past. These may be accomplishments to benefit humankind, such as discovering a cure for a deadly disease or an invention that could be used around the world. Or these may be accomplishments of personal significance such as learning to walk again after a debilitating accident or winning first place in a pie-baking contest. These victories are the things we must all work for and earn.

I pray for the time when people focus on showing each other what they are capable of accomplishing, rather than concentrating on what color they are or from where their family originated. In such an era, we will gain personal respect from our deeds and the pre-designated color of our skin won't matter. We should never be ashamed of what is God-given, such as our skin color. We can only be proud of what we become through our own given endeavors.

This book is by no means a how-to manual providing the solution to the racial plague on our planet—it is but one man's pioneering approach. Now, I can only hope that someone after me improves upon my method by using it as a springboard to launch a rocket that will soar into the future in the quest to improve race relations. Perhaps my experiences will shed more understanding and others will be inspired to seek out and eradicate racial prejudice with education, not only the academic type one receives in school, but the kind we attain when we learn about our fellow human beings from one-on-one, non-confrontational encounters. It is my dream, that through this new discourse, in a new millennium of brotherly love and friendship, we will overcome hatred and prejudice.

Epilogue

While everyone I have encountered on my journey to find the roots of racism has significance, some have impacted my experiences, views and memories more than others.

Matt Koehl: Moved his headquarters from Arlington, Virginia and relocated to Cicero, Illinois.

Roger Kelly: Continues to be the Imperial Wizard of the Invincible Empire Knights of the KKK. His views have modified somewhat since coming to know me. His Klan organization remains one of the least violent. Roger, his second wife, and their first child, my godchild, are my close friends.

Vernon Naimaster: Retired from the Klan and was content to live out the rest of his life enjoying fishing and smoking his pipe. He passed away in October of 1992. I miss him.

Daryl Davis

Tony LaRicci: Remains retired and content to live out his life peacefully with his wife, Frances. He has minimal contact with Klan members. He is proud of what he has done and what he has tried to do, but has now put those days behind him. He plans to spend more time with his children—who are now grown—and his grandchildren. I visit with him often and we play guitar together after dinner in his home.

Bob White: Retired. The Grand Giant has become a good friend. He often comes to my gigs with his girlfriend and since he doesn't do much dancing, I dance with her.

David Black: Became an ordained Southern Baptist Minister. He is now married and has two sons. He preaches at a church in Maryland and does not oppose integration, but remains opposed to miscegenation between races, as he believes that it is not what the Bible intended. David now has many friends of different races. He still has very loose affiliations with the Right-Wing. He maintains that he joined the Klan for political more than racial reasons and became disillusioned with their false Christian message.

Chester Doles: Within months of his recent release from prison, Chester severely beat the husband of a woman with whom he had begun an affair. He is back in jail. This time his victim was White. We communicate frequently. He hopes to reorganize a Klan group upon his release from prison.

Raymond Pierson: Currently remains incarcerated.

Bob Tweed: Arrested and convicted of running drugs across state lines with the intent to distribute. He is currently incarcerated.

Tom Tarrants: Active in his church and organizing projects in inner cities, it shames and pains him to think about the former life he once led and will rarely discuss it. I especially appreciate his discussing those days with me and thank him for all the good deeds he has since done.

Karen: Works hard and still practices astrology. She remains a silent member of a Klan group.

Roy Frankhouser: Recently got out of prison again. This time he was convicted of Obstruction of Justice in the case of a White Power Skinhead from Boston who was suspected of conspiring to blow up a synagogue. I continue to communicate with him.

Daryl Davis: Continues playing music and battling prejudice.